D1165423

The Closing of the Middle Ages?

A History of Medieval Britain

General Editor
Marjorie Chibnall

Advisory Editor
G. W. S. Barrow

This series covers the history of medieval Britain from the Roman withdrawal in the fourth century to 1529. The books combine the results of the latest scholarship and research with clear, accessible writing.

Already published

The Closing of the Middle Ages? England, 1471–1529
Richard Britnell

Anglo-Norman England, 1066–1166
Marjorie Chibnall

Angevin England, 1154–1258
Richard Mortimer

In preparation

The Age of Settlement, c.400–c.700
Philip Dixon

The Emergence of the English Nation, c.650–c.920
Richard Abels

Late Anglo-Saxon England, c.920–1066
Robin Fleming

England under Edward I and Edward II, 1259–1327
J. H. Denton

England from Edward III to Richard II, 1327–1399
Barrie Dobson

Lancastrian England, 1399–1471
Simon Walker

Medieval Wales, 1050 to the Death of Owen Glyn Dwr
Ifor W. Rowlands

Scotland, 400–1100
David Dumville

Later Medieval Scotland
Norman A. T. MacDougall

The Closing of the Middle Ages?

England, 1471–1529

Richard Britnell

BLACKWELL
Publishers

The right of Richard Britnell to be identified as author of this work has been asserted in accordance with the Copyright, Designs and Patents Act 1988.

First published 1997

Blackwell Publishers Ltd
108 Cowley Road
Oxford OX4 1JF
UK

Blackwell Publishers, Inc.
350 Main Street
Malden, Massachusetts 02148
USA

British Library Cataloguing in Publication Data

A CIP catalogue record for this book is available from the British Library.

Library of Congress Cataloging-in-Publication Data

Britnell, R. H.
The Closing of the Middle Ages?: England, 1471–1529 / Richard Britnell.
   p.   cm. — (A History of medieval Britain)
Includes bibliographical references and index.
ISBN 0-631-16598-3. — ISBN 0-631-20540-3
   1. Great Britain—History—House of York, 1461–1485. 2. Great Britain—History—Henry VIII, 1509–1547. 3. Great Britain—History—Henry VII, 1485–1509. 4. Civilization, Medieval—14th century.
5. England—Civilization. 6. Fifteenth century. I. Title.
II. Series.
DA425.B8   1997
942.04—dc21   96-51565
                                                         CIP

Typeset in 11 on 12.5 pt Sabon
by Graphicraft Typesetters Ltd, Hong Kong

This book is printed on acid-free paper

Voluala barchin heman la lauoluola dramme pagloni

Contents

List of Plates

List of Figures

List of Tables

Acknowledgements

I am grateful to the University of Durham for research leave in 1993 and 1996 that enabled me to work on this book. It has benefited considerably from the comments of those friends and colleagues who have checked my misunderstandings, given me new ideas, and suggested things I should read, and in particular I am grateful to Ian Blanchard, Christopher Brooks, Christine Carpenter, Margaret Harvey, John Hatcher and Anthony Pollard. The text has been greatly enriched by their help, and those who know them and their work will probably be able to spot where. Marjorie Chibnall read the penultimate draft of the whole text closely, and the final version benefits extensively from her most helpful observations. Jennifer Britnell, my wife, has been of invaluable assistance, not only because of her comments and suggestions, but also because her book collection complements mine.

RICHARD BRITNELL

Introduction

The period 1471–1529 is often seen as an epilogue to the Middle Ages, or a prologue to the Early Modern period, for reasons that have much more to do with the way in which historians specialize than with any intrinsic characteristics of these particular years. Fortunately the point is now sufficiently widely recognized not to need labouring, but there remains a special duty on a book that aims to introduce the period not to treat it in terms of the problems of another age. These years correspond to the lifetime of people, like Cardinal Wolsey (1472/3–1530), who experienced neither the collapse of government under Henry VI nor its assertive centralization under Thomas Cromwell, and knew nothing of either the mid-fifteenth-century economic recession nor the sixteenth-century recovery. The present study therefore deliberately avoids an interpretation of the events and concerns of these years that would imply an old age was ending and a new one beginning, since such a claim is no more appropriate for this period than for any other of equivalent length between 1066 and 1529.

Chapters 1 and 2 are designed to give a chronological shape to the period, first with reference to the dynastic problems and then to foreign policy. Although these narratives are highly selective, between them they provide a sufficient framework for the location of events discussed elsewhere in the text. They also supply bibliographical details of recent works where the events of the period are discussed in more circumstantial detail. Good narrative history necessarily requires a good deal of space, and to have developed it further in this book would have meant squeezing out other approaches equally deserving of inclusion. The third chapter comments on aspects of kingship that do not fit well into a narrative framework, namely the various resources peculiar to a king that supported his exercise of power. The thinking in this

chapter leads into both part II of the book (which examines political institutions that gave scope to a king's activities and limited
his power) and into part III (which examines how nationhood,
the church and the law supported a king's authority while imposing particular obligations upon him).

Part II concerns the institutions through which the king related
directly to his subjects. These, following Dr Harriss, are defined as
the separate dimensions of court politics, country politics, parliamentary politics and popular politics.[1] Each of these has its particular problems and historical debates, some of which are bitterly
fought. In particular, there is an ongoing debate about the place
of factions in court politics and another about the importance of
county institutions in country politics.

Part III concerns institutions of central importance to the education, values and allegiances of people at the time. The church
and the law are obvious candidates for discussion here because
they offered sophisticated structures of though of general significance. Both, too, had specialized institutions of higher education
and presented opportunities for professional employment. In addition, this section includes a discussion of nationality. In so far as
nationhood is expressed in linguistic affiliation, it would be fair to
see nationality as an elaborate cultural construct distantly analogous to religion and law. The real reason for including nationality
here, however, is its close interaction with religion and law in
forming political values and encouraging a habit of allegiance to
the crown. Nationality, law and religion may be thought of as
three aspects of social awareness that were logically independent
of the character of the English monarchy, but which nevertheless
served to buttress support for it and thereby encouraged political
obedience.

The final part examines some aspects of the society and economy
of the period. Although money and trade were everyday features
of late medieval life, their operation can only be understood within
the context of a society where much was defined by tradition.
Three aspects of traditional thought are examined in particular
in chapter 10, one relating to the structure of social ranks, the
second relating to the family, and third relating to the political
concept of social justice. All these traditions inculcated values
that were opposed to purely financial calculation, and they can

---

[1] G. L. Harriss, 'The Dimensions of Politics', in R. H. Britnell and A. J. Pollard, *The
McFarland Legacy: Studies in Late Medieval Politics and Society*, Stroud and New York
1995, 1–20.

be thought of as defining non-market relationships. Chapter 11, by contrast, examines relationships that were brought about by trade, and some of the problems that market dependence created. The final chapter is an assessment of the extent to which the economy was growing through the period.

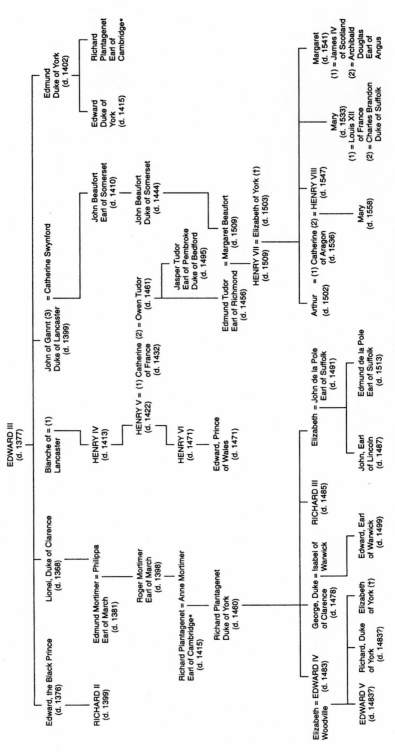

FIGURE 1.1 The descent of the Yorkist and Tudor kings

Part I

Kings and Kingship

I

Kings and Dynasties

This is a book framed by dynastic crises. In 1471 Edward IV seized the English throne from Henry VI for the second time, and so set the Yorkist dynasty on the throne for the next fourteen years. In 1529 Cardinal Wolsey was dismissed from his post as chancellor, and the Reformation Parliament first met, because the kingdom faced dynastic disaster in the absence of a male heir to Henry VIII. Reports of births, deaths, alliances and quarrels in the royal family fill a good deal of the space in contemporary annals, and a survey of them introduces much of the matter of late medieval politics.

Edward IV's Second Reign, 1471–83

When Edward IV returned to London on 21 May 1471, he was accompanied by his leading supporters and a large number of his mounted men. The previous October, within ten years of his first becoming king of England, he had been confronted by rebellion, and had been driven into exile in Burgundy. Henry VI, the last of the Lancastrian kings, had then been temporarily restored to the throne. Now, at the age of twenty-nine, Edward had regained his kingdom with the help of Charles the Bold, duke of Burgundy. He had landed on the Yorkshire coast with about 1200 men on 14 March, and had advanced rapidly because nobody opposed him. When Lancastrian forces were eventually raised, Edward had defeated them decisively at the battles of Barnet on 14 April and Tewkesbury on 4 May.[1]

With him at his entry to London rode his two younger brothers,

---

[1] Waurin, v, 674; Scofield, *Edward the Fourth*, i, 537–93; Ross, *Edward IV*, 145–77.

George, duke of Clarence,[2] aged twenty-six, and Richard, duke of Gloucester, aged eighteen. Edward had very different obligations to the two of them. In 1470 Clarence had conspired with Richard, earl of Warwick, and together they had deposed Edward and restored Henry VI as king. Having succeeded, they had pushed through parliament legislation to disinherit Edward as a traitor and make Clarence heir to the throne in the event of Henry VI's dying childless. Following Edward's return, Clarence had eventually betrayed Warwick and joined his brother in the midlands. Richard, by contrast, had been with Edward in exile and distinguished himself in battle in the recovery of the kingdom both at Barnet, where King Henry VI was captured, and at Tewkesbury, where Henry VI's only son, the young Prince Edward, was killed in the pursuit that followed the collapse of the Lancastrian army.[3]

The day following the Yorkist entry into London, there was another procession, coming from the Tower and through the busy centre of the city. This time the focus of interest was a coffin containing the body of Henry VI, accompanied again by a large company of armed men.[4] Henry lay in state overnight in St Paul's, with his face exposed to the public gaze to make sure people knew he was really dead. Next morning the corpse was taken to the Blackfriars church, and some time later it was conveyed by boat along the Thames to Chertsey Abbey for burial. Although one pious report had it that Henry had died merely of rage and disappointment,[5] common sense suggested that he had been murdered during the night of 21–22 May.[6] Edward banked on a continuing sense of military crisis to convince the citizens that this was a politically necessary death. Since Henry's son was also dead, there was no longer an obvious Lancastrian claimant to the throne. This tactical brutality demonstrates the deep chasm that existed between medieval doctrines of kingship and political realities.

One lesson to be drawn from Edward's temporary deposition in 1470 was that he had failed to restore the authority of the English monarchy from the abyss into which it had fallen in the mid-fifteenth century. At the time of Edward's coronation on 28 June 1461, many people had had high expectations that he would

[2] This title, given to him in 1461, signified a royal runner-up. Previously held by the second surviving son of Edward III and by the second son of Henry IV, it derived from Clare Castle in Suffolk, which the first duke of Clarence had held by marriage.

[3] Hammond, *Battles*, 123–6.

[4] *Great Chronicle*, 220.

[5] *Arrivall*, 38; Waurin, vi, 675; Basin, ii, 90.

[6] *Crowland Continuations*, 128; Warkworth, 21.

restore good government and prosperity, but within a few years he was blamed for continuing civil dissension, high taxes and disrupted overseas trade.[7] The problems had been too great to be rapidly resolved, and the events of 1470 had clearly demonstrated the continuing political and military weakness of the crown.

The recent crisis also demonstrated the fragility of the Yorkist alliance. The Lancastrians and Yorkists were aristocratic factions, and there were strong emotions of loyalty in play. Lord Hastings, Edward's leading councillor, was a fine example of loyalty to the Yorkist cause, and John de Vere, earl of Oxford, had similarly stood by the Lancastrians. But aristocratic factions were not political parties. They did not exist to promote corporately formulated policies. Each of the noblemen or gentlemen who supported Edward IV had his own interests to protect, and this was often best achieved by political inaction. Even the extensive family connections of the Yorkists could not guarantee political cohesion. Of the two enemies who had recently deposed Edward, the earl of Warwick was his cousin and the duke of Clarence was his brother.

Edward IV's second reign was to be more successful than his first, partly because he had learned to face problems more intelligently. However, he had great difficulty in managing the Yorkist alliance. Rivalries amongst his followers were more than a domestic matter, and for many years after 1471 severely compromised his credibility as restorer of good government. The dukes of Gloucester and Clarence both expected to benefit from the share-out of estates confiscated from Lancastrians, and they were not disappointed. Yet within a few months of the victories of 1471 there was an unseemly conflict between them. Clarence had married Isabel Neville, the elder daughter of the defeated earl of Warwick, and hoped in time to receive all the extensive lands her mother held in her own right. Gloucester, however, wanted to marry her sister Anne, so that he could share in this particular bonanza. Already, by February 1472, the dispute was severe enough to be brought before the king's council for a hearing. Soon afterwards Gloucester abducted the fifteen-year-old Anne and then married her. It was said that Clarence had concealed her in London dressed as a kitchen-maid, but that Gloucester had tracked her down and removed her to sanctuary in the collegiate church of St Martin-le-Grand, and thence to Middleham Castle.[8] The level of animosity was such that in 1473 many people feared civil war; it is difficult

[7] Warkworth, 3, 12.
[8] Ross, *Richard III*, 28–9.

otherwise to understand the number of portents of disaster reported in that year. The most dramatic was a headless man seen
on Dunsmore Heath between Leicester and Banbury crying 'Bows,
bows'. In February 1474 the Milanese ambassador in France was
expecting civil war in England as Gloucester prepared to fight his
brother.[9] Edward used parliament to force a solution of the problem. A session of May 1474 was summoned primarily to impose
a settlement that involved dividing the lands of the countess of
Warwick between the two contestants 'as if the said countess were
now naturally dead'.[10]

Within a few years, an even more serious conflict had opened up,
this time between Clarence and the king. When Clarence's wife
died in 1476, the king sabotaged his chances of a spectacular
remarriage to the heiress of the duchy of Burgundy. Edward was
disinclined to involve himself in Burgundy's quarrels with France,
and too suspicious of his brother's loyalty to want him as an independent neighbour. Clarence was outraged, and displayed such a
degree of hostility to his brother that he became politically dan-
gerous. Edward proceeded against him in a session of parliament
early in 1478. Having been attainted as a traitor and condemned,
Clarence was put to death in the Tower of London, probably by
drowning in a butt of Malmsey wine, and perhaps because this
was the form of death he himself chose. Edward, who was not
a vindictive man, had acted under extreme provocation. Amongst
other things, Clarence was said to have 'falsely and untruly noised,
published and said that the king our sovereign lord was a bastard
and not begotten to reign upon us'. In other words, Clarence had
considered himself to be the rightful king of England, and had let
this be known.[11]

Throughout Edward IV's reign the influence of the queen's family, the Woodvilles,[12] was a source of political disquiet. Edward's
secret marriage to Elizabeth Woodville at Grafton (Northamptonshire) in 1464 had been politically damaging because of the comparatively low ranking of her family within the English nobility.
Having raised their status by this marriage, the Woodvilles had
thoroughly integrated themselves into the upper nobility by an impressive series of further marriage alliances. Their influence in the
country at large derived more from office-holding than from land-
ownership, and this limited their capacity to form an independ-

[9] Warkworth, 24; *Milanese Papers*, no. 255, p. 178.
[10] *Rot. Parl.*, vi, 100.
[11] *Rot. Parl.*, vi, 194; Hicks, *False, Fleeting, Perjur'd Clarence*, 128–41, 200–4.
[12] The name Woodville is often spelled Wydeville.

ent power base. Nor did their envied position preclude regular cooperation in the government of the realm with other members of the nobility. Much of their reputation for causing divisions in the royal family is the direct result of the fact that in 1483 they were the chief obstacle to the wishes of Richard of Gloucester, and there is no evidence of political hostility between them and Richard up to that point.[13] However, they were locked in personal antagonism with other distinguished figures at court, notably with William, Lord Hastings. In addition, the queen herself, her brother Anthony, Earl Rivers,[14] and her son Thomas, marquess of Dorset, acquired a reputation for acquisitiveness, though in reality they were hardly more acquisitive than the king's two brothers.[15]

Despite such jealousies, Edward's later years were politically stable. Barring accidents, the succession to the throne was then more secure than at any other time between 1422 and 1603. Edward IV's first son, Edward, was born in 1470, and a second son, Prince Richard, in 1473.[16] There were no Lancastrian claimants except Henry Tudor, who was abroad with scant resources of any kind. The fact that the succession to the throne became problematic again in the 1480s, was largely the consequence of Richard of Gloucester's unwillingness to work with the Woodvilles in 1483, and of his eventual decision to make himself king.

Edward V and Richard III, 1483–5

Edward IV's death on 9 April 1483, at the age of forty, was sudden. Had he lived only a few years longer his elder son, then twelve years old, would probably have been crowned King Edward V without question. As it was, the young king was still too young to rule, and some interim arrangement was needed. The determination of his thirty-year-old uncle Richard that he would mastermind that arrangement led to one of the most astounding crises in English political history – Richard's usurpation of the throne and the disappearance of Edward V and his younger brother. England once more justified its reputation abroad for political instability,

---

[13] Horrox, *Richard III*, 80–1, 90–6, 121–7; C. E. Moreton, 'A Local Dispute and the Politics of 1483: Roger Townshend, Earl Rivers and the Duke of Gloucester', *The Ricardian*, viii (1989), 305–7.
[14] The title of Lord Rivers was revived for Richard Woodville, the queen's father, in 1448, for reasons that are not now understood, and he was created an earl in 1466.
[15] Mancini, 64–5; Hicks, *Richard III and his Rivals*, 221–8, 247–79, 297–316, 323–35; Lander, *Crown and Nobility*, 112–18.
[16] Ross, *Edward IV*, 166, 248.

though in fact Richard's usurpation was quite unrelated to any of the more usual causes of royal weakness.

About the time of the late king's funeral, and before the arrival in Westminster of Richard of Gloucester, a council meeting fixed the coronation of Edward V for 4 May. However, Gloucester, working together with the duke of Buckingham, took an independent line by taking custody of the young king at Stony Stratford on 30 April and placing under arrest four of those who were looking after him. On Gloucester's authority, these four, including the king's uncle, Anthony, Lord Rivers, and his half-brother, Sir Richard Grey, were sent for confinement in Yorkshire. The queen mother, hearing the news, went into sanctuary in Westminster with her younger son and her daughters. On 4 May the young king entered London in Gloucester's protection, and Gloucester justified his intervention, which had delayed the coronation, by alleging a Woodville conspiracy against him. A meeting of the council on 10 May appointed him Protector of the realm, and postponed the king's coronation until 22 June. So far there was no overt doubt about Edward V's right to the throne.[17]

During April and May Gloucester claimed powers as Protector to enhance his personal security. He replaced the greater officers of state and gave extraordinary powers in the shires to some of his supporters, notably to the duke of Buckingham, who was given authority in Wales and the Welsh Marches. By the end of the month the extension of Richard's personal power had gone far beyond what his formal duties implied. Then on 13 June, alleging that Lord Hastings was conspiring against him, he accused him of treason at a council meeting in the Tower of London, and had him immediately arrested and beheaded without trial on Tower Hill. On 16 June he arranged for the king's younger brother to be removed from sanctuary in Westminster Abbey and sent to the Tower of London. Orders were then sent for the execution of three of those arrested on 30 April; Earl Rivers, Sir Richard Grey and Sir Thomas Vaughan were beheaded at Pontefract on 25 June. Meanwhile, on 22 June Richard III's claim to the throne was expounded in a sermon at St Paul's Cross in London, and two days later Buckingham put the same case to the mayor and aldermen of London. The following day Buckingham took advantage of the fact that a small number of nobles and gentlemen had arrived for Edward V's coronation, not having received notice of

---

[17] Horrox, *Richard III*, 89–99; Pollard, *Richard III and the Princes*, 90–3; Ross, *Richard III*, 65–76.

its cancellation, to address them on the same theme. They were intimidated into accepting Buckingham's arguments and agreed to petition Richard to accept the throne. The next day, 26 June, this petition was presented at Baynard's Castle in London by these nobles and gentlemen, together with the mayor and aldermen of the city, and Richard, after a show of reluctance, accepted the invitation. He was crowned king on 6 July.[18] The deposed king and his brother had stopped appearing in public by mid-July 1483, and by the end of that month it was generally supposed in London that they were either dead or doomed.[19]

It is improbable that Richard, ruthlessly acquisitive though he was,[20] had seriously planned to make himself king at any time before 1483, since he could not have predicted that his brother would die young. To become king in 1483 he had to take different groups of people by surprise. Yet his success was so spectacular that an Italian resident in London at the time, Dominic Mancini, thought it worth writing up as a literary work. Richard's justifications for his actions involved three areas of argument – higher and lower social rank, just and unjust title, loyal and treacherous dealing. His adoption of the title of Protector, formally approved at a council meeting on 10 May, was an assertion of the right to higher status than any of the Woodvilles.[21] His subsequent claim to the throne rested partly on the suggestion that Edward IV himself had been illegitimate, implying that Clarence had been right after all. But he placed his main stress on the illegitimacy of the two princes, alleging that under canon law (the law administered by the church) Edward's marriage to Elizabeth Woodville was technically invalid.[22] Finally, Richard's extreme ruthlessness against his political opponents required the allegation that the Woodvilles and Lord Hastings had conspired to conceal the truth about the bastardy of the princes, and had plotted against him.

Richard had split the precarious balance of interests on which the Yorkist alliance had been built. The rebellion that broke out against him in the autumn following his coronation seems, in origin, to have been a protest in favour of Edward V, though it rapidly changed its form with the spread of the suspicion that the

[18] Horrox, *Richard III*, 89–137; Pollard, *Richard III and the Princes*, 93–6; Ross, *Richard III*, 76–95.
[19] Mancini, 92–3; *Great Chronicle*, 234; Pollard, *Richard III and the Princes*, 121–3.
[20] Hicks, *Richard III and his Rivals*, 247–321.
[21] Humphrey, duke of Gloucester was Protector of England between Henry VI's accession to the throne in 1422 and his coronation in 1429.
[22] For a clear statement of Richard's legal case, see Helmholz, 'Sons of Edward IV', 91–103.

young prince and his brother were dead. The bulk of support came from Edward IV's servants, dismayed at the way his sons had been treated. The duke of Buckingham's participation in the revolt is more difficult to explain, since he had so far contributed much to Richard's success, but the best guess seems to be that he was as opportunistic as the king, and was playing for personal advantage. The rebels failed, and Buckingham was beheaded in Salisbury on 2 November 1483. Yet the rebellion cast a shadow over the next couple of years because it exposed antagonism towards Richard within the former Yorkist camp.[23] Margaret Beaufort – perhaps with John Morton, bishop of Ely, as her intermediary – had successfully brought to the attention of dissident Yorkists the political usefulness of her son, Henry Tudor, as an enemy of Richard III, and it was in this context that his dynastic claims were first canvassed.[24] Meanwhile, the challenge to Richard's authority in the southern English counties drove him into closer dependence upon northern supporters, and his favour to these outsiders further jeopardized his claims to be maintaining continuity with the past.[25]

Following his defeat of the rebellion of 1483, Richard's main task was to reconstruct the foundations of committed support for his kingship. He probably had the political abilities to achieve this, had he been able to rule for long enough. Some peers who had formerly worked closely with Edward IV, like Lord Ferrers and Lord Audley, became Richard's councillors and gave him faithful service.[26] Moreover, he was still young. He lost his only son, Edward, and his wife Anne in the course of 1484, but he was expected to remarry. It is conceivable that, despite the violent start to his reign, Richard might have ruled for many years and restored political stability to the kingdom.

The fact that his reign was so short was the result of Henry Tudor's risky, but successful, invasion from abroad in August 1485, at a time when Richard's hold on the loyalties of his subjects was still insecure. Henry had only a few hundred English supporters with him in exile, of whom the best known were members of the Woodville family, notably the queen's son, the marquess of Dorset, and three of her brothers. There were also former servants

---

[23] Horrox, *Richard III*, 138–77; Pollard, *Richard III and the Princes*, 109–14; Ross, *Richard III*, 105–24.

[24] C. S. L. Davies, 'Bishop John Morton, the Holy See, and the Accession of Henry VII', *EHR*, cii (1987), 5; Griffiths and Thomas, *Making*, 91–6.

[25] A. J. Pollard, 'The Tyranny of Richard III', *JMH*, iii (1977), 147–65.

[26] Ross, *Richard III*, 160–1.

of Edward IV and William Lord Hastings. Many of Henry's followers were political refugees who had fled abroad after the failure of the 1483 rebellion. The returning exiles were too weak in numbers and resources for independent action, however, and Henry was able to confront Richard III at the battle of Bosworth on 22 August 1485, only because of military support from the king of France and some additional forces gathered on his progress through Wales. The outcome of the battle turned on the allegiance of Sir William Stanley, who came in on the side of Henry, his son-in-law, in the nick of time. Richard was killed in battle, and his army was defeated. Like Henry VI in 1471, Richard was exposed to public view in Leicester to advertise the reality of his death, and then unceremoniously buried there.[27]

Henry VII, 1485–1509

Following his victory at the battle of Bosworth, Henry Tudor entered London in triumph on 3 September 1485. Unlike Edward IV in 1471, he had few close male relatives. He was crowned king on 30 October. Like Henry IV in 1399, Edward IV in 1461, Henry VI in 1470 and Edward IV in 1471, he had obtained the throne as the result of a successful invasion from abroad. This, then, was a more characteristically English crisis than that of 1483. Henry's title to rule by descent was nowhere near as good as that of the king he deposed. On his father's side he had no claim at all. His mother, Margaret Beaufort, was the great-great-grand-daughter of Edward III, but since the Beaufort line descended from an illegitimate son of John of Gaunt, Edward III's third son, Henry's legal claim had several things wrong with it.[28] In the eyes of the French he was king merely 'by the grace of Charles VIII of France'.[29]

After the death of Richard III, the only surviving heir of Edward III by direct succession from father to son was Edward, earl of Warwick, the son of the recently executed duke of Clarence. Warwick's title, indeed any Yorkist title, was better than that of Henry Tudor, since the Yorkists descended legitimately (and by direct male descent) from Edward III's fourth son, Edmund, duke

[27] Griffiths and Thomas, *Making*, 105–9, 117–65.
[28] See figure 1.1, p. 4.
[29] A. V. Antonovics, 'Henry VII, King of England, "By the Grace of Charles VIII of France"', in Griffiths and Sherborne, *Kings and Nobles*, 169–70.

of York. Yet ever since the death in battle of Prince Edward, Henry VI's only son, in 1471, Henry Tudor had been regarded as the heir to the Lancastrian claim to the throne simply because, through his mother, he was the nearest heir of Henry VI. From July 1483, once Edward V and his brother were presumed dead, Henry had also received the attentions of Richard III's opponents from within the Yorkist camp. It was important that Henry had royal blood, but none of the details of his title amounted to much in comparison with victory by force of arms.

Henry's earlier life, though parts of it make a good story because of occasional moments of danger, had been an inappropriate one for a future king. For the first fourteen years of his life, up to 1471, nobody expected him ever to claim the throne, and he had spent a secluded life in Wales. In 1471, within a fortnight of Edward IV's triumphant entry into London, he had fled from Tenby to the Continent in the care of his uncle Jasper Tudor, an active Lancastrian, and he spent the following fourteen years in exile, mostly in Brittany.[30] At the time of his victory at Bosworth few of his friends could be expected to give reliable political advice about handling the day-to-day government of a kingdom, but they included some able men, notably John Morton, bishop of Ely, who became chancellor in 1486. Sir William Stanley, whose help had been so vital at Bosworth, became chamberlain of his household. In addition, Henry was able to count on the considerable experience of his mother, whose advice was important to him to the end of his life.[31]

The Tudor dynasty was built, in this way, on shaky foundations. To shore it up, Henry did what he had sworn to do, and what friends and enemies alike expected him to do, in marrying Edward IV's daughter, Elizabeth of York, on 18 January 1486. Papal dispensation for the marriage, which was necessary because Henry and Elizabeth were related within prohibited degrees of kinship, had been issued two days before.[32] In itself this marriage could do nothing to strengthen Henry's own title, but it bore fruit only eight months later with the birth of prince Arthur on 19 September, so ensuring that a legitimate heir to the throne combined the Lancastrian and Yorkist claims. A second son, Henry, was born on 28 June 1491.[33] So far, at least, the idea that the

---

[30] Griffiths and Thomas, *Making*, 58–60, 75–8.
[31] Jones and Underwood, *King's Mother*, 66–93.
[32] Davies, 'Bishop John Morton', 14–15.
[33] Chrimes, *Henry VII*, 65–7.

Tudors were divinely favoured to found a line of kings was more or less confirmed.

Henry VII did not pursue a vindictive policy against others of royal blood, though he responded relentlessly to any evidence of active disloyalty. He allowed Clarence's son to live in the Tower of London, and he initiated no persecution of Edward IV's nephews, who bore the family name de la Pole because Edward's sister, Elizabeth, had married John de la Pole, duke of Suffolk. This policy was close to that of Edward IV, who was similarly reluctant to destroy potential rivals without evidence of active conspiracy against his rule. The main domestic challenges to Henry's kingship, though framed in a dynastic context, were ingenious attempts by neighbouring powers to destabilize the English crown by supporting impostors, and will be discussed more fully in the context of Henry's foreign relations. Here it is necessary only to assess the extent to which Yorkist loyalism was a real problem after 1485.

There were three principal challenges to Henry's title, of which the first two were very early in the reign. The first was the rebellion of Francis, Viscount Lovell, one of Richard III's closest confidants, together with Humphrey and Thomas Stafford at Easter 1486. All three had fought for Richard at Bosworth and then fled to sanctuary. It is not clear whom the rebellion was intended to benefit since it was rapidly abandoned by its leaders; the followers of the Staffords were probably confined to their friends and tenants in the west midlands.[34] It is inconceivable that the earl of Warwick, the likeliest Yorkist candidate for the throne, was knowingly involved in the plot, since he survived unscathed.

The second challenge to Henry's rule came from a ten-year-old boy from Oxford, known as Lambert Simnel, who in 1487 was set up by a young priest named Richard Simons to impersonate the earl of Warwick. The fact that Warwick was alive in London, and could be paraded through the streets to prove it, casts doubt on the perspicacity of the plot's originators, but it nevertheless achieved a surprising measure of success. This was chiefly because Simnel was adopted as king by Gerald Fitzgerald, eighth earl of Kildare, and most of the other Anglo-Irish lords, in an attempt to enhance their independence of the English crown. Simnel was crowned King Edward VI in Dublin. A second wing

[34] Hall, 419, 427; D. Luckett, 'Patronage, Violence and Revolt in the Reign of Henry VII', in R. E. Archer (ed.), *Crown, Government and People in the Fifteenth Century*, Stroud 1995, 151–2.

of this rebellion was created by John de la Pole, earl of Lincoln, who obtained military support from his aunt, Margaret of Burgundy. Simnel received little backing within England; his troops probably numbered fewer than 8000, and were deficient in heavy cavalry, billmen and archers. The rebellion was decisively defeated at the battle of Stoke, near Newark, on 16 June 1487. Henry VII was so confident that he had nothing more to fear from Simnel that he took him into his household as a kitchen boy.[35]

The most difficult of the conspiracies to assess is the third, that of Perkin Warbeck, son of a townsman of Tournai in Flanders, whose backers had the wit to promote him as someone who could not readily be paraded in London. He was rehearsed, origin-- ally by the French, in the role of Richard, duke of York, Edward IV's younger son, and in accordance with good precedent, was launched in the susceptible ambience of Ireland in 1491. With the support of an impressive series of patrons, he remained a thorn in Henry VII's flesh until his capture in 1497. He was treated humanely after his capture, and was condemned and hanged only in 1499, in the wake of his teaming up in a plot with the earl of Warwick. At a given moment, however, he had posed more of a dilemma to Henry than ever Lambert Simnel had done because he had attracted more support within England. He twice contributed to crises in internal politics, first in 1495 and then in 1497. In the former year the king's intelligence agents brought to light an internal conspiracy in Warbeck's favour involving Sir William Stanley, the king's step-uncle and chamberlain, who was tried and beheaded for treason. It is very difficult to imagine what Sir William hoped to gain, given the amount of political favour the king had shown him. The second occasion was quite different. On this occasion, having lost the backing of James IV of Scotland, Warbeck hitched his fortunes to a Cornish uprising against taxation, and persuaded some of the insurgents to accept him as King Richard IV. Although both in 1495 and 1497 some of Warbeck's supporters had at some stage been loyal to the Yorkist kings, the same could be said of most people who had reached adulthood before 1483. It is more likely that the rising of 1497 was a protest against Henry VII – partly because of royal taxes, partly because of the numerous south-western families disappointed by Henry's narrow distribution of favours – than that it was primarily a revival of a dormant Yorkist cause.[36]

[35] Bennett, *Lambert Simnel*.
[36] This assessment goes against the opinion of the most important recent studies of the rebellion: I. Arthurson, 'The Rising of 1497: A Revolt of the Peasantry?', in J. Rosenthal

Few of Henry VII's subjects supported him out of old family loyalty, since the Tudors had never had that sort of following in England. Henry VII's usurpation lacked the advantage that Henry IV had derived from his Lancastrian connection, Edward IV from his Yorkist connection or Richard III from his Neville connection. Nor could Henry's legal title to the throne command much more than tolerant acquiescence. His appeal was essentially to pragmatism, in that through his victory at Bosworth and his marriage to Elizabeth of York he offered a political solution to a dynastic dilemma. It should cause no surprise if some old loyalties persisted,[37] but in fact there was very little trouble of that sort. The English political establishment played for political stability, and the Yorkist challenge (like the Jacobite cause of 1688–1745) found its warmest support either from neighbouring states or amongst magnates antagonistic to the idea of being ruled from Westminster.

In 1499 the earl of Warwick was beheaded on Tower Hill after trial before the earl of Oxford as constable of England. It was a miserable conclusion to his fourteen years of imprisonment, but he was convicted of having been involved with Warbeck in an attempt to escape from the Tower. There was perhaps, too, diplomatic pressure from Spain to eliminate this potential claim to the throne in preparation for the marriage of Catherine of Aragon to Prince Arthur, though the bride's father, King Ferdinand of Aragon and Castile, in fact allowed the marriage negotiations to be completed before Warwick was dead.[38] Even then, however, the king was not free of rival claimants to his throne. Edmund de la Pole, earl of Suffolk – brother of John de la Pole who had been killed in the battle of Stoke – chose in 1499 to ape the imprisoned Perkin Warbeck by going to Flanders as champion of the Yorkist cause, thereby creating big problems for his family and friends. He was later joined in exile by his brother Richard. Henry VII succeeded in getting hold of Edmund and imprisoning him in the Tower in 1506, following negotiations with King Philip of Castile in his capacity as duke of Burgundy, but Richard de la Pole remained a royal dissident at large.[39]

Meanwhile, to the end of his days Henry VII could not be sure

---

and C. Richmond (eds), *People, Politics and Community in the Later Middle Ages*, Gloucester 1987, 1–18; Arthurson, *Perkin Warbeck*, 163–5. Cf. Luckett, 'Patronage, Violence and Revolt', 155–60.

[37] K. Dockray, 'The Political Legacy of Richard III', in Griffiths and Sherborne, *Kings and Nobles*, 214–22; Hicks, *Richard III and his Rivals*, 383–7.
[38] Ross, *Edward IV*, 284n.
[39] Chrimes, *Henry VII*, 94.

that a Tudor would succeed him. His third son, Edmund, died in
June 1500 at the age of sixteenth months. Then, on 2 April 1502,
Prince Arthur died at the age of fifteen, after only five months of
marriage; the marriage is unlikely to have been consummated.[40]
The queen died the following year, and Henry never remarried.
This left him with his second son, only ten at the time of his
brother's death, as sole male heir. It is not surprising that there
were whisperings in some quarters about possible alternative heirs
to the throne.

Henry VIII's Reign to the Fall of
Cardinal Wolsey, 1509–29

When Henry VII died on 21 April 1509 at the age of fifty-two,
his death was kept secret for two days, in anticipation of political
crisis arising from conflicting political values within the existing
staff of royal servants.[41] In the event, however, Henry VIII succeeded his father smoothly, and this in itself contributed to confidence in the future of the Tudor dynasty. He was crowned the
following 24 June. The fact that no invasion was attempted by
any usurper during his reign was partly because there were few
potential claimants to the throne, partly because of the complacency with which the Tudor dynasty was now viewed. A young
king enjoying public confidence, persuaded on all sides that his
kingship was divinely favoured, could reasonably expect to be
the father of kings.

To this end, shortly after his coronation, he married his deceased brother's widow, Catherine of Aragon. This was the end
result of a long and complex set of negotiations going back to the
time of Arthur's death. Henry VII and Ferdinand of Aragon had
agreed promptly in 1502 that the substitution of Prince Henry
for Arthur was a convenient settlement, even though she was
five years older than he was. Nevertheless, canon law, which controlled all questions concerning the validity of marriages, did not
permit a man to marry his brother's widow, so that authorization
had to be obtained from the pope. The necessary dispensation had
eventually been obtained from Julius II, but even then Henry VII had
delayed the marriage for a number of years because of disagreements with Ferdinand.[42] In the event the decision to go ahead with

---

[40] Chrimes, *Henry VII*, 67, 284–5, 302; Scarisbrick, *Henry VIII*, 8, 188–9.
[41] S. J. Gunn, 'The Accession of Henry VIII', *HR*, lxiv (1991), 278–88.
[42] Below, p. 36.

the marriage was the bridegroom's own, taken after his father's death, even if in accordance with his father's dying wish.[43]

There was no pressing urgency for Henry to have an heir, though the difficulties Catherine had in childbearing presumably started to trouble Henry within a few years of the marriage. A son born in on New Year's Day 1511 died seven weeks afterwards, and this was just the first of a string of miscarriages, still births and infant deaths.[44] Mary, born in February 1516, was strong enough to survive infancy, but there was no clear precedent for a daughter inheriting the crown. Henry's thoughts on the subject are unrecorded, and were probably complex, since he remained confident of the divine appointment of the Tudor dynasty and appreciative of the virtues of the queen. The absence of a male heir was nevertheless an increasing source of tension,[45] and as Catherine grew older it required more faith to suppose that the divine favours bestowed on the Tudors in the past were going to be continued. Eventually, after seven years in which no child was conceived between them, Henry stopped sleeping with Catherine in 1524.[46]

One sign of mounting dynastic insecurity as time went on was the destruction of Edward Stafford, duke of Buckingham. Buckingham was descended through his paternal grandparents from both John of Gaunt, Edward III's third son, and Thomas of Woodstock, his fifth son. He could reasonably claim to be the nearest male heir to the throne. Buckingham did not overtly threaten Henry VIII, however, and it was only through disloyal leakages of information by the duke's own servants that the king came to hear of his expectation, even intention, of becoming king. He was reported to have made several payments of money to Nicholas Hopkins, a Carthusian monk who had prophesied that the king would leave no male heir, and that Buckingham would become king. Amongst his fellow peers, he had spoken of his title to succeed to the throne in the event of the king's death, and had made similar comments to his servants. Since the only royal infant at the time of Buckingham's arrest was Princess Mary, it would have been many years before even a female heir could accede to the throne without the need for a Protector. If that Protector should be Buckingham, and if Buckingham expected to be king, the realm would be in real danger of a close repetition of Richard

---

[43] Chrimes, *Henry VII*, 297; Scarisbrick, *Henry VIII*, 12–13.
[44] Scarisbrick, *Henry VIII*, 27.
[45] E.g. *SP*, i, 1–2.
[46] Ives, *Anne Boleyn*, 99.

III's usurpation. Buckingham was charged with treason, tried by twenty of his peers, who understood much of the king's predicament, and beheaded on Tower Hill on 17 May 1521.[47]

It is impossible to say what would have happened had the king died during the 1520s. The situation was similar to that between 1120 and 1135, when Henry I had a legitimate daughter, Matilda, but no legitimate son. Probably in the event the nobility would have rallied to the cause of the infant Mary, and there would have been a difficult period of conciliar government in her name. There were proposals to strengthen Mary's claim by marrying her to some appropriate king or prince. Yet there was no appropriate marriage partner who would be unobjectionable as king of England, and the only precedent for a married heiress – Matilda again – was unpromising. Sir John Fortescue, the chief justice of the court of king's bench in Henry VI's reign, had been prepared to argue that the succession of a woman to the throne of England was uncustomary, inconvenient and unlawful.[48] An alternative that must have had some attraction was to prepare the way for the king's illegitimate son Henry Fitzroy, who was born in 1519. His mother, Elizabeth Blount, had been the king's mistress for several years. In June 1525 the boy was made duke of Richmond – the title held by Henry VII before his accession to the throne – with the further provision that he should have precedence over every nobleman in the realm except any future legitimate son of the king's. In March 1527 the Spanish ambassador reported that the king wanted to make Richmond the king of Ireland.[49] This may indicate one way the king's mind, and the speculations of his subjects, were working between 1525 and 1527, their logical conclusion being the legitimizing of Richmond and an Act of Succession to recognize his title to succeed. Yet Henry had good grounds for doubting whether this strategy was wise, since in this period illegitimate birth counted as a personal defect as well as an impediment in law, and this would count against Richmond being acceptable as a proper king. Henry I, in similar circumstances, had not attempted to secure the succession for his illegitimate son, Robert of Caen, though he made him earl of Gloucester.

None of the current possibilities satisfied Henry. His dynastic plans took a new turn in the spring of 1527, when he decided to divorce Catherine of Aragon and start again.[50] Since all issues

[47] Harris, *Edward Stafford*, 180–209.
[48] Chrimes, *English Constitutional Ideas*, 62.
[49] Hall, 703; Ives, *Anne Boleyn*, 100; Scarisbrick, *Henry VIII*, p. 425n.
[50] Ives, *Anne Boleyn*, p. 101.

concerning the validity of marriage were a matter for canon law, Henry was obliged to pursue his divorce through church courts if he wanted an unambiguously legal solution. However, by resting his case for a divorce on a point of theology, he adopted from the beginning a confrontational stance towards the papacy. He had convinced himself that the absence of a male heir was a sign that his marriage to his brother's widow was contrary to divine law. A narrowly legalistic analysis of his marital status could not explain why he had no son, when all previous indications of divine favour to the Tudors implied that he was entitled to one. Nothing was ever to shake Henry's theological interpretation of the problem, which he based on two verses from the book of the Old Testament called Leviticus:[51]

> You shall not uncover the nakedness of your brother's wife; it is your brother's nakedness.

> If a man takes his brother's wife, it is impurity; he has uncovered his brother's nakedness; they shall be childless.

Henry used these texts in a particular way, to make 'childless' mean 'without a male child'. He ignored texts with a contrary indication from elsewhere in the Bible. He argued that Pope Julius II had acted wrongly in authorizing his marriage in defiance of these texts, and so directly challenged the papal power of dispensation in such cases. Catherine herself persistently rejected the idea that her marriage was invalid, and valiantly refused to accept proposals that she should simplify the king's project by volunteering to become a nun.[52]

In the meantime, Henry was 'struck with the dart of love' for Anne Boleyn, probably about February 1526. For over two years he had been having an doubly adulterous affair with her elder sister Mary (wife of William Carey, a gentleman of the king's privy chamber who was distantly related to the king through the Beaufort family), but Anne's elegance and exceptional talents had made a big impression at court. Henry's original decision to divorce Catherine is unlikely to have been the consequence of this new affection, since there is no reason to suppose that he was interested in Anne as any more than a possible mistress until the summer of 1527. By the August of that year, however, Henry and Anne had agreed to marry once the divorce from Catherine was

---

[51] *Leviticus* 18:16, 20:21.
[52] Scarisbrick, *Henry VIII*, 163–4, 214, 218, 224.

completed, and from that time on Anne became an independent driving force behind the protracted divorce proceedings.[53]

Henry VIII himself took an active part in promoting the case for his divorce, and was largely responsible for managing the propaganda that accompanied his campaign.[54] The legal proceedings, meanwhile, were entrusted to the king's chancellor and chief councillor, Thomas Wolsey, one of the most eminent churchmen in Europe; he was archbishop of York (1514–30), bishop of Durham (1523–9), and had been a cardinal since 1515.[55] Wolsey was one of the first to know about the king's wish for a divorce in the spring of 1527. He held a secret preliminary investigation of the issues at Westminster on the 17 May following, even before the queen herself knew what was afoot. He decided, at that point, that the points of law were too problematic for a decision to be taken as a matter of routine, and that negotiations to establish a legal commission with appropriate authority would have to be opened with the papacy.[56] The failure of these negotiations, and the consequent inability of Henry VIII to solve his dynastic problem by recognized means, had the direst consequences for English politics. It led directly to the discrediting of Wolsey, and to his dismissal from the office of chancellor on 17 October 1529.[57] It also inaugurated a new phase of policy in which the king sought to get his way by bullying churchmen, using a new parliament summoned to meet on 3 November 1529 as one of his instruments.[58] The ultimate consequences of this policy – not yet perceptible in 1529 – were of profound significance for the later history of church and state in England.

[53] Ives, *Anne Boleyn*, 109.

[54] V. Murphy, 'The Literature and Propaganda of Henry VIII's First Divorce', in MacCulloch, *Reign of Henry VIII*, 135–58.

[55] The two best studies of Wolsey (which are very different in their opinions of him) are Gwyn, *King's Cardinal* and Pollard, *Wolsey*.

[56] Gwyn, *King's Cardinal*, 501–2.

[57] E. W. Ives, 'The Fall of Wolsey', in Gunn and Lindley, *Cardinal Wolsey*, 286–315.

[58] S. E. Lehmberg, *The Reformation Parliament, 1529–1536*, Cambridge 1970, 1–7.

2

Neighbours

There are direct analogies between the external policies of late medieval governments and those of modern states in so far as they concerned peace and war, as well as freedom or restriction of the movement of people and goods. Yet the principles by which external affairs are conducted have changed radically. In the Middle Ages, the primary concern of governments and their servants abroad was dynastic interest. The pretext for war was more likely to be a family claim to titles and territory, or the redress of slighted royal honour, than anything that would be acceptable to a democratic government today. Indeed kings went to war, or switched alliances, for reasons that now look absurdly frivolous. External policy of the period 1471–1529 accordingly needs to be studied as a field of activity whose norms are not self-evident to a modern observer.

This is not because there were no concepts equivalent to 'national interest' in this period. Governments recognized the importance of overseas trade as a source of precious metals, without which the circulation of money in the kingdom would run dry. They recognized, too, that the interruption of trade caused unemployment in parts of the kingdom, especially in areas of textile manufacture. The economic importance of England's increasing exports through Antwerp was a strong argument for peace with the duchy of Burgundy. These concerns were not ignored, but the fact remains that issues of external policy, and decisions concerning war and peace, were not predominantly national in character and that in the short term kings were often prepared to sacrifice important sectors of the economy to their personal concerns.

Because diplomacy was conducted primarily as a matter of relationships between families, many aspects of overseas affairs are inexplicable in terms of relations between states. An important illustration of this point concerns the activities of Edward IV's sister Margaret, who married Charles the Bold, duke of Burgundy, in 1468. After her husband's death in battle against the French at Nancy in 1477, she remained a great lady, and her palace at Malines was the focus for Yorkist resistance to the Tudors until her death in 1503. Acting in conjunction with the Habsburg rulers of the duchy of Burgundy, she conducted a vendetta against the Tudors, and raised troops to support Yorkist invasion attempts in 1487 and 1495. In his campaign against Perkin Warbeck, Henry VII was obliged to maintain a diplomatic stance towards her quite separate from that towards the Archduke Philip, ruler of Burgundy from 1493, who claimed that she had full authority in her own lands and was working independently.[1] Amongst the foreign noblemen who played an independent role in English foreign affairs was the Scottish peer, John Stuart, duke of Albany, who engaged in vigorously anti-English activities at every opportunity between 1515 and 1524. Another was Charles, duke of Bourbon, who was prepared to ally with Henry VIII against the king of France in the years 1523-4.[2]

Between 1471 and 1529 the territorial possessions of the English monarchy changed little. The principal long-term territorial gain was on the Scottish border, where Richard of Gloucester regained Berwick from the Scots in 1482.[3] No other wars or marriage alliances of the English crown in this period resulted in significant gains or losses. This was uneventful indeed in comparison with the kaleidoscopic developments amongst the ruling dynasties of continental Europe. The most spectacular gains were those of the Habsburg dynasty, which in the course of the period expanded its interests in the Burgundian Netherlands and in Spain as a result of two important marriage alliances – the first, in 1477, of Maximilian, son of the Emperor Frederick III (reigned 1440-93) to Mary, daughter and heiress of Duke Charles the Bold of Burgundy, and the second, in 1496, of their son, the Archduke Philip, to Princess Juana of Spain, who by 1500 had become heiress of the kingdoms of Castile and Aragon. These titles all came together under Charles, son of Philip and Juana, who became duke of Burgundy in 1506, king of Spain in 1516, and eventually succeeded in being elected Holy Roman Emperor as Charles V (reigned 1519-58). In addition, to this accumulation of inheritances, towards the end of the period imperial troops were achieving great successes in Italy, culminating in the defeat

[1] Weightman, *Margaret of York*, 148-86.
[2] Gwyn, *King's Cardinal*, 82, 213, 380, 384-6.
[3] Ross, *Richard III*, 47.

of the French at the battles of Pavia in 1525 and Ladriano in 1529. Meanwhile the Valois dynasty of France consolidated its hold over the territory of modern France, notably through the military take-over of parts of the Burgundian Netherlands between 1477 and 1482, the reversion to the crown of rights in Anjou, Maine and Provence in 1481, and the acquisition of Brittany by war and by the marriage in 1491 of Anne of Brittany to Charles VIII of France (reigned 1483–98).

The absence of effective territorial aggrandizement under the English kings is attributable not to any commitment to pacifism but to the lack of available resources for war. The primary question of external policy for English kings was how to benefit from antagonism between their better-resourced neighbours, as conflict between the Valois kings of France and the Valois dukes of Burgundy[4] broadened into conflict between the Valois and Habsburg dynasties. By comparison with Habsburg and Valois resources, the Yorkist and Tudor kings were lightweights, and this explains why England was so rarely committed to warfare between 1471 and 1529. English campaigns were minor, brief and spaced out. Some of them, such as Henry VII's French campaign of 1492 or Henry VIII's French campaign of 1522, were undertaken tardily in accordance with treaty obligations.[5] Nothing in English history compares with the commitment of Habsburg and Valois troops to campaigns in Italy, a theatre of war in which England took no direct interest. A distinction may be made between Henry VIII and his three predecessors, to the extent that he was more eager than they had been to compete for honour abroad. The period 1471–1509, though not without a few aggressive gestures, is chiefly interesting for its defensive policies; between 1509 and 1529, by contrast, the English crown had more obvious competitive intentions. Even Henry VIII, however, was obliged to content himself with brief episodes of martial display rather than with the sustained pursuit of military objectives necessary for a convincing conqueror.

Edward IV

An obvious worry for the governments of England in the late fifteenth century was the ease with which a king of England

---

[4] Jean II, the second Valois king of France (1350–64), was the father of both Charles V of France (1364–80) and Philip the Bold, duke of Burgundy (1363–1404). The latter had become count of Flanders in 1384 through his marriage to the heiress.

[5] Chrimes, *Henry VII*, 281–2; Scarisbrick, *Henry VIII*, 94–6.

could be turned off his throne. Recent events had demonstrated the effectiveness of a simple tactical recipe for would-be kings. The basic programme was to invade England from a continental base, preferably at a point on the coast where support could be expected to concentrate, and then to force battle on the reigning king before he had time to get his forces together. The annual budget of English kings was not enough to sustain any sort of standing army or police force. For raising troops in a hurry the king relied upon the leading noblemen and gentlemen of the shires, who might just as well be foes as friends in a period of political crisis.[6] In the course of 1471, troops had been raised against Edward IV by the earl of Warwick in Warwickshire during March and by Thomas Fauconberg in Kent in May.[7] Even if noblemen remained loyal, they could not be depended upon to assemble troops rapidly at some unpredictable spot chosen by the invader. The security of the monarchy depended on the idea that rebellion would not succeed, and by 1471 such confidence had been repeatedly undermined. A slight subvention from France had been enough to overthrow Edward in 1470, and only modest help from Burgundy had restored him. The point was obvious to all onlookers. On 18 April 1471, Sir John Paston speculated that God could easily reverse the marvels he had brought about, and probably soon would. Looking back on Edward's triumphal return, the French observer Philippe de Commynes shrugged his shoulders: 'So you see what English changeability is like .... Of all the world's nations the English are the most prone to these battles.'[8]

The threat of invasion, even by minuscule armies and improbable claimants to the throne, was not one that the government could afford to take lightly. The best hope was to deter such expeditions by responding to them promptly. It seems likely that the withdrawal of Thomas Fauconberg's pardon and his execution in September 1471 were a response to the fear that he might assist such invasion plans. There was another invasion scare in September 1473 when the earl of Oxford, who had gone into exile after the battle of Barnet, seized St Michael's Mount in Cornwall and held it. He was presumably hoping to hold it as a bridgehead for a Lancastrian invasion in the winter of 1473–4, but no invasion came. Oxford was captured there in February

[6] Lander, *Limitations*, 14.
[7] *Arrivall*, 8, 33.
[8] *Paston Letters*, i, 438; Commynes, i, 217.

1474, and spent the rest of Edward's reign as a prisoner at Hames, near Calais.[9] Fear of invasion subsided for a few years, only to return with renewed force after Richard III's usurpation.

War was not always a good idea for a medieval English king. It was expensive, and parliaments rarely contributed generously even when they recognized an obligation to pay something. It was possible, too, for a king to lose reputation through incompetence or misfortune, especially when neighbours were large, wealthy and populous. On the other hand, if all went well, a military expedition could have positive advantages for royal authority. External aggression could enhance not only a king's international prestige but also his position at home. On this latter pattern of reasoning – interwoven with the additional consideration that the French king supported the Lancastrian cause – Edward IV decided early after his return to the throne in 1471 that he would try to emulate the achievement of Henry V.

France at this time was united in a way it had never been in the days of Henry V's invasions earlier in the century, but an encouraging feature of the 1470s, that had some parallel with the 1410s, was the running conflict between the dukes of Burgundy and the kings of France. It was in the course of this aggression that each side had so wantonly intervened in English politics in the crises of 1470–1. After Edward's victory in 1471, one of his first acts was to send an embassy to Charles the Bold to prepare the ground for a great scheme to invade France and lay claim to the throne.[10] In Edward's first parliament, which opened in 1472, he sought finance for this venture, stressing the insecurity of the realm in the midst of its enemies, by which he meant the kings of France and Scotland. After the battles of Barnet and Tewkesbury, Edward had a recent military reputation, which no doubt helped his rhetoric. Parliament was responsive, and granted funding for 13,000 archers in the form of an extraordinary tax of 10 per cent of the annual income from land, rents and fixed annual incomes of certain other kinds, to be collected by February 1473 and set aside for the king's campaign. The plan at this stage was for an invasion within two years.[11]

In the event it was closer to three years before the campaign was able to start. This was partly because of problems in raising adequate funds, and partly because the duke of Burgundy was

[9] R. H. Britnell, 'Richard, Duke of Gloucester, and the Death of Thomas Fauconberg', *The Ricardian*, x (1995), 174–84; Ross, *Edward IV*, 192.

[10] *Crowland Continuations*, 130.

[11] *Rot. Parl.*, vi, 4–6.

heavily committed with ambitions of his own, and wanted negotiated guarantees that he would receive territory in north-eastern
France in exchange for supporting England. A new timetable,
agreed with Charles the Bold by the treaty of London, entailed
Edward's army moving into France by 1 July 1475. Edward himself crossed to France on 4 July, but shipping the whole army
took about three weeks. By the time the English forces were
ready for action the chances against their achieving anything had
greatly narrowed. Charles, who had undertaken to support the
English invasion with 10,000 men, was now otherwise occupied,
and left the English to manage on their own. At the same time,
Louis XI of France (1461–83) showed himself to be well prepared to meet the invaders. Edward backed off. On 12 August he
opened negotiations with the French, and by 29 August the two
sovereigns were able to meet at Picquigny to compose a seven-
year truce. Edward was to take his army home in return for a
down-payment of 75,000 crowns and an annual pension of 50,000
crowns to be paid in London. It was agreed that the dauphin,
Charles, should marry Edward's daughter Elizabeth.[12] Contemporary observers could not agree whether this was an intelligent
outcome or whether both kings had made fools of themselves.[13]

   Edward was financially better off as a result of his aborted war.
The settlement of 1475 was a turning point in his career, and its
implications governed his approach to foreign affairs for the rest
of his reign. He had a strong interest in maintaining peace with
Burgundy, since the dislocation of normal trading relations would
cause economic recession in sectors of employment dependent on
the Antwerp market – especially the cloth industry – and would
reduce royal income from customs dues. On the other hand, because the pension from France made such a significant contribution to his annual income, he had a reason for not offending
the French. These two considerations implied that Edward's best
course was to stay out of the conflict between the two rivals.
In 1477, as we have seen, the duchy of Burgundy was brought
into the Habsburg domains. The dowager duchess, Margaret of
Burgundy, eventually succeeded in drawing her brother into a
perpetual alliance with Burgundy and the Empire in 1480, but
this was not a belligerent alliance, since the emperor was making
peace with France the same year. Yet Edward's passive stance left

   [12] Ross, *Edward IV*, 210, 226–34; Scofield, *Edward the Fourth*, ii, 129–45; R. Vaughan,
Charles the Bold, London 1973, 340, 348–50.
   [13] *Paston Letters*, i, 486; *Crowland Continuations*, 136; Commynes, ii, 70; Basin, ii,
240–4.

him without leverage on the course of events. In the last years of his reign, he was left as a bystander, and when Louis XI and Maximilian, duke of Burgundy made the treaty of Arras in December 1482, by which Louis XI accepted a marriage between the dauphin and Margaret of Austria, Edward's dynastic and financial interests were altogether thwarted; his pension from France was stopped, since Louis no longer had need of his friendship, and his hope of marrying his daughter Elizabeth to the French dauphin was dashed.[14] A dossier of information on the French betrayal, issued in time for the parliament of January 1483, is the first known piece of printed propaganda issued by an English government.[15]

Edward's judgement in making peace in 1475 had been sound, even if ignominious.[16] The honour to be achieved by warfare was uncertain, and he did not have the revenues to afford it. By contrast, the advantages of healthier royal budget were plain. By 1480 the average annual income of the crown was higher than it had been in the 1460s, largely owing to an expansion of customs revenues (which would have been jeopardized by war with Burgundy) and by the pension from Louis XI (which would have been forfeited in the event of war with France). The only other appreciable source of increased income was the revenue from the duke of Clarence's estates, forfeited to the crown at the time of his attainder. One of the advantages of peace, combined with an increased normal income, was that Edward did not need to ask parliament for grants of taxation between 1475 and 1483.[17] Since shortage of funds, and dependence on the goodwill of reluctant parliaments, had become a major source of the crown's weakness by 1471, it is arguable that Edward had done something to remedy the situation.

The diplomatic isolation of Edward in his last years may have owed something to his ill health, and this may also explain why in 1480 he allowed his brother, stirred by territorial ambitions, to lead a raid against Scotland in the novel role of lieutenant-general of the north. Gloucester conducted another invasion of Scotland in 1482 with the object of replacing the king of Scots, James III, by his brother Alexander, duke of Albany. In the event, though Gloucester was able to take Edinburgh, Albany wisely decided

---

[14] Ross, *Edward IV*, 292.

[15] *John Vale's Book*, 71, 253–5.

[16] For an argument to the contrary, however, see C. R. Richmond, '1485 and All That, or What Was Going On at the Battle of Bosworth', in Hammond, *Richard III*, 186–91.

[17] Ross, *Edward IV*, 381, 384–5.

that it would not be an easy matter to rule Scotland as a puppet of the English crown, and came to terms with his enemies. The ostensible purpose of the campaign was thereby undermined. Gloucester's successes nevertheless consolidated his high reputation in the north, especially when he succeeded in taking Berwick for the English on 24 August.[18]

Richard III

It took some time to wean Richard from his preoccupation with Scotland, and a state of war continued until the negotiation of a three-year truce in September 1484. This came about partly because of intensive Scottish overtures for peace, and partly because of the financial difficulty of pursuing a northern war with any vigour, but also because of the increasingly obvious need for finesse in England's diplomacy on the Continent. Relations with duke Francis II of Brittany were especially critical, because he was acting as host to enemies of the Yorkist regime in exile, whose number was augmented in 1483 by refugees fleeing from England after rebellion had failed. Since England and Brittany were engaged in prolonged disputes over responsibility for the maritime piracy committed by ships from both sides of the Channel, the duke of Brittany was willing to make the most of any embarrassment he could inflict on the English king. This meant that throughout his reign Richard was aware of a claimant to his throne, patronized by his enemies, and waiting only for the opportunity to invade. Indeed, in November 1483 Henry Tudor attempted such an invasion somewhere on the south coast with 5000 men supplied by the duke of Brittany, though he was too late to coincide with the internal uprising that year; his enterprise was reduced to a fiasco by a combination of bad weather and the readiness of Richard's coastal defences.[19]

Richard responded to the threat from Brittany by stepping up aggression against Breton ships and merchants. Commissions were issued to royal servants to take to sea in pursuance of this naval war of attrition. The use of force was backed up by diplomatic overtures to Duke Francis to persuade him to abandon Henry Tudor's cause. This policy had positive effects in the autumn of 1484, when Francis was ill and the government of the duchy was

[18] Pollard, *North-Eastern England*, 235–44.
[19] Chrimes, *Henry VII*, 26–7.

in the hands of his treasurer, Pierre Landais. The Breton government needed support against its own political opponents in France and Brittany, and this was just what Richard was offering Francis, along with the title and estates of Henry Tudor's own earldom of Richmond. Henry was luckily informed by Bishop Morton, then in Flanders, that the Bretons were about to extradite him to England, and with a small retinue he escaped secretly from Vannes to the French court before he could be arrested, probably in September 1484. Duke Francis then allowed the remaining English exiles to join Henry in France.[20]

The decision by the French court to adopt Henry Tudor's cause and support another invasion of England was an unpredictable turn of good fortune for the Tudor cause. Following the death of Louis XI on 30 August 1483, leaving a thirteen-year-old heir, the government of France was contested between the young king's elder sister, Anne of Beaujeu, whose party won the political struggle, and his brother-in-law, Louis duke of Orléans (later King Louis XII of France), who lost it. In September 1483 the opposition Orléans party had established a common cause with duke Francis of Brittany, who was simultaneously cementing better relations with England. The decision of the French government to support Henry Tudor's invasion was therefore a temporary expedient to weaken the alliance between the duke of Orléans, the duke of Brittany and the king of England.[21]

Henry VII

In contrast to the failed attempt of 1483, Henry's invasion plan in 1485 worked without even the benefit of internal rebellion. He took between 3500 and 4500 men from the River Seine in northern France to Mill Bay in Pembrokeshire.[22] Between the time when he landed on 7 August and his conflict with Richard III at Bosworth on 22 August he picked up perhaps between 500 and 1500 additional men. He was lucky to defeat Richard with such a small and miscellaneous force, but his success confirmed, for all to see, the defencelessness of English monarchy.[23] The next

---

[20] Griffiths and Thomas, *Making*, 110–18.
[21] F. J. Baumgartner, *Louis XII*, Stroud 1994, 24–8; Griffiths and Thomas, *Making*, 118–19.
[22] Commynes, ii, 234; Chrimes, *Henry VII*, 39–40.
[23] His total force at Bosworth, excluding Sir William Stanley's 3000 men in the wings, is said to have been 5000: Chrimes, *Henry VII*, 47–8.

attempt at the same ploy came within two years, aiming to restore the Yorkist cause in the person of Lambert Simnel, with financial backing from Margaret of Burgundy. A force of between 1500 and 2000 German mercenaries, supplemented with a unknown number of miscellaneous Irish troops, sailed from Dublin to Furness in Lancashire, where they landed on 4 June 1487. They attracted little support on their advance southward through Sedbergh, Masham, Boroughbridge and Doncaster. Even so, Henry's victory in the battle of Stoke on 16 June was not a foregone conclusion.[24]

There was a danger of further invasion attempts of the same sort so long as there were claimants to the throne at large. The way Perkin Warbeck could conspire with England's neighbours again demonstrated their confidence that this was a sure way to embarrass an English king. Since Henry was disseminating evidence about Warbeck's true origins by the summer of 1493, and since the French and the Burgundians were at least as well positioned as Henry to establish the truth, it is unlikely that Warbeck's success as a Yorkist prince from that time was more than a diplomatic ploy. He was first adopted by the French, at a time when Henry VII threatened France in an attempt to preserve the independence of the duchy of Brittany. In 1491 his claims first became known to a wider public when he was temporarily welcomed in Cork. He was momentarily accepted as a prince in France, until England and France made peace at the Treaty of Etaples in November 1492. He was then taken up by Margaret of Burgundy. After she had no more use for him, in the summer of 1495 he turned to Ireland, where he was welcomed again by the earl of Desmond. However, he then found a more promising backer in James IV of Scotland, at whose court he stayed from November 1495 to July 1497.[25]

During the course of his wanderings Warbeck tried to invade England three times. The first proposal, supported by Margaret of Burgundy and the Emperor Maximilian I (reigned 1493–1519),[26] was for a small force to invade in 1495 backed by insurrection within England. Henry's intelligence system enabled him to scotch the internal rebellion before the plan could be put into effect, so that when Warbeck eventually attempted to land on the coast at Deal in July his forces were easily destroyed. The second invasion, with Scottish forces in September 1496, advanced no more

[24] Bennett, *Lambert Simnel*, 63, 68–9, 71, 87, 98–9; Chrimes, *Henry VII*, 76–7.
[25] Arthurson, *Perkin Warbeck*, 50–1, 53–9, 113–16, 121, 170–2.
[26] Maximilian I was duke of Burgundy by marriage.

than a few miles beyond the Scottish border before turning back. After having been abandoned by James IV of Scotland, Warbeck then made his third and last invasion attempt by lending his name to the Cornish uprising of September 1497. It was in the course of that campaign that he was captured.[27]

In international diplomacy Henry's main task was to reduce the perils from abroad. This, together with his financial situation, recommended a predominantly non-interventionist policy on the continent. Only once was Henry drawn into engagement with France, and that was because of an obligation to the duchy of Brittany under the treaty of Redon of 1489. Francis II, duke of Brittany, Henry's former protector, had died in 1488 leaving a twelve-year-old heiress to succeed him. She was promptly claimed as a ward by Charles VIII of France, who had designs to reduce the independence of the duchy. Increasing French control of the Channel coast was against English interests and met with diplomatic opposition. Despite military threats by England and the Empire, however, Charles took over the duchy and married Anne in December 1491. In this situation Henry took to arms, though his campaign was little more than a gesture of disapproval. An army crossed from England to Calais in October 1492, laid siege to Boulogne, then promptly accepted proposals for peace. Charles VIII, who wanted to be free for campaigning in Italy, was willing to buy Henry off for a money payment of 745,000 crowns payable at the rate of 50,000 crowns a year, part of which was for arrears due under Edward IV's treaty of Picquigny. He also promised not to help rebels against Henry, and promptly broke off relations with Perkin Warbeck.[28]

The opening of the Italian Wars, with the invasion of northern Italy by Charles VIII of France in 1494, benefited Henry VII to the extent that it turned the focus of diplomatic and military concern away from north-western Europe, and made it easier for Henry to pursue an honourable policy of neutrality. The support or neutrality of England was worth cultivating by rulers who sent armies southwards. Once Henry had successfully dealt with the challenge from Warbeck, he was in a strong position to negotiate for dynastic recognition from his neighbours. A principal wing of this policy was the negotiation of marriages which integrated the Tudors into other royal dynasties and confirmed a structure of alliances that would minimize the support future claimants

---

[27] Arthurson, *Perkin Warbeck*, 108–20, 140–9, 169–90.
[28] Chrimes, *Henry VII*, 82–3, 281–2; A. Grant, *Henry VII*, London 1985, 39.

of the throne could expect. To this end, Henry forged new ties with the Habsburg and Stuart families. In 1501, in accordance with the treaty of Medina del Campo (1489), his elder son, Arthur, was married to Catherine of Aragon, a younger sister of the heiress to the thrones of Aragon and Castile. Henry's daughter Margaret married James IV of Scotland (reigned 1488–1513) in 1503. Arthur died in 1502, but, as we have seen,[29] both the English and Spanish courts immediately set about maintaining the connection by negotiating for the marriage of Catherine to Arthur's younger brother. Henry VII was also determined in the last years of his reign to maintain a friendly attitude towards France. He resisted the attempts of the Spanish court to negotiate him into hostility to Louis XII of France (reigned 1498–1515) in 1503, and in 1505 he proposed a marriage alliance between the French and English royal families. By such means, he succeeded in maintaining good diplomatic relations with his neighbours while avoiding involvement in the affairs of northern Italy. In 1508, when the League of Cambrai was formed against Venice, Louis XII of France, the Emperor Maximilian, the Archduke Charles, Ferdinand of Aragon and the pope were all members, but Henry VII was left out. He was nevertheless in the strong position of being neither isolated nor overcommitted.[30]

The chief diplomatic problem of Henry VII's last years illustrates well the dynastic issues that shaped international diplomacy. In 1504 Queen Isabella of Castile died, and her kingdom was inherited by her daughter, Princess Juana. Juana's husband, the Archduke Philip, leapt at the chance of becoming king of Castile. The crowns of Castile and Aragon, which had been temporarily united by the marriage of Isabella to Ferdinand of Aragon in 1469, were now once more divided, and remained so until Ferdinand's death in 1516. Since there was antagonism between Philip of Castile and Ferdinand of Aragon, Henry VII had some complex decisions to make. The marriage alliance under discussion between Prince Henry and Catherine of Aragon implied friendly relations with her father, Ferdinand, but at the same time England's commercial interests implied maintaining friendly relations with Philip as ruler of the Burgundian Netherlands. Henry succeeded in balancing the claims of both parties, though this particular dilemma contributed to the long delay in finalizing the Anglo-Aragonese marriage settlement.[31]

[29] Above, p. 20.
[30] Wernham, *Before the Armada*, 60.
[31] Chrimes, *Henry VII*, 295–6.

The details of Henry VII's diplomatic relations with Spain, Burgundy and Denmark all illustrate his awareness of English trading interests. Commercial prosperity was to his private advantage, in fact, because of the importance of customs revenues for royal income. The principal area of his concern was inevitably the Netherlands. A major treaty with the Archduke Philip in 1496 created the foundation for rising English exports in the early sixteenth century.[32]

Henry VIII

Henry VIII took a more interventionist part than his predecessors in the affairs of western Christendom. His external policy was founded on an assumption of internal stability, and was more outward-looking and spasmodically aggressive than his father's. It would be misleading to speak of Henry's wanting to dominate his neighbours, since he was never in a position to do this, and well knew it. On the other hand, passivity had no appeal for him, he tended to exaggerate his chances of military gains, and the years from 1509 to 1529 may be analysed as a series of initiatives intended to enhance his reputation amongst his fellow kings and princes.[33]

The course of Henry's policy oscillated between different strategies, and historians have had difficulty in defining any consistent goals. Between 1509 and 1513 he was set on war with France, following the pattern of Henry V. He fought a minor French campaign in 1512 and a more extended one in 1513. In this latter year, Henry brought England as close as it ever came to military glory between 1471 and 1529. In that year the king's armies crossed to Calais, fought a minor skirmish, grandiosely known as the battle of the Spurs, at which a number of important prisoners were taken, and then occupied Thérouanne and city of Tournai on the borders between France and the Burgundian Netherlands. The chief reason for taking territory so separated from other English lands was diplomatic pressure from the Emperor Maximilian. Instead of handing over Tournai to the Empire, however, English forces occupied it and the surrounding countryside. Meanwhile, James IV of Scotland led a large army into northern England, taking advantage of the absence of the

---

[32] Wernham, *Before the Armada*, 62–76; below, p. 230.
[33] On the goals of Henry's foreign policy, see in particular Gunn, 'French Wars', 28–51; Gwyn, 'Wolsey's Foreign Policy', 755–72.

king and his armies abroad. On 9 September 1513, James encountered an English army under the earl of Surrey, and in the
drawn-out battle of Flodden, lasting from four in the afternoon
till nightfall, suffered a devastating defeat in which he himself
was killed.[34]

Having made peace with France in August 1514, the following few years were a period of relative disengagement. However,
the English crown entered vigorously into European affairs again
from the summer of 1517 in order to exploit a period of respite
in the antagonism between the Habsburg and Valois dynasties.
The years 1517–21 were years of universal peacemaking, in which
Cardinal Wolsey's intermediary role was diplomatically important.
By the treaty of London of October 1518 the kings of England
and France agreed to terms of peace. This was promptly followed
by a broadening of the peace to include Spain, the Emperor and
the papacy, all of whom pledged themselves to perpetual amity,
with a professed aim of cooperating against the Turks in eastern
Europe.[35] In February 1519, under the terms of the treaty of London, Tournai was unceremoniously returned to the French, and
in June the following year the courts of England and France held
a joint celebration of peace. This was the famous meeting known
as the Field of the Cloth of Gold, an event, lasting sixteen days,
which took place between Guines, a village administered by the
English at Calais, and Ardres, which was on the territory of the
king of France.[36] Another major peacekeeping operation of this
period was the Calais Conference between August and November
1521. By this time the peace between Habsburg and Valois was
breaking down, though at Calais Wolsey was prominent in the
unpromising attempts to shore it up again.[37]

The attempt failed, and once conflict had again broken out
between Habsburg and Valois forces England reverted to its traditional hostility to France, in alliance with the Emperor Charles V.
Henry VIII's armies fought the French in 1522, and with greater
force in 1523, though he no longer led them in person. By comparison with the victories of 1513, the French campaign of September 1523, led by Henry's brother-in-law, the duke of Suffolk,

---

[34] Cruikshank, Henry VIII and the Invasion; Cruikshank, English Occupation; Nicholson, Scotland, 600–6.

[35] Gwyn, King's Cardinal, 92–103; G. Mattingley, Renaissance Diplomacy, Harmonds-worth 1965, 159–60; Wernham, Before the Armada, 93–7.

[36] Hall, 603–20; Cruikshank, English Occupation, 263–4; J. G. Russell, The Field of the Cloth of Gold, London 1969.

[37] Gwyn, 'Wolsey's Foreign Policy', 755–72; Russell, Peacemaking, 93–132.

was an inglorious business, though not sufficiently disastrous to damage Henry's reputation. An army of 10,000 failed to capture Boulogne but advanced to within fifty miles of Paris. However, Henry was let down by his allies, the weather turned foul, and the mutinous English troops scrambled back towards the coast as fast as they could.[38] Neither in 1522 nor 1523 did English troops receive the expected support from their allies, and the government's enthusiasm for the imperial alliance cooled in the face of repeated snubbing by the emperor.

In 1524 and 1525 external policy gradually moved towards an alliance with the French against the imperialists, a shift that was hastened after the battle of Pavia on 24 February 1525. In that battle French forces in Italy were defeated, and the French king captured, but Charles V made plain that all the advantages of the situation were going to be his. This further snub pushed England into a series of treaties with France, the treaty of the More (August 1525), the treaty of Hampton Court (August 1526), the treaty of Westminster (April 1527) and the treaty of Amiens (August 1527).[39] From that time onwards English external policy was dominated by determination to obtain a divorce for Henry VIII, and this reduced Wolsey's freedom of manoeuvre. When the Habsburg–Valois conflict was again drawn to a halt at the Peace of Cambrai in 1529, the English negotiators were an unwelcome presence and a complicating factor in the negotiations rather than prime movers, though English commerce benefited from the peace, and there were appropriate celebrations.[40]

Many historians, following contemporary satires and polemics, have attributed this changeableness of policy to Wolsey, and have looked to fluctuations in his private ambitions to explain changes of course. This, however, is a counsel of despair, since we know very little about Wolsey's personal ambitions, and argument along these lines rapidly becomes circular. In any case, it is unlikely that Wolsey ever exercised the sort of freedom of action that the argument implies. There are various versions of the Wolsey-centred explanation of foreign affairs, none of which works well. It has been variously argued that he was peace-loving (in contrast to Henry VIII), that he was always concerned to toe a papal line, that he was driven by a desire to become pope, and that he was

---

[38] Gunn, 'Duke of Suffolk's March', 596–634.

[39] Bernard, *War, Taxation and Rebellion*, 9–40; Giry-Deloison, 'Diplomatic Revolution?', 77–83.

[40] S. J. Gunn, 'Wolsey's Foreign Policy and the Domestic Crisis of 1527', in Gunn and Lindley, *Cardinal Wolsey*, 153; Russell, *Diplomats*, 124–5, 129–31, 136.

influenced by the bribes of foreign powers. Wolsey was indeed at times prominent in peacemaking operations, amid floods of pacifist propaganda; he was specially commissioned as a papal legate *a latere* in 1518 for the purpose of promoting the papal policy for peace within Christendom and furthering plans for a crusade.[41] On the other hand, he makes an unconvincing pacifist. His aversion to standing on the diplomatic sidelines is well attested.[42] When he had the money and occasion for war, he showed no aversion to vigorous personal commitment. His promotion by Henry VIII was accelerated because of the efficiency with which he planned the logistics of maintaining an army in France in 1513, and he was involved in the development of royal shipping at this time.[43] In 1523 Henry VIII valued his comments on handling the invasion of France, and it was Wolsey rather than the king who recommended a rapid advance towards Paris late in the year.[44] Wolsey's concern for the papacy has been much exaggerated; he followed a papal lead only when it suited him to do so. Though he was negotiating for peace as papal legate in 1518, the pope's concern to combine forces against Turkish advances in the Middle East was not reflected in his aims. Nor does the evidence support the idea that he was motivated by an ambition to become pope.[45] The idea that English foreign policy was directed by bribes to Wolsey is merely an extension of other criticisms of his acquisitiveness,[46] and ignores the extent to which the payment of pensions to foreign dignitaries was a normal feature of European diplomacy.[47]

It would have been surprising if Wolsey had been allowed to conduct English external policy to his own advantage, since this was the area of policy most closely associated with the king's standing among the crowned heads of Christendom, as well as having great implications for royal income and expenditure.[48] Foreign affairs were also an area of policy in which the king showed personal interest. Henry's talents, personal appearance and lifestyle were all matters for jealous comparison with those

---

[41] Gwyn, *King's Cardinal*, 102. A legate *a latere* ('from the side', i.e. of the pope) was commissioned as a special envoy from the pope: Pollard, *Wolsey*, 165–71.

[42] Gwyn, *King's Cardinal*, 358.

[43] Cavendish, 13–15; Wolsey had a three-masted ship reproduced on the almoner's seal: D. J. Starkey (ed.), *Henry VIII: A European Court in England*, London 1991, 174.

[44] More, *Correspondence*, 275–99.

[45] Chambers, 'Cardinal Wolsey', 20–30; Gwyn, *King's Cardinal*, 100.

[46] Vergil, 232–9, 246–9, 266–9, 274–5, 284–5, 296–7, 322–5; Skelton, 283.

[47] Gwyn, *King's Cardinal*, 95–6; Potter, 'Foreign Policy', 128–30.

[48] Potter, 'Foreign Policy', 124–6.

of his contemporaries. He was eager to inaugurate his reign with campaigns in France, following the example of Henry V. On the very first day of his reign, according to the Venetian ambassador, he promised to undertake war against France.[49] He personally led his army in the French campaign of 1513. When his father-in-law, Ferdinand of Aragon, proved himself an unreliable ally against France, Henry was so enraged that he hungered for revenge, and there were stories that he intended to divorce Catharine of Aragon. Following the accession to the throne of France of the nineteen-year-old Francis I (reigned 1515–47), Henry displayed an irresistible competitive urge. The following May, in a conversation with Piero Pasquaglio, the Venetian, Henry even showed himself concerned to make physical comparisons between himself and the French king.[50] The Field of the Cloth of Gold, in 1520, exemplifies his personal involvement in interdynastic relations. The previous year, Henry and Francis I had both sworn not to shave until they should meet, though Henry did shave, and the English ambassador in France had to make his apologies.[51] The divorce issue, again, was one driven forward by the king's personal obsession. Henry was kept informed about diplomatic affairs; he had correspondence read to him by his secretaries, he received direct communications from abroad, and he sometimes held personal interviews with both English and foreign ambassadors.[52]

Henry VIII was ambitious for military fame, and usually more eager for war than his councillors.[53] Nevertheless, the bounds of his ambitions were set by his income. This constraint will be examined in greater detail elsewhere, but it is worth observing that in the 1520s Henry VIII reached the limits of what his subjects were willing to afford. In his satirical poem 'Why Come Ye Not to Court', written around November 1522, John Skelton was already able to assume that the level of government exactions was causing discontent.[54] The following year, the government's request for funds for the pursuit of war was met in the commons by hardline resistance to keep down the cost, and the money granted was spread over four years. In 1525 the attempt to fund a possible invasion of France, in the wake of the battle

---

[49] Giry-Deloison, 'Diplomatic Revolution?', 77.
[50] A. F. Pollard, Henry VIII, illustrated edn, London 1951, 68–9.
[51] Russell, Field of the Cloth of Gold, 16.
[52] E.g. SR, i, 3–4, 12–14, 140, 209, 213, 282–3, 284–5, 325, 330–1, 331–3, 337, 339–40, 345–6.
[53] Gunn, 'French Wars', 43–4.
[54] Below, p. 237.

of Pavia, provoked widespread resistance and rebellion, and forced the king to back down.[55] It is difficult to see how the king could have been more belligerent in these years than he actually was. Failing an opportunity for military success, ostentatious peace-making maintained a high royal profile without costing much money. This was the overt goal of policy between 1517 and 1521 and again between 1525 and 1527. Peace precluded glory by force of arms, but it supplied ample opportunity for the safer, and cheaper, alternative of vying in court ceremonial and hospitality, and the English court was prepared to go far in trying to impress its neighbours. Wolsey himself was responsible for funding international receptions and ceremonies on an extravagant scale, as in his house party for an embassy of between sixty and eighty French visitors to Hampton Court in October 1527.[56]

The things to avoid, for the honour of the crown, were military disgrace, diplomatic subservience and diplomatic isolation. Henry VIII never came very close to the first of these, though he risked it in 1523. He was constantly in danger of the second, however, given the relative weakness of English diplomatic and military resources, and in 1529 he incurred the third. If direct involvement in war was too expensive, and if war between England's neighbours ruled out a general peace policy, there was little to be done but hope to show well as an honoured ally. This was often an uncomfortable position. England's trading interests and royal claims against France prejudiced Henry in favour of an alliance with the Habsburg dynasty through most of the period 1509–27, but he then risked being dragged into wars he did not have the resources to fight, as in 1522, or of having his interests disregarded, as in 1523–5. It was usually in the Habsburg interest to have England as a friendly bystander, but never to further specific goals of English policy. This weakness in England's position was a recurring source of frustration, and accounts for the switch into alliance with France after 1525, when it became clear that Charles V was far too independent of English assistance to have anything to offer. Even that, however, was to lead nowhere. England's isolation in 1529 was reminiscent of that at the end of Edward IV's reign, but the stakes were much greater as a result of Henry VIII's matrimonial dilemma.

[55] Below, pp. 121–2.
[56] Cavendish, 67–74; Potter, 'Foreign Policy', 116–18.

3

Kingship

A narrative of English political events between 1471 and 1529 is one of recurrent perils and uncertainties in which the very foundations of political stability seem at times to be under threat. Behind that eventful narrative, however, there is a much less changeable history of customs, institutions and beliefs that were tenaciously maintained throughout dynastic crises, supplying the apparatus through which these crises occurred and the language in which they were expressed. It is only through the interpretation of normal ways of acting and thinking that we can understand the tensions that came to the fore in times of political crisis. One of the best places to start is to appreciate the inherent conflict, constantly re-enacted in the rituals of political life, between the mundane financial and military limitations on the king's power to act and his exalted status as a man set above his subjects.

Financial Resources

One of the most interesting English works of fifteenth-century English political thought, Sir John Fortescue's treatise *The Governance of England*, discusses the limitation of royal resources in the 1470s. It describes the kingdom of England as 'a lordship royal and politic' in which the king might not impose laws on his subjects nor tax them without their assent. In other words, he made the existence of parliamentary politics, and the right of parliament to approve of taxation, a defining feature of a distinctively limited monarchy. This he regarded as a matter for national self-congratulation, since it meant that the people, free from excessive taxation, were prosperous, and well able to defend the realm against its enemies. Fortescue was simultaneously aware, however, that the English crown was underfunded, and consequently

vulnerable to being challenged by overmighty subjects. His recommended solution was to have the best of both worlds, holding
back taxation but building up the independent resources of the
crown.[1] This was, indeed, a policy the Yorkists and Tudors adopted
and their subjects accepted, not because they had all been reading
Fortescue, but because the problem was a generally recognized
one and the proposed solution was one in accord with the past
traditions of the kingdom.

We know little about fluctuations in the level of royal income
between 1471 and 1529, partly because of serious losses of government records, and partly because medieval kings did not organize an annual budget. They kept no single central record of their
income, but had several sets of accounts that were audited in different places at different times – some in the exchequer, some
in the royal household, some in the separate estate offices of the
duchies of Lancaster, Cornwall and elsewhere. They often made
payments directly out of estate incomes or tax revenue at source
rather than from their central accounts, so that gross receipts
are difficult or impossible to establish. For these reasons historians of royal finance cannot supply tables of royal income and
expenditure year by year.[2] On the other hand, there is no doubt
that the income of the crown increased between 1471 and 1529.

Henry VII, as a result of his inheritances and acts of attainder,
was from 1485 onwards 'the greatest royal landowner in England since the Norman Conquest'.[3] The king's normal income
remained many times larger than that of his leading subjects. For
example, the duke of Buckingham, who was England's wealthiest
landowner, received about £5000 a year from his estates at the
time of his execution in 1521, and only two other noblemen – the
earl of Derby and the earl of Northumberland – could obtain
more than £3000. At that time the king's income from land
alone, excluding revenues from the duchy of Lancaster estates,
was about £25,000.[4] Not only was the king's income from the
crown lands at least five times larger than Buckingham's, but he
also had an income from customs that, though dependent upon
parliamentary grant, had come to be recognized as a normal part
of royal revenue. As a result of royal policies to improve the
royal demesne, and of improvements in the volume of overseas
trade, the gap between the king's normal income and that of the

[1] Fortescue, *Governance*, 18–20, 109–16, 127–40.
[2] Gunn, *Early Tudor Government*, 144–56; Hoyle, 'War', 75.
[3] T. B. Pugh, 'Henry VII and the English Nobility', in Bernard, *Tudor Nobility*, 83.
[4] Gunn, *Early Tudor Government*, 114; Harris, *Edward Stafford*, 104.

leading nobility widened appreciably after 1471. To this extent the sort of policies that Fortescue recommended had had positive results. Nevertheless, the regular income of the crown was inadequate to support many of the things kings wanted to do. Henry VIII was no more able than his predecessors to fund warfare out of normal income, and his continental involvements depended upon his ability to raise extraordinary revenues.

The royal income between 1461 and 1470 had averaged about £72,000 a year.[5] By 1502–5, this had risen to about £105,000,[6] and by 1522–7 to about £180,000.[7] Allowing for the effects of rising prices in the early sixteenth century, the king's income had increased by about 80 per cent in real terms. The scale of this achievement was reduced, however, by the extent to which Henry VIII's income came to depend on precarious sources of funding. Some of the increase was the result of greater efficiency in managing the king's income from land and feudal dues, which had risen from about £30,000 in the 1460s to about £40,000 in 1502–5 before dropping back again in Henry VIII's earlier years.[8] Revenue from customs rose from about £25,000 a year in the 1460s to about £40,000 between 1500 and 1520 before dropping to about £35,000 in the 1520s. This implies that the gains between the 1460s and 1502–5 were largely independent of extraordinary taxes, since three-quarters of it derived from the increased incomes from land and customs duties.[9] The increases in Henry VIII's first twenty years were quite different, however, since income from land and customs duties had fallen, so that the increase in royal income between 1502–5 and 1522–7 was based on extraordinary revenues – mostly grants of lay and clerical taxation – that could not be levied every year.[10] This increased dependence upon parliament meant that the estimated royal income in 1522–7 was more politically contingent than that of the earlier years, and that the level of government funding had become more volatile.

Even if the whole of the royal income in the 1520s had been guaranteed from year to year it would not have allowed Henry VIII to operate on equal terms with Francis I of France or the Emperor Charles V, whose annual incomes were equivalent to

[5] Ross, *Edward IV*, 371–3.
[6] Wolffe, *Crown Lands*, 217, 223.
[7] This figure allows £80,000 a year from regular income and £100,000 from extraordinary income: Hoyle, 'War and Public Finance', 77, 89.
[8] Ross, *Edward IV*, 373; Wolffe, *Royal Demesne*, 219; Wolffe, *Crown Lands*, 76–7.
[9] Grant, *Henry VII*, 41–6.
[10] See below, pp. 112–16.

about £800,000 and £1,100,000 respectively.[11] The Marignano campaign of 1515 alone cost Francis I about 7.5 million *livres tournois*, equivalent to about £750,000 in sterling, which was perhaps over six times Henry's income for that year.[12] These differences are relevant to understanding the king's authority at home, since they illustrate how dependent he was upon his subjects to be able to put up any sort of show in European affairs. The aim of foreign policy was necessarily to make as much of a mark as possible with sums of money too small to support prolonged military campaigns.

Military Resources

Perhaps the most striking consequence of the restraints on royal funding was the absence of a permanent armed force in Yorkist and Tudor England except in a few scattered defensive positions. There were permanent garrisons on the northern border at Berwick and Carlisle, and another at Calais, all told amounting probably to between 2000 and 3000 men. The Yorkist kings had small bodyguards in times of military tension, and Henry VII made this a permanent feature of the royal establishment by creating the yeomen of the guard. Though this has been interpreted as a sign of insecurity on Henry's part, it was a very tiny force. Between 1510 and 1515, Henry VIII added a small corps of fifty noble-born 'king's spears', each with three attendants.[13] None of these troops was sufficiently mobile to constitute the basis for a field force.

Military support for the monarchy depended closely on the effectiveness of administration and lordship in the shires. One system of military recruitment, whose origins go back to the Saxon *fyrd*, rested upon the ancient obligation of all able-bodied adult men between the ages of sixteen and sixty to serve in a county militia in times of danger. Commissioners of array, or sheriffs in times of emergency, were specially appointed to raise a stated number of men, and for this purpose they would use information supplied by constables from the villages and towns of their area. Recruits had to be supplied with suitable clothing and weapons,

[11] Ross, *Edward IV*, 387. The total income of Francis I (ordinary and extraordinary) was 7.8 million *livres tournois* in 1523: Knecht, *Renaissance Warrior*, 196. See also D. Potter, 'Foreign Policy', in MacCulloch, *Reign of Henry VIII*, 111–12.

[12] Knecht, *Renaissance Warrior*, 185. Henry's income in 1515 is here estimated as £25,000 from crown lands, £40,000 from customs, £7000 from wards and liveries and £45,000 from parliamentary taxes, a total of £117,000.

[13] Lander, *Limitations*, 14–15, 63; Cruikshank, *Henry VIII and the Invasion*, 164–5.

and in some cases local communities were expected to give financial support to the men taken on the king's service.[14] County militias served chiefly as a home guard to resist rebellion or repel invasion. This did not necessarily mean that they stayed close to their homes. In October 1523, for example, the king ordered his subjects of every degree in Staffordshire, Nottinghamshire, Derbyshire and Shropshire to be ready at a day's notice to go north to serve under the earl of Surrey in the war against the Scots.[15] Forces of this sort had definite value where they could be swiftly levied and securely led, but there were serious limitations on their reliability. Conscription by the arrayers was often unwelcome, particularly when village communities had to bear the costs, and the unpopularity of Edward IV in 1470 was increased by the resentment of people being called to battles 'far out their countries at their own cost'.[16] A second disadvantage of the system, particularly in the event of rebellion, was that the king's enemies could sometimes take over local troops to use them against him. The ability of local officers to raise troops supposedly in the king's name, and then involve them in civil war, was another feature of mid-fifteenth-century disturbances that had bred hostility to the system. In 1487, uncertainties about Sir Edmund Bedingfield's authority to array troops in Norfolk hampered his ability to do so.[17] Those arrayed from county militias did not expect to serve for long, and troops levied in this way were not therefore suitable for campaigns abroad.

Service of this kind was most valuable near the borders. In the north, the crown appointed members of the nobility as wardens of the marches to supervise border defence and to monitor cross-border relations. Whenever the wardens required it, northern landlords had to muster their men to fight the Scots, so that in this region the obligation of men to perform military service became akin to an incident of tenure. Tenants had to maintain a horse and appropriate equipment. Money rents were kept low in order to accommodate this military obligation.[18] Such tenures could

---

[14] Cruikshank, *Henry VIII and the Invasion*, 169–70; Goodman, *Wars of the Roses*, 137–8.

[15] *Tudor Royal Proclamations*, i, no. 97, pp. 142–3.

[16] Warkworth, 12.

[17] For county militias in the late fifteenth century see Goodman, *Wars of the Roses*, 137–51.

[18] S. G. Ellis, *Tudor Frontiers and Noble Powers: The Making of the British State*, Oxford 1995, 39, 98; R. W. Hoyle, 'An Ancient and Laudable Custom: The Definition and Development of Tenant Right in North-Western England in the Sixteenth Century', *P&P*, 116 (1987), 25.

provide substantial numbers of troops for northern campaigns. A survey of the Percy estates in Northumberland compiled in the 1530s reported that 'there be of tenants and able men, resident and inhabiting with[in] the said lordships and manors, ready to serve the king, having jack-coat (= jacket) of fence (= defence) and harness with long spears, bows and other weapons in a readiness whensoever they shall be called upon, to the number of 1967, whereof horsemen 849, footmen 1118'. In theory a further 3310 horsemen and 5964 foot-soldiers could be raised from the earl's estates in Cumberland and Yorkshire.[19]

The commonest form of military service, meanwhile, was contractual, and this was the universal form of armies taken on campaigns into France (as in 1475, 1492, 1512–13 and 1522–3), Scotland (as in 1482, 1513, 1522–3) or Ireland (as in 1520). When the king raised troops, noblemen and gentlemen were chosen to serve as captains in the army and were obliged to recruit a certain number of men to serve under them. The detailed arrangements might be the result of personal negotiation and the drawing-up of formal indentures between king and captain, but Henry VIII abandoned the use of this form of recruitment after the first years of his reign. In preparation for his invasion of France in 1513 he merely wrote to people telling them how many men to recruit and where they should assemble for embarkation. It was taken for granted that noblemen had friends, dependants and tenants whom they could call on for the purpose.[20] Richard III and Henry VII both committed some of their more trusted supporters, both noble and non-noble, to maintaining a predetermined number of men in readiness.[21] Captains had to supplement this core of trusties by recruiting among neighbours and tenants, since they could not possibly have afforded to maintain permanently all the hundreds of men they led on campaign. The number of men sent to France and Brittany reached at least 13,000 in 1475, 26,000 in 1492, 25,000 in 1513, 15,000 in 1522 and 11,000 in 1523.[22] The importance of the landlord–tenant link for the raising of these armies is emphasized by Wolsey's General Proscription of 1522, an ambitious government fact-finding

[19] M. James, Society, Politics and Culture: Studies in Early Modern England, Cambridge 1986, 60, 76.

[20] Cruikshank, Henry VIII and the Invasion, 171; H. Miller, Henry VIII and the English Nobility, Oxford 1986, 133–4, 136.

[21] Gunn, Early Tudor Government, 40.

[22] Guy, Tudor England, 107; Ross, Edward IV, 221; R. B. Wernham, Before the Armada: the Growth of English Foreign Policy, 1485–1588, London 1966, 36, 85, 102.

exercise that aimed to record all the men in England capable of bearing arms, together with the name of the lord from whom each held land.[23] Soldiers recruited on contract with the king in this way were paid a regular wage out of royal funds so long as they were in service, but they were led by a member of the nobility or gentry to whom they were commonly attached by some tenurial or service connection.

Authority, Tradition and Myth

The fact that the financial and military resources of late medieval English kings depended on the cooperation of their subjects was plain for all to see. Edward IV and Henry VII had done something to expand the crown's independent power base by increasing the amount of income that did not depend upon parliamentary assent. Yet the significance of such policies can easily be exaggerated. The authority of the crown in 1529 remained dependent upon parliament for the slightest expansion of its activities and upon aristocratic cooperation for the most minimal use of armed force, and in this respect nothing had changed significantly in the course of the previous sixty years. Underlying royal power was a long-standing habit of obedience on the part of the king's subjects, and the build-up of independent royal income under Edward IV and Henry VII did little more than reduce frictions that would have arisen had the crown depended more heavily on taxation.

Between the 1440s and the 1460s, confidence in the king's power to enforce law and order or to defend the realm against its neighbours had been undermined, and one of the achievements of Edward IV and Henry VII was to raise the authority of the crown from the depths to which it had sunk. They were able to do this because of the deep-seated commitment to monarchical government on the part of their subjects, and it would be impossible to explain their success without reference to a general prejudice in their favour. The fundamental proposition that kings depended upon being supported and obeyed out of habit is needed to account for such regularity and order as the realm possessed between 1471 and 1529. Accounts of the period that stress the constructive activities of kings are inclined to overlook this other side of the relationship.

One powerful claim to obedience, deeply rooted in traditional

---

[23] Goring, 'General Proscription', 681–705.

values, was ancestry. Kings had this in common with their leading subjects, whose titles to status and property were characteristically founded on inheritance from their forebears. But the royal
family surpassed all, and a strong genealogical sense was inseparable from royal status, since despite all the disputes over the royal
succession that had disturbed fifteenth-century politics, the hal-
lowed status of royal blood remained uncompromised. The three
sons of York venerated their family tree, and an important part of
their political mythology involved appealing to it. Under Edward IV
genealogists were employed to carry the Yorkist line beyond the
historically legitimate, tracing Edward IV's ancestry from Adam,
through the Trojans and Britons. This form of dynasticism has been
described as old-fashioned by comparison with the symbolism of
the Burgundian court, which was more geared to the emblematic
value of classical heroes.[24] Yet it is surely significant, given the
recent history of the monarchy, that the Yorkists should appeal
to such traditional criteria of authority. The emphasis on British
descent, with the implied rejection of Anglo-Norman, had further
propaganda value in emphasizing the nationalism of the Yorkists.
They simultaneously emphasized the illegitimacy of Lancastrian
rule between 1399 and 1461, and the extent to which this had been
divinely punished through the illness of Henry IV, the wasting of
the kingdom under Henry VI and the victory given to Yorkist arms
in 1461.

Because of the circumstances of their accession, Tudor legitimizing mythology differed from that of the Yorkists in stressing
the union of rival claims rather than the purity of a primeval
claim. Royal blood remained as important to the Tudors as to
their predecessors, but they stressed the coming together, in Henry
VII's marriage to Elizabeth of York, of different flows of royal
blood, and the consequent concentration of regal status in the
Tudor children. When historians refer to the 'Tudor myth' they
signify an interpretation of history that has remained influential
to this day, chiefly because it became so much part of the thinking
of sixteenth-century England. In essence, the Tudors were believed
to have ended generations of dynastic strife (whose horrors grew in
the telling) by uniting the houses of Lancaster and York. This interpretation of the past led, in the hands of even the best sixteenth-
century historians, to a distortion of historical narratives of the
years 1450–85, and became deeply embedded in English cultural
tradition through Shakespeare's history plays. The horrors of the

[24] Ross, *Edward IV*, 301.

Wars of the Roses were described in such exaggerated terms that modern historians have had a major task in demythologizing them, and Richard III's character was so blackened that he is the only medieval English king to have a society dedicated to defending his reputation.

Henry VII did not need a propaganda machine. The Tudor myth was powerful because it was what people wanted to believe.[25] The nobility and gentry could not be secure in a world where rival dynasties repeatedly demanded their loyalty, and they were more than willing to settle for stability. The nobility had not diminished in numbers through fratricidal strife to the point that there was no one able to resist the crown. On the contrary, failure of succession in the English nobility was no more marked between 1450 and 1475 than in the preceding quarter-century.[26] But after a generation of apathy towards political conflict because of the hazards of getting involved in partisan battles, with all the associated risks of being judged a traitor for having chosen the losing side, leading families turned out in force to protect the 1485 settlement. When Henry VII set out from Nottingham to meet the earl of Lincoln's forces on 15 June, 1487, he had with him an impressive array of nobles, including Jasper Tudor, duke of Bedford, and the earls of Oxford, Derby, Shrewsbury, Devon and Wiltshire.[27] Eighteen noble retinues supported him at Blackheath in 1497.[28] It was this groundswell of commitment that enabled the Tudors to depend upon legal procedures in defending their dynastic position against all potential dangers. Firm acceptance by the nobility of the Tudor solution sealed the fate of the earl of Warwick in 1499, when he showed signs of wanting to rock the boat, and that of the duke of Buckingham in 1521. The Tudor myth was not a mendacious propaganda stunt imposed by a despotic monarchy on a divided people, but a reading of events rapidly adopted after 1485 amongst subjects of the English crown as a solution to a generally recognized problem.[29] It effectively compensated for any defects in the Tudor title to rule by inheritance.

To demonstrate the traditional force of habits of obedience is to explain how royal government and other continuities of institutional tradition survived the challenges they encountered. This

---

[25] Elton, *Studies*, iv, 89.
[26] K. B. McFarlane, *The Nobility of Later Medieval England*, Oxford 1973, 148–9, 172–6.
[27] Bennett, *Lambert Simnel*, 83.
[28] Arthurson, *Perkin Warbeck*, 166.
[29] It is already fully fledged before 1490 in Rous, 212–19.

does not mean that the habit of obedience was always unqualified. People shared loyalties and value systems other than the one that inculcated obedience to the crown. Ideas of law, religion and nationality were all double-edged to the extent that they might sometimes furnish better arguments for opposing the political establishment than for supporting it. The king's subjects also had both individual and collective material interests of their own, some of which led to rebellion, crime or simple evasion of responsibility. There is no self-contradiction, therefore, in describing the institutions and patterns of thought that normally induced loyalty to the crown while also recording examples of individuals and groups of people who, in particular circumstances, rebelled. However, the normal habit of obedience gave kings the means to resist rebellion and crime when it occurred. They expected to use force to back their government in many different contexts, and they were usually well able to do so. When, for example, disturbances broke out in East Anglia in May 1525 over the levying of the Amicable Grant, the dukes of Norfolk and Suffolk raised a force of 4000 men within two days, and the mere threat of violence was enough to subdue the resistance.[30] Most of the powerful men of the kingdom obeyed the king most of the time, and enforced his will against dissidents, even when they were being asked to endorse policies that reduced their autonomy.

Symbolic Resources

The general assumption that the king should be obeyed was expressed through a complex structure of institutionalized practices and traditional concepts. Loyalty to the king's person was orchestrated through rituals and symbols that expressed his special standing. Although the king was not mistaken for a god, or even for a priest, he partook of the sacred. The overlap between sacred and royal symbolism and ritual was considerable, and clearly points to analogies between earthly and heavenly kings that were built into contemporary ways of thought. The king was crowned and anointed in a special religious service, so this requires some attention as a royal initiation ceremony. The distinctive linguistic terminology used of the king is of interest as a feature of the way he was set apart from ordinary men, and so

[30] G. W. Bernard, *War, Taxation and Rebellion in Tudor England: Henry VIII, Wolsey and the Amicable Grant of 1525*, Brighton 1986, 81–2.

PLATE 3.1   A symbolic representation of the coronation of Henry VIII, from the unique copy of Stephen Hawes's poem 'A Joyful Meditation' (1509) in Cambridge University Library. Both Henry and Catherine are being crowned with imperial crowns. Henry has above him a large Tudor rose, and Catherine a large pomegranate (*by permission of the Syndics of Cambridge University Library*)

are the visual symbols of kingship used on buildings, coins, costumes and elsewhere. Finally, since the importance of the king's dynastic allegiance has already been illustrated in discussing events at home and abroad, it should come as no surprise that genealogical symbols were in constant use. They had the interesting property that they drew attention to the king's whole family rather than to the king as an individual. Since the habit of loyalty rested on past tradition, kings had nothing to gain by radical innovation, and most of the symbolic resources at the disposal of the Yorkists and early Tudors had been around for a long time.

Many of the symbols of kingship which the Yorkists and Tudors maintained were predictably linked with the sacred. Coronations, the grandest of all royal ceremonies, were an obvious case in point. The ceremonial, then as now, included a grand procession to and from Westminster Abbey. Having sworn a solemn oath, the new king was ritually anointed with sacred oil, then dressed in cloth of gold and crowned in accordance with a highly formalized tradition. The coronation was a public and visual expression of the honour and obedience due to a king. Yet the proportion of the population who had seen such a ceremony, let alone learned any lesson from it, was tiny. Cardinal Wolsey, whose lifetime (from 1472 or 1473 to 1530) spanned the period of this volume almost exactly, could not possibly have seen more than three coronations, and probably saw only one.

How, in everyday practice, could a king appropriate the sacred qualities attached to him at his coronation? One way was by the routine assertion that each king was king 'by the grace of God' (*Dei gracia*), a formula repeated both in documents issued by the crown and on the coinage. Other effects were achieved by special modes of address that exploited the wide overlap between divine and royal attributes and symbols. When Stephen Hawes wrote a poem on 'the coronation of our most sovereign lord King Henry the Eight' he made the most of these analogies in his address to the Almighty:

O God, alone in heaven wearing crown,
In whose inspect [= sight] is every regal see [= throne],
Both to enhance [= raise up] and for to cast down
(Such is the power of thine high majesty),
Neither hardiness, treasure nor dignity
May withstand thy strength, which is in every place,
So great and mighty is thy divine grace.

Apart from the visual representation of God as a crowned king in the first line of this stanza – parallelled later in the poem by a description of God as enthroned in Heaven – the allusions to God's 'high majesty' and to his 'grace' had their analogies in normal forms of reference to the king as 'the king's highness' and 'the king's grace' (or 'his highness' and 'his grace'). 'The king's majesty' (or 'his majesty') was another expression used, though not yet as frequently as it was from the mid-1530s.[31] Hawes cites the obedience due to both as another analogy between God and the king: 'England be true and love well each other / Obey your sovereign and God omnipotent.'[32] The expressions 'our sovereign', or more commonly 'our sovereign lord', were not new in this period, but they were adopted as standard form by Henry VII

[31] OED, under Majesty²; LP, *Richard III and Henry VII*, i, 220–1, 243, 246, 250–2, 426–30; *Tudor Royal Proclamations*, i, nos. 110, 141, 144, 150–1, 153–7, pp. 155, 211, 214, 221, 224–9.
[32] Hawes, 85–91.

PLATE 3.2 A gold sovereign of Henry VII, 1489, showing the king seated and crowned with an imperial crown (obverse) and a large Tudor rose (reverse) (*Ashmolean Museum, Oxford*)

from the beginning of his reign,[33] and he gave the name sovereign to a new gold coin first minted in 1489.[34] In conversation the king was addressed as 'your grace', 'your highness' or 'sir'.[35]

The reverence due to the king also paralleled to some degree the honour paid to God. Some features of court ceremonial exalted the king in this way. The king's principal dining-room, also known as the presence chamber, was always supplied with an upholstered throne, positioned opposite the entrance under a canopy of rich brocade, called the cloth of estate. No one other than the king was entitled to go near the throne or stand under the cloth of estate, so marking that area as taboo. Furthermore, those passing through the room when the king was absent were expected to reverence the throne and cloth of state in the same way as if he were present, 'everyone standing on foot with his cap in his hand'.[36] There was some similarity here between the royal presence in the presence chamber of a palace and the divine presence in the sanctuary of a church.

Other effects were achieved by routinely associating the king with bishops, churches and saints in the course of royal ceremonies, and all the kings of the period were dutifully pious.[37] A

[33] *Tudor Royal Proclamations*, i, nos. 3–8, pp. 4–10.
[34] The sovereign was valued at £1 (i.e. 20s): Challis, *Tudor Coinage*, 47.
[35] E.g. Cavendish, 184.
[36] Cavendish, 93; D. R. Starkey, 'Intimacy and Innovation: The Rise of the Privy Chamber, 1485–1547', in D. R. Starkey (ed.), *The English Court from the Wars of the Roses to the Civil War*, London 1987, 73; D. R. Starkey, 'The King's Privy Chamber, 1485–1547', unpublished Ph.D. thesis, Cambridge 1973, 5–6; Thurley, *Royal Palaces*, 122.
[37] For Richard III, see A. F. Sutton, '"A Curious Searcher for our Weal Public": Richard III, Piety, Chivalry and the Concept of the "Good Prince"', in Hammond, ed., *Richard III*, 63–70.

good example of the search for sanctity by association was Henry
VII's promotion of the case for recognizing Henry VI as a saint.
By 1492 the king was promoting his cause in Rome, and within
a few years he made moves to have Henry VI's body reinterred
in Westminster Abbey. Both these projects continued to occupy
him till the end of his life, though neither of them was brought
to fruition. To gain further benefit from Henry VI's sanctity, the
story was put into circulation that, by divine inspiration, he had
prophesied in 1470 that Henry Tudor would become king.[38]

Of royal symbols, the crown was always the chief, and was
used to denote the king's royal status on the coinage, which for
the first time under Henry VII (about 1504) attempted a portrait
of the king rather than an icon. Although such a time-honoured
symbol of royalty, the crown was still capable of being developed
under the Tudors. Since Henry V's coronation, and particularly
under the Yorkists, English kings had been represented as wearing an arched crown, of a type associated with the emperor. This
imperial crown became the normal image under Henry VII. In
1489 it was used for the first time on the coinage, notably on the
sovereign, whose minting was inaugurated on the same day that
England ratified the treaty of Medina del Campo. The use of this
symbol indicated that English kings, like those of the Continent,
had rejected the doctrine that the German emperor had a higher
status than themselves. When Charles V entered London in 1522
he and Henry were both presented with a sword and a an imperial crown by a figure representing Charlemagne.[39] A coin called
a crown, minted in gold, with an imperial crown and a Tudor
rose on the obverse, was introduced in 1526.[40]

Like kings elsewhere in Christendom, the Yorkists and Tudors
alike made use of family symbols as royal devices. This often
meant dispensing with the full heraldic paraphernalia available to
them to concentrate on one or two easily recognizable motifs.
Under the Yorkists the white rose of the houses of York was
frequently used, as when, following his coronation, Richard III
changed into a gown decorated with white roses and the insignia
of the Order of the Garter.[41] As a royal emblem, the rose had the
great advantage that it could be contrasted with the lily used for
centuries by the French monarchy. There is no comparable evid-

---

[38] Griffiths and Thomas, *Making*, 69–71.
[39] Hoak, 'Iconography', 57–70, 83.
[40] It was initially valued at 4s 6d, but this was changed to 5s before the end of the year:
Challis, *Tudor Coinage*, 69.
[41] Ross, *Richard III*, 140.

PLATE 3.3 Royal armorials from the west end of King's College Chapel, Cambridge, sculpted in the years 1508–15. Below three imperial crowns are a portcullis (left), a Tudor rose (right) and the royal arms supported by a dragon (left) and a greyhound (right). The portcullis and the greyhound symbolise Henry VII's claims to royal descent through the Beaufort family. The red dragon was a royal device specially favoured by the early Tudors because of its resonance in both Welsh and English tradition (*The Conway Library, the Courtauld Institute of Art*)

ence that the Lancastrians used a red rose. Henry VII seems to have invented this device for his own use by analogy with the white rose of York, but it was already well established by 1486.[42] It was a clever invention, and permitted the iconographic innovation of the Tudor rose, in which white and red petals were combined to symbolize the united blood of the houses of York and Lancaster in the Tudor children. The power of the Tudor myth is well demonstrated by the ubiquity of this symbol from early in Henry VII's reign. When Henry VIII became king in 1509 the Tudor rose symbolized his right to rule, and the point was laboured by the poets. John Skelton started his laudatory verse for the occasion with the observation that 'The rose both white and red / In one rose now doth grow',[43] and Stephen Hawes said it all:

[42] J. Ashdown-Hill, 'The Red Rose of Lancaster?', *The Ricardian*, x (1996), 406–20; Scattergood, *Politics and Poetry*, 215–16.
[43] Skelton, 110.

England be glad; the dew of grace is spread.
The dew of joy, the dew wholesome and sweet,
Distilled is now from the rose so red
And of the white, so springing from the root,
After our trouble to be refute and boot [= deliverance
                                        and remedy].
This royal tree was planted, as I know,
By God above, the rancour down to throw.

Who is the flower that doth this grace distill
But only Henry the VIII, king of his name
With golden drops all England to fulfil.[44]

In addition to roses, both Yorkist and Tudor families also used emblems of their ancestors. The Yorkists used the lion badge of the March family.[45] They also employed the sunburst, previously used by Richard II, an emblem that caused disaster for the Lancastrians at the battle of Barnet in 1471. In the heat of battle Lancastrian troops mistook men coming to their assistance wearing the earl of Oxford's blazing star for enemy troops wearing the Yorkist blazing sun, with the result that they turned on their friends.[46] The Tudors used the Beaufort portcullis, the greyhound, which was associated with their Lancastrian forerunners, and the red dragon, which signified Henry Tudor's descent from Welsh princes, though this latter connection was not one that he chose to emphasize.[47] Such emblems lacked the significance of the Tudor rose, and were often used more for decoration than with political intent. However, under the Tudors the proliferation of royal personal and family emblems, often in non-royal contexts, was carried to unprecedented lengths, and the very profusion of such motifs may have served to enhance the status of the royal family.

Not all the tokens of the king's exalted status used set imagery. Magnificence in itself registered the king's special position, and in Skelton's play, *Magnificence*, the title role represents the king himself.[48] Magnificence was perhaps most aptly reserved for visitors to court, where the royal capacity to impress depended upon the availability of appropriate buildings, furnishings and organizational skills. To Edward IV fell the costly task of restoring the dignity of the English court after the tribulations of the 1450s. The

---

[44] Hawes, 86–7.
[45] Gunn, *Early Tudor Government*, 197; Hammond, *Battles*, 117.
[46] Ashdown-Hill, 'Red Rose of Lancaster?', p. 410. Hammond, *Battles*, 77.
[47] Anglo, *Images*, 34–5.
[48] Fox, *Politics and Literature*, 237.

1460s saw the beginnings of reconstruction, but the court splend-
our became even greater after Edward's return in 1471 from exile
in the Low Countries. Chroniclers held the reconstruction of royal
palaces to be one of his chief claims to fame. Edward also raised
the standard of furnishings in the royal household. The continu-
ator of the *Crowland Chronicle* speaks of his achievements in
'the collection of gold and silver vessels, tapestries, and highly
precious ornaments, both regal and religious'. Inspired by his
time in Flanders in 1470–1, Edward built up the royal library,
purchasing some books and commissioning others, so that by the
time of his death the royal collection was worth the admiration
of foreign visitors.[49] New heights of magnificence were achieved
under the Tudors, who increased the number of palaces and increased the splendours of court entertainment both at Westminster and when the king toured the country.[50]

The most lavish expenditure at court was reserved for special
occasions, and it is these that receive the greatest attention in
contemporary descriptions. Some spilled out into the streets of
London and provided entertainment for thousands of the king's
subjects. In preparing for the wedding of Prince Arthur and Catherine of Aragon in 1501, Henry VII appointed Richard Pynson,
a leading London printer, to advertise the celebrations throughout
London.[51] The beneficial political consequences of such display are
open to doubt because of the restricted number of people likely
to see or hear them.[52] Nevertheless there was clearly an interest
in reading about them amongst the reading public, and in com-
piling his chronicle during the 1540s, Edward Hall was able to
find an extraordinary amount of detailed information relating to
the court ceremonial of the period.

Symbols, Rituals and Power

According to some anthropologists the extent to which a monarchy deploys symbolic resources is inversely related to its effective
coercive strength, and late medieval English kingship has been
interpreted in this way. This line of argument needs handling
with discretion, since in fact medieval English kings were moderate in their exploitation of sacred imagery. For the most part, the

[49] Rous, 211; *Crowland Continuations*, 138–9; Ross, *Edward IV*, 260, 264–8.
[50] Samman, 'Progresses', 59–61, 70–1.
[51] Jones and Underwood, *King's Mother*, 77.
[52] Anglo, *Images*, pp. 109–12.

relationship between God's majesty and the king's majesty was left to impress itself on the king's subjects by analogy and without great labouring. Many opportunities for exalting the person of the king – such as the proliferation of royal portraits or statues – were ignored. No kings of the period doled out literary patronage to poets in order to boost the image of authority. Much of the symbolism that has been discussed was confined to royal buildings, furnishings or court entertainments that would only be seen by people who had many material reasons for obeying the king. Even in its more commonly available forms, such as the royal portraiture on the coinage, it is not obvious that the king's subjects were all aware of the meaning of the symbolism presented to them.

The Yorkist and Tudor kings were not afraid of letting humanity show through, and did not exploit the trappings of divinity as much as they might have done. Royal personalities were not hidden under masks of office.[53] Edward IV's concern to re-establish the authority of the crown did not imply a commitment to personal remoteness and austerity. He earned a reputation, in fact, for 'conviviality, vanity, drunkenness, extravagance and passion',[54] not to mention self-indulgent sexuality, and it may be that he should be credited with loosening up the formalities that had characterized the courts of his predecessors.[55] Henry VII did not share this reputation for *bonhomie* or hedonism, but he was no recluse. He played chess, cards, dice, archery and tennis, and lost money at all of them. In the course of jousts held at court in 1494 to celebrate the creation of Prince Henry as duke of York, one of his gentleman ushers rode a horse whose trapper, made of paper, was painted with 'two men playing at dice and certain oaths written not worthy here to be rehearsed', and he did it 'to cause the king to laugh'.[56] Henry VIII in his youth was prepared to risk his court looking puerile in order to maintain the sort of carefree lifestyle that he preferred, and was taken to task by his councillors for lowering the tone of the court.[57]

Like royal financial and military resources, the symbolic resources of kingship that have been discussed here supply only a superficial explanation for the authority of the crown, though

[53] Elton, *Studies*, iii, 46–9.

[54] *Crowland Continuations*, 152–3.

[55] D. Loades, *The Tudor Court*, 2nd edn, Bangor 1992, 22.

[56] Anglo, 'Court Festivals', 14; S. J. Gunn, 'The Courtiers of Henry VII', *EHR*, cviii (1993), 39.

[57] Below, pp. 71, 128.

they well illustrate its traditional character. They were effective only as part of a much broader construction of authority in which many elements played a part, some of them significantly more closely related to everyday life. The authority ascribed to kings, in other words, can be understood only by looking beyond the monarchy itself to other institutions of society. The themes of this chapter will accordingly be picked up and developed on a broader scale through those that follow. Limitations on the power of the monarchy are examined in further detail in part II on the dimensions of politics, which discusses the different areas of political activity in which kings had to operate. Traditional grounds of obedience to the king are explored more extensively in part III on religion, law and nationality, three areas of English culture that buttressed the authority of the king both institutionally and intellectually. Although it is no longer fashionable to treat the development of parliament as the central theme in medieval English history, these tensions were more overtly formalized in meetings of parliament than on any other occasions, since parliaments acted both a check on the power of the king and as a representation of his unique authority at the head of the commonwealth of the realm.

Part II

Dimensions of Politics

4

Court and Council

The centre of power in Yorkist and Tudor England was wher-
ever the king happened to be, except in the reign of Edward
V, when the king was inside the Tower of London and his Protector was outside. There were those during the 1520s who professed to believe that Henry VIII's household had been upstaged
by Wolsey's, but Wolsey himself never doubted that the balance
of power lay with the king. At no point between 1471 and 1529
was any king trammelled by the formal conciliar constraints that
had been a mark of incompetent or irresponsible kingship since
the thirteenth century.

The king's household was the largest single unit of salaried and
fee-earning employment in England.[1] Accommodating it required
exceptional resources of imagination and flexibility because the
king had so many open-ended commitments towards visitors, and
the financial side of household organization was inevitably problematic. Nevertheless, the court remained migratory, and the number of royal palaces multiplied to increase the scope for choosing
where it should go. Where the king happened to be was rarely predictable without access to recent court news. Around Christmas
he was likely to be at Westminster, and he was often in Windsor
on 23 April to celebrate the feast of St George. But there was
little consistency of pattern from year to year, and moves were often
made at quite short notice. At the beginning of reigns, and in
moments of political crisis, kings travelled exceptional distances
to make their presence felt, often staying in other people's houses,
or in the larger abbeys. Even in quieter times, kings moved about
in the course of the year, especially in the summer months when
they went on progress, often with reduced households. In the
course of twelve months in 1478–9, Edward IV moved from

---

[1] Elton, *Studies*, iii, 41.

place to place about sixty times.[2] The concentration of royal houses in the south-east nevertheless suggests that this mobility was not chiefly for political reasons. Frequent changes of residence were desirable on grounds of health. In 1517 Henry VIII's moves were governed by his determination to escape the sweating sickness that had killed some of his pages.[3] The king's seasonal recreations, as in earlier centuries, also helped to determine his whereabouts. Edward IV, for example, was often in Woodstock (Oxfordshire) for the hunting, even in his later years, and he enlarged the parks at Eltham (Kent). Henry VII, another very keen huntsman, enlarged the park adjoining his new palace of Richmond (Surrey), and made a new park at Greenwich. Henry VIII used his hunting activities as a way of getting to know the gentry of the shires where he travelled.[4]

Different kings had their favourite houses but most of them preferred the south-eastern shires. Richard III as king was unusual for the amount of time he spent farther north; the only places where he settled for more than a fortnight outside London and Westminster were Nottingham, York and Pontefract, and he went south of the Thames only once, for a few weeks in November 1483 in response to Buckingham's rebellion. Edward IV favoured his palaces in the Thames valley, and in his later years his movements were chiefly between Westminster, Windsor (Berkshire), Eltham (Kent), Greenwich (Kent) and Sheen (Surrey). The first three of these saw some of his biggest building projects.[5] Henry VII was fond of Sheen, which his predecessor had not visited once during his reign. Between 1495 and 1501 he spent probably over £20,000 there building a palace which became a model for later Tudor palace architecture, and he called it Richmond to celebrate the title he had held from birth.[6] He would command more affection from students and tourists alike had his palace survived.

The number of royal palaces reached a peak under Henry VIII. He inherited Westminster Palace, and Baynard's Castle in London, and other residences at Windsor (Berkshire), Eltham and Greenwich (Kent), Richmond (Surrey), Clarendon (Wiltshire),

---

[2] *Household of Edward IV*, 21, 236. Henry VIII's moves in the summer were announced in advance: Samman, 'Progresses', 62.

[3] Gwyn, *King's Cardinal*, 88; Starkey, *Reign of Henry VIII*, 73.

[4] Ross, *Edward IV*, 271–2; Samman, 'Progresses', 65; Scofield, *Edward the Fourth*, ii, 439; Thurley, *Royal Palaces*, 68.

[5] R. Edwards, *The Itinerary of King Richard III, 1483–1485*, London 1983; Ross, *Edward IV*, 271, 273; Scofield, *Edward the Fourth*, ii, 429–30.

[6] Colvin, *History of the King's Works*, iv, 1, 11.

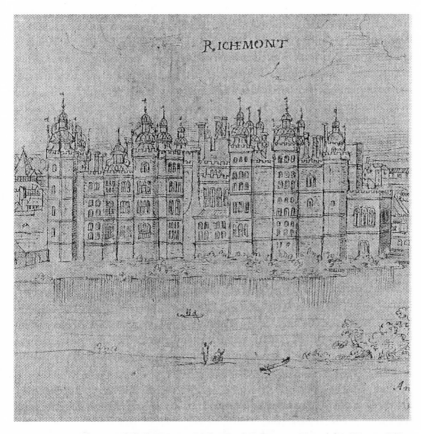

PLATE 4.1 The royal lodgings at Richmond Palace, restored by Henry VII
at the royal manor of Sheen after fire gutted an earlier house there in 1497
(*from a drawing by Anthonis van den Wyngaerde dated 1562,
Ashmolean Museum, Oxford*)

Woodstock, Langley and Minster Lovell (Oxfordshire), Ditton
(Buckinghamshire), Collyweston (Northamptonshire), Tickenhill
(Worcestershire), Havering and Wanstead (Essex), Woking (Surrey) and Hanworth (Middlesex) – as well as a number of smaller
hunting lodges. Henry himself became obsessed with the accumulation and rebuilding of houses. The residential parts of Westminster Palace burned down in 1512, and what was left was then
abandoned to accommodate lawyers, administrators and meetings of parliament. But Westminster Palace was replaced by several new London palaces – one at Bridewell, just beyond London
city wall to the west, built between 1515 and 1523, a second at
Hampton Court, given by Wolsey in 1527, and a third at Whitehall, confiscated from Wolsey after his downfall. In addition, by

1529 Henry had acquired new country houses at New Hall (Essex) in 1516, Ampthill (Bedfordshire) in 1524, Hunsdon (Hertfordshire) in 1525 and Grafton (Northamptonshire) in 1526. Some royal properties remained unused for long periods. The Tudors abandoned Clarendon (Wiltshire) and allowed it to decay, and Minster Lovell (Oxfordshire) was similarly never visited, though kept in repair.[7]

These houses were all of different size, and few had been originally built with the royal household in mind. Yet the basic structural principles of the court are easily stated. At the time when Edward IV's *Black Book* was compiled in 1471, the court had two divisions, responsibilities being divided between the household, directed by the king's steward, and the chamber, directed by the king's chamberlain. The first of these divisions catered for royal servants and visitors at court; the second looked after the king's own accommodation and entertainment. From about 1495 the court became a tripartite structure when the chamber was divided into two areas of responsibility. One part – still under the chamberlain – was responsible for attending to the king's more public activities. The other, the privy chamber – managed by the groom of the stool – was now responsible for the his private affairs.[8] These distinctions are now worth examining in more detail.

The king's steward in 1471 was responsible for accommodating at least 300 people entitled to set meals, and the variable number of extras could amount to several hundreds more. The household therefore needed a large number of rooms for royal servants and guests, together with a great hall, with all its attached kitchens, stores and sculleries, for feeding the household and for court entertainments. The steward's officers had the task of allocating chambers. If there were not enough to go round, people had to make other arrangements locally.[9] There was some embarrassment – not to the king, needless to say – when Wolsey turned up at Grafton in 1529 and there was no spare room.[10] Under Henry VII the newly-formed yeomen of the guard were employed to keep undesirable people out of the hall as well as to

---

[7] Loades, *Tudor Court*, pp. 194, 198. Whitehall had previously been York Place, the London house of the archbishops of York.

[8] Starkey, 'Court and Government', 31–2; D. R. Starkey, 'The King's Privy Chamber, 1485–1547', unpublished Ph.D. thesis, Cambridge, 1973, 171–3.

[9] Loades, *Tudor Court*, pp. 39–40; K. Mertes, 'The *Liber Niger* of Edward IV: A New Version', *BIHR*, liiii (1981), 37; D. A. L. Morgan, 'The House of Policy: The Political Role of the Late Plantagenet Household', in Starkey, *English Court*, 32–3.

[10] Cavendish, 92–3.

add dignity to state occasions. Corporate dining was going out of favour as an everyday event and most of the king's servants were more likely to eat in their rooms or elsewhere.[11] The king's attendant staff nevertheless had to be accommodated and catered for, and this remained a large part of the court complex, under the lord steward's supervision. Table 4.1 shows some contemporary estimates of the basic supplies needed for Henry VIII's household; the annual cost of these alone was about four times the duke of Buckingham's annual income at the time of his execution in 1521.

Where there was a hall, the king's private quarters led from it. He needed at the very least a guard chamber, a large dining-room, and a private chamber. Edward IV, and probably Henry VII too, often had to be content with three chambers on this pattern. A household ordinance of 1471 refers to the 'middle or upper chamber' and the 'inner chamber', and lists three doors to be guarded daily.[12] The more public of these rooms, which changed little in the course of the period, was variously known as the dining chamber, the present chamber, the chamber of presence or the chamber of estate. It had to be appropriate for meeting councillors and for the formal reception of visitors, and even in the smallest palaces, it contained a throne and cloth of estate.[13] By contrast, the king's private lodgings were being made significantly more elaborate. The privy chamber became a separate royal suite, including, beside a bedchamber, a drawing-room, a dressing-room and various other amenities. The best illustration of this proliferation of chambers is the arrangement of the royal quarters at Greenwich, which were reconstructed both by Henry VII and Henry VIII.[14] For the queen there was a matching hall, dining chamber and private quarters, either adjacent to the king's or on the next floor, sometimes designed in such a way that her bedroom connected to the king's. Queens had their own numerous household staff parallel to that of the king, including officers to handle their private estates and the considerable income arising from it. The surviving accounts for queens' households show that

[11] Starkey, 'King's Privy Chamber', 5.
[12] *Household of Edward IV*, 31-2, 201; Colvin, *History of the King's Works*, iv, 11-13; D. R. Starkey, 'Intimacy and Innovation: The Rise of the Privy Council, 1485-1547', in Starkey, *English Court*, 73.
[13] See above, p. 55. Cavendish, 93; Starkey, 'Intimacy', 73; Starkey, 'King's Privy Chamber', 5-6; Thurley, *Royal Palaces*, 122.
[14] Starkey, 'King's Privy Chamber', 6; S. Thurley, 'Greenwich Palace', in Starkey, *Henry VIII*, 20-5.

Table 4.1 Estimates of the consumption of basic foodstuffs and beverages in the king's household, with their total cost for four years, 1518–1527

Years	Wheat (quarters)	Oats (quarters)	Wine (tuns)	Ale and beer (tuns)	Beef (carcases)	Mutton (carcases)	Total cost (£)
1518–19	2640	3749	301	1249	1421	7650	20,378
1520–1	2952	2489	342	1393	1470	8323	21,568
1521–2	2897	3506	317	1401	1467	7751	21,666
1526–7	2928	3482	277	1405	1343	7666	20,254

Source: LP, iv (2), 1383

Elizabeth Woodville's annual income in 1466–7 was £4541 and that of Elizabeth of York in 1502–3 was £3586.[15]

Under Henry VII the administration of the king's private quarters became more distinct from the rest of the household. Successive kings increased the number of household knights and esquires, but in the process they reduced the intimacy between the king and his entourage. Around 1495, Henry made his personal quarters more private by restricting access to a small number of servants headed by the groom of the stool, whose duties included waiting on the king while he relieved himself.[16] Henry VIII maintained these divisions, and early in his reign they were formalized. Being of a different temperament from his father he elaborated the staff of the privy chamber, adding to it a number of gentlemen companions who in 1518 became known as gentlemen of the privy chamber. In the short term this arrangement provoked criticism from councillors who said that the king's chosen companions were not suitably grave, and in 1519 the king's 'minions' were temporarily expelled in favoured of gentlemen thought to be more suitable. Four 'knights of the body in the privy chamber' were appointed to serve as councillors attendant on the king. Innovations and reforms in 1518–19 decisively established the privy chamber as a separate department of the household with sixteen stipendiary officers, and in the process raised the social levels from which its staff were drawn. Seven years later, the Eltham Ordinances of 1526 separated the staff of the privy chamber even more decisively from that of the chamber, and established fifteen recognized posts.[17] Historians are divided between those who ascribe these formal reorganizations of the king's privy chamber primarily to Wolsey's jealousy of its independent influence, and those who see them primarily as royal concessions to the need for decorum and economy.[18]

Household and Administration

Government in the later Middle Ages was still a very limited activity by modern standards. The king was committed to giving

[15] *Household of Elizabeth Woodville*, 209, 450; *Privy Purse*, ciii, 111; Thurley, *Royal Palaces*, 140–1, 143.
[16] D. Luckett, 'Crown Officers and Licensed Retinues in the Reign of Henry VII', in Archer and Walker, *Rulers and Ruled*, 224–6; Starkey, 'Introduction', in Starkey, *English Court*, 4, 75–6.
[17] Starkey, 'King's Privy Chamber', 121–3, 158–9, 177–8; Starkey, 'Court, Council and Nobility', 184–7.
[18] Compare Starkey, *Reign of Henry VIII*, 76–89, with Gwyn, *King's Cardinal*, 555–64.

justice, maintaining law and order, and defending the realm. The civil service required to perform these various tasks was insignificant in proportion to the total population of the country. Quite apart from the very limited scope of government, many of its activities were performed away from court as voluntary activities by local dignitaries. Even most of the central activity of government had long been hived off from the household, since it was unthinkable that all the operations of day-to-day administration should move around with the king. The central royal law courts all met in various parts of Westminster Hall during the legal terms. The exchequer, which was the oldest institution of royal finance as well as a court of law, also had its headquarters in Westminster. The keeper of the privy seal, who remained a hub of the administration because of his importance in authorizing routine procedures, had long been detached from the household.[19] All these branches of government were administered in accordance with professional expertise which the king himself lacked. Their leading officers were not members of the king's household, though they might need to visit the court from time to time.

Even some of the branches of administration still in the hands of household officials were not in fact based on the household. While Thomas Vaughan was treasurer of the king's chamber between 1465 and 1483 the chamber became a leading financial department, with its own staff trained in estate management, law and accounting, responsible for a large portion of the king's normal revenue. This was both to increase the king's control of available funds and, in the longer term, to help raise the crown's income from the dismal level to which it had fallen under Henry VI. An increasing number of royal estates were removed from the normal auditing procedures of the exchequer and made subject to special auditors who could investigate how well they were being managed. In Richard III's reign all receivers on the king's estates, other than those responsible for Elizabeth Woodville's former rents, paid their balances into the king's chamber treasury and had their accounts audited by 'foreign' auditors – that is, auditors outside the exchequer system. The combination of improved management and an increase in the size of the royal estate under the Yorkists led to a larger income passing through the chamber. Its total net receipt under Richard III was at least £25,000 a year. Henry VII at first abandoned this development, probably because it required more royal direction than he was capable of giving,

[19] G. R. Elton, *The Tudor Revolution in Government*, Cambridge 1953, 14, 31.

with the result that during the 1480s the exchequer recovered some of its former responsibilities. But such were the advantages of the chamber system that from the early 1490s Henry returned to it wholeheartedly, and the chamber soon rose to greater prominence than ever before. Some surviving audited accounts of the early sixteenth century show that between 1502 and 1505 chamber receipts averaged nearly £105,000, the major part of the crown's income.[20] This scale of operations was not maintained under Henry VIII. Early in his reign the normal income of the chamber was reduced by reassignment of income to the household and wardrobe, by the restoration of crown lands to former owners, and by grants of land and annuities to his friends. The chamber's expenditure settled down to an average of £73,644 between 1515 and 1520, only about three-quarters of what it had been in Henry VII's last seven years.[21] Even so, responsibility for the collection of such sums could not be exercised by travelling household officers.

Chamber finance required its own auditing, which involved much more than simply checking the books, since it implied assessing rents, investigating arrears and, when necessary, initiating action against defaulting tenants. As the crown estates grew, the burden of work increased. In Henry VII's reign John Heron, as treasurer of the chamber, had an office in the sanctuary at Westminster, where payments were received and where the chamber archive was housed. A loosely-structured audit department, manned by royal councillors, was in existence in the years 1505–8. Then, in the last months of his life Henry VII established a larger, rather more formal court of audit that met at the Dominican house of Blackfriars or in Westminster Palace.[22] After a couple of years when auditing income from the crown estates was reabsorbed into the exchequer, in 1511 Henry VIII cautiously reconstructed his father's separate court of audit under two general surveyors of crown lands, confirming to them the use of a room in Westminster Palace. He gave these auditors the respectability of statutory authority in 1512, 1515, 1516 and 1523. By

---

[20] B. P. Wolffe, 'The Management of English Royal Estates under the Yorkist Kings', *EHR*, lxxi (1956), 20; B. P. Wolffe, 'Henry VII's Land Revenues and Chamber Finance', *EHR*, lxxix (1964), 233–46.

[21] F. C. Dietz, *English Public Finance, 1485–1641*, 2nd edn, 2 vols, Urbana 1964, i, 85, 90; Wolffe, *Crown Lands*, 83–4.

[22] J. A. Guy, 'A Conciliar Court of Audit at Work in the Last Months of the Reign of Henry VII', *BIHR*, xlix (1976), 289–91; W. C. Richardson, *Tudor Chamber Administration, 1485–1547*, Baton Rouge 1952, 160, 410.

these measures the chamber was publicly recognized as a financial department separate from the king's household.[23]

The royal court nevertheless remained the centre of government to the extent that the king himself held meetings, made decisions and authorized the preparation of documents. When necessary, the king met at court officers whose everyday business was conducted elsewhere. Here he saw advisers individually or in small groups, received foreign ambassadors and made innumerable decisions about matters great and small. When Henry VIII was at Greenwich, Wolsey would go and visit him there once a week, and even when the king was in the country during the summer months, Wolsey travelled long distances to visit him, often residing as close as he could to the court. Sir Thomas More, on succeeding Wolsey as chancellor in 1529, was given the great seal by the king himself in the king's inner chamber at Greenwich Palace.[24]

The king required clerks constantly about him to handle administrative business and correspondence. He received many petitions for legal redress from poor suitors, to be considered by the councillors attendant on the king, and these implied routine clerical work. From the reign of Edward IV it became more common for kings to authenticate documents with their own signatures, but they rarely wrote out the text of a letter. Their correspondence often required a high level of linguistic, literary or legal competence. The king's secretary, who had custody of the king's signet seal, was the obvious household officer for the more demanding letter-writing, but it was by no means a foregone conclusion that he would be sitting in the king's palace with pen poised. A lot depended upon what else the king called on him to do. William Hatclyffe, Edward IV's secretary from 1464 to 1480, was an experienced diplomat, and was often away from court for some ambassadorial purpose. During his period as the king's official secretary between 1522 and 1526, Thomas More was usually with the king, but he was at times away from court on council business, or as speaker of the house of commons in May 1523, or as a member of Wolsey's oyer and terminer commissions, or as a member of a diplomatic commission. He was sent to France in August 1525.[25] In these circumstances the king required proficient deputy secretaries to be in residence.

---

[23] Elton, *Tudor Revolution*, 45–8; Richardson, *Tudor Chamber Administration*, 216–17, 410–11; Wolffe, *Crown Lands*, 78–81.

[24] Guy, *Public Career*, 32; Gwyn, *King's Cardinal*, 207–8; Samman, 'Progresses', 72–3.

[25] Guy, *Public Career*, 16, 18–20; F. M. G. Higham, 'A Note on the Pre-Tudor Secretary', in A. G. Little and F. M. Powicke (eds), *Essays in Medieval History presented to Thomas Frederick Tout*, Manchester 1925, 365.

The king employed some of the best brains in the country to do his work. He had to do so in order to get men capable of coping with the exacting and varied tasks that the administrative system demanded. The staff employed in chamber finance, and that employed about the king's chapel, can properly be described as one of professional careerists. Employment at court was the goal of ambitious young men from the universities or the inns of court who hoped for a lucrative career in politics or the professions. Often men got into court by way of outstanding service in the households of the king's own entourage, so that they were already of proven capacity in a variety of different tasks. Once there, their duties tested their capabilities yet further. Laity and clergy, for all the differences of their initial training, overlapped in the sort of work they did. The linchpin of Henry VII's chamber auditing in between 1503 and his death in 1508 was Roger Layburne, bishop of Carlisle, who also belonged to the council learned in the law.[26] The work that household servants might be asked to take on would vary according to their abilities, and the shape of their careers was unpredictable. They were often called on to participate in tasks relating to diplomacy and war. Wolsey told a garbled tale of how, as a chaplain to Henry VII, he was sent as an ambassador to the emperor Maximilian near Calais, and completed his mission faster than the king supposed possible.[27]

These features of service in the king's household demonstrate that late medieval officialdom was not a rigid structure. Administrative roles, both in the household and outside, were not tightly defined, and could be combined in ways that cut across departmental specialization. It has been usual to contrast the conservatism of the older agencies of government with the greater responsiveness of household departments to the king's requirements, and it is true that institutions like the exchequer often had routines that did not serve the interests of either precision or speed. Nevertheless, even the exchequer's practices were revised from time to time. A tough code of rules from 1484 was designed to speed up the collection of revenue and to tighten auditing procedures.[28] Henry VII reformed the workings of the treasury of receipt late in his reign; he downstaged the treasury chamberlains in favour of the under-treasurer and tellers, and discontinued the production of some sets of accounts that were no longer useful.

[26] Guy, 'Conciliar Court', 290; R. Somerville, 'Henry VII's "Council Learned in the Law"', *EHR*, liv (1939), 429.

[27] Cavendish, 7–10; D. A. L. Morgan, 'The King's Affinity in the Politics of Yorkist England', *TRHS*, 5th ser., xxiii (1973), 15–16.

[28] *Harley 433*, iii, 118–20.

In 1508 he added to the under-treasurer's tasks the obligation to produce an annual 'declaration of the state of the treasury'. Moreover, members of the exchequer staff were not isolated in a private world from the rest of the king's administration. At least two early sixteenth-century exchequer tellers are known to have served concurrently as clerks in the chamber under Sir John Heron. Sir John Daunce in 1514 was an exchequer teller, a treasurer of war under Wolsey, the receiver-general of wards, and a customs collector in London.[29]

Besides the careerists, chosen for professional ability, the king's court always found employment for men chosen for their social virtues. Key positions were given to the king's closest and most trusted friends, who were sometimes elevated to the peerage in recognition of their services. The chamberlains of the royal household illustrate well the importance of these personal ties. Edward IV's regime relied heavily upon William Hastings, whose family had a long record of service to the Yorkists, and who had fought with them at Towton. He was made chamberlain of the king's household in 1461, and summoned to parliament as a baron the same year. Through his office at court, he was reputed to be 'partner of his privy pleasures', and 'secretly familiar with the king in wanton company'.[30] The chamberlain in Richard III's household was Francis Lovell, created Viscount Lovell by Edward IV early in 1483, who had been with Richard at Middleham and Sheriff Hutton as a teenager and had campaigned with him in Scotland in 1481–3.[31] Sir William Stanley, whom Henry VII appointed chamberlain in 1485, was an unusual choice, in that the king hardly knew him. His intervention had won a Tudor victory at Bosworth, and as brother of the king's step-father he could be supposed to have some continuing interest in upholding Tudor rule. However, Sir William was never ennobled, and his execution for treason in 1495 implies that the appointment was a mistake.[32] Henry replaced him with Giles Daubeney, a former servant of Edward IV, who had fled to Brittany after the failure of Buckingham's rebellion, and had returned to fight against Richard III at Bosworth. He had been created a baron in 1486 and had served the king assiduously as a councillor and in numerous other

---

[29] J. D. Alsop, 'The Structure of Early Tudor Finance', in Starkey, *Revolution Reassessed*, 146–7.
[30] Mancini, 68–9; More, *Richard III*, 11; Ross, *Edward IV*, 73–5.
[31] Ross, *Richard III*, 8, 49–50.
[32] Griffiths and Thomas, *Making*, 163, 165; Chrimes, *Henry VII*, 85.

capacities ever since.[33] After Daubeney's death in 1508, he was replaced by Charles Somerset, another servant whose record went back to the days in exile before 1485. He was an illegitimate son of Henry Beaufort, third duke of Somerset, and so Henry VII's second cousin. He had been recognized as a baron, with the title lord Herbert, from about 1504, and Henry VIII created him earl of Worcester ten years later. He remained as chamberlain of the household until 1526.[34]

The king's own part in government was one that permitted variations. It was not expected of medieval kings that they should spend all their time doing administrative chores; they employed servants for the purpose. Each king had his particular style of government, based to a large extent upon personal likes and dislikes. Edward IV has a reputation for leading a life of pleasure, but he managed to combine this with an adequate attention to the problems of government. Henry VII was unusually committed to supervising the operations of government, and was not averse to a certain amount of paperwork. He was given to going through the chamber accounts and, at least until 1503 when his eyesight was deteriorating and business was increasing, he used to put his monogram by each item of payment.[35] In this attention to business he was very different from his son, who was capable of getting obsessive about particular problems while ignoring everything else. Henry VIII's decision to employ Wolsey as an *alter ego* is usually held against him – as it is also, less justifiably, held against Wolsey – but it was a direct implication of his idle temperament. In reality this was a remarkably successful experiment in government that worked for fifteen years, and it illustrates well how little royal duties were prescribed in detail. Henry VIII's inclinations were closer to the normal medieval pattern than those of his father.

The King's Council

Amongst those primarily responsible for keeping an eye on the king's finances and giving him financial and legal advice were the king's councillors. In this respect the royal council operated like that of any nobleman in the land. The council had a definite

[33] Chrimes, *Henry VII*, 111; Griffiths and Thomas, *Making*, 100, 107, 179; Gunn, 'Courtiers', 29.
[34] Chrimes, *Henry VII*, 138–9; T. B. Pugh, 'Henry VII and the English Nobility', in Bernard, *Tudor Nobility*, 80, 98, 109.
[35] Chrimes, *Henry VII*, 131 and plate 8.

membership, some members being drawn from the household itself and some from outside. Kings were free to appoint any councillors they thought appropriate, and were concerned to get the ablest men that they could. On retaking the crown in 1471 Edward IV appointed to his council the former Lancastrian lord chief justice, Sir John Fortescue, even though he was at least seventy-six years old, had no legal or administrative office, and had been in exile for most of the previous ten years. Analysis of the list of Edward IV's eighty-eight known councillors between 1471 and 1483 shows that there were twenty-one noblemen, thirty-five ecclesiastics, twenty-three royal officials and nine others. It is not obvious from this that Edward IV was concerned to exclude the nobility, and indeed there was no reason why he should, given the usefulness of having them to consult.[36]

Surviving documentation relating to the council is very imperfect, partly because of archival losses, but also because of the nature of conciliar procedures. The administrative documents required to implement the council's recommendations did not need to allude to the its participation in events; often they were issued under the king's signature, which was authority enough. But close examination of different types of evidence has established that it sat frequently as an advisory body throughout the period 1471–1529. Much of its business related to the king's finances. Under Edward IV the council is known to have discussed the administration of the royal estates, the appointment of estate officers, problems in the administration of customs, the organization and finances of the king's household, the funding of war in 1475 and the sources of payment for the garrison at Calais.[37] Many of these matters were things that the council could attend to in the king's absence. From time to time, indeed, individuals or groups of councillors were commissioned to exercise a standing responsibility for some aspect of estate administration or government. Henry VII, it has been said, 'turned naturally to a conciliar solution for every administrative problem'.[38] The development of a conciliar court for auditing the accounts of the chamber has already been noted.

The most notorious of Henry VII's conciliar experiments was the council learned in the law, which operated between about 1500 and 1509 partly to enforce a medley of statute laws and

---

[36] Fortescue, De Laudibus, lix, lxvi–lxvii; Lander, Crown and Nobility, 205–6.
[37] Lander, Crown and Nobility, 173–5, 191–204.
[38] Condon, 'Ruling Elites', 132.

partly to enforce the king's financial rights; the two were obviously connected to the extent that the court could impose fines for breach of statute. The king was entitled, as the feudal overlord of many of his subjects, to a number of lucrative customs, and notably to the right to administer the estates, and control the marriages, of tenants who died leaving heirs too young to inherit. The heirs themselves became wards of the king's court. The king's right to arrange the marriages of the widows and wards, and to collect payments, called reliefs when his feudal tenants entered into their inheritance, were two other rights which tenants sometimes tried to evade, but which the king's 'council learned in the law' was commissioned to track down. This council was also responsible for maximizing the king's income from treasure trove and forest fines. As its title implies, the council was predominantly made up of lawyers, who became more prominent on Henry VII's council than they had been before.[39] Though the court sometimes convened in one of the royal palaces, it more commonly sat in the council chamber of the duchy of Lancaster in Westminster. It was through the operations of this court in Henry's latter years that Richard Empson and Edmund Dudley became notorious for their unscrupulous exploitation of the king's rights.[40]

The king's council also discussed political matters, and was sometimes a theatre of political events. Councillors observed at first hand some of the conflict that led to the condemnation of Clarence in 1478.[41] Some accounts of Wolsey imply that his use of the council was authoritarian;[42] he always took his duty to represent the king more seriously than any one else could. As intermediary between the council and the king from early in 1514 onwards, he was able to shape its business, to lead its discussions, and often to act unilaterally. But even under his presidency the council was expected to discuss weighty matters, and it met frequently. A document drawn up in 1519, presumably after discussion between Henry VIII and Wolsey, lists a number of big issues that the king intended 'in his own person to debate with his council' – the enforcement of law and order, administrative reform at the exchequer, the establishment of royal control in Ireland, the reduction of unemployment and the defence of the realm.[43]

[39] Condon, 'Ruling Elites', 130-1.
[40] Somerville, 'Henry VII's "Council Learned in the Law"', 427-42.
[41] Lander, Crown and Nobility, 189, 249.
[42] Skelton, 283-4, 288-9, 295-6.
[43] British Library, Cotton MSS, Titus B.i, fo. 191r; J. A. Guy, 'Wolsey and the Tudor Polity', in Gunn and Lindley, Cardinal Wolsey, 60-2.

The importance of councillors to the king was not restricted to the advice he received from their formal deliberations. Not all the king's councillors were his close associates or in a position to chat to him, but some of them were, and did. There was an inevitable overlap between the king's councillors and his family and friends. The overlap can be seen at its most striking in the court of Edward IV, whose family constituted in itself an inner ring of councillors. Kings were liable to discuss their private affairs, as well as affairs of state, with favoured individuals at court. Having become a councillor in 1517, Sir Thomas More spent much of his time near the king, who liked his company. Henry would invite him to dinner for the sake of his conversation, and was known to take him on to the palace roof for star-gazing.[44]

Competition and Faction

The court existed to serve the king, and it was maintained by his expenditure. Its officers were his appointees, and its movements about the country were at his discretion. Here, if anywhere, the king was master of his own. Yet even casual acquaintance with the king's court was enough to expose practices that owed nothing to the king's personal choice. The court was a world in its own right, fascinating and alarming both to those in it and to those outside. Especially to those out of favour it could look like an institution that limited the king, even shaping his values and controlling his mind. An old tradition of conventional political mythology that transferred blame for unpopular political decisions from the king to those around him, remained sufficiently influential in this period to affect all surviving literary and narrative sources to some degree. Throughout the period the political role of court needs to be investigated with care, though the problems are exceptionally acute for the reign of Henry VIII.

It was only to be expected that those connected with the court should pursue private purposes. The most important aspect of court life to be considered in this context is its inevitable association with competition for royal favour. The hopes of ambitious individuals centred on catching the king's ear and earning his consideration, either to win some legal argument, to gain some desired employment, or to direct the marriage of one of the king's

---

[44] Guy, *Public Career*, 15; R. Marius, *Thomas More*, Glasgow 1985, 192.

wards. Not surprisingly, therefore, the court was a hub of scheming and intrigue, and is represented as such in much of the literature of the age.[45] Those with influence at court, like William, lord Hastings, in Edward IV's reign, received presents and fees from suitors whose position was weaker.[46]

Much of this was of little political importance, even when it concerned employment, which was usually allocated according to personal connections and personal knowledge. Henry VII, for example, was observed to have taken over 'the most party of his guard' from the ranks of Lord Hastings's servants.[47] Many household positions were sufficiently remote from the king to have no political implications of any sort. Henry VII did not put Lambert Simnel to work in his kitchens because he wanted to discuss affairs of state with him. Posts nearer the king were a rather different matter, however, because they carried possibilities both of greater current influence over the course of events and of future advancement in power and wealth. Political ambition cannot be sharply distinguished from individual careerism. For example, clerical appointments in the household, as elsewhere in the king's administration, were an avenue of vital importance for the higher ranks of ecclesiastical promotion. A string of bishops of Exeter – John Booth (1465–78), Peter Courtenay (1478–87), Oliver King (1493–5) – were former royal secretaries.[48] Clerical promotions were given as rewards for political services, and clerks needed courtly arts to win the king's regard even if they were not interested in political influence in the long term. On the other hand, there were some formidable clerical politicians. George Cavendish gives a characteristically candid description of Wolsey on his way to the top, 'full of subtle wit and policy, perceiving a plain path to walk in towards promotion'.[49] Successful administrative careerists made attractive allies for those further from the king who had objectives to be achieved at court.

Court politics involved more than competition between rival administrators. It also extended to questions of policy. On issues where alternative courses of action were under discussion between the king and his councillors, court groupings might range themselves on either side. Contemporary observers were well aware

[45] Barclay, *Eclogues*; A. Fox, *Politics and Literature in the Reigns of Henry VII and Henry VIII*, Oxford 1989, 37–55.
[46] Morgan, 'House of Policy', 61–3; Ross, *Edward IV*, 317.
[47] Gunn, 'Courtiers', 29.
[48] Ross, *Edward IV*, 320–1.
[49] Cavendish, 11.

of such divisions, though often so badly informed about them that truth and rumour were indistinguishable. For most of the time the way in which kings took counsel and formed policy is unrecorded, though court politics undoubtedly contributed to the outcome. It is difficult to assess the significance of court factions in the determination of policy, if factions are understood to be long-standing alignments of political interest rather than temporary groupings on single issues. The question has been fiercely debated. Some authors see faction fighting as an intrinsic feature of monarchical government; 'faction is characteristic of personal rule whether by Henry VIII or by Stalin'.[50] Others see faction more as a feature of certain royal personalities, such as that of Henry VIII; 'the chief cause of the continued faction strife lay . . . in the King himself'.[51] Others, again, consider struggles at court to be the exception rather than the rule, even under Henry VIII, and are suspicious of the sort of evidence, often nebulous, that is used to link people together as fellow-schemers.[52] This is one of those complex historical disagreements where ambiguities in the available information are complicated further by problems of definition; faction is not a very precise word.[53]

The most convincing instances of faction at work, as in earlier periods of medieval history, are from situations where a royal consort had distinct family interests. Two good examples of this were the Woodville faction in the years 1471–83, and the Boleyn faction in 1527–9. The Woodvilles were essentially a courtier family, owing their status in the kingdom to the king's marriage to Elizabeth Woodville, and as such they provoked jealousies amongst other members of the nobility. While Edward IV was alive they were perceived as an independent interest at court. Edward was capable of resisting the Woodvilles when it suited him – as in his political and personal dependence upon Hastings – so presumably their influence was strongest in matter he regarded with indifference. They were probably not the principal force behind the destruction of Clarence, who was his own worst enemy, though they were widely supposed to have influenced the king's decision. However, their political identity acquired a determining influence on major events after Edward's death, and that was

---

[50] E. W. Ives, 'The Fall of Anne Boleyn Reconsidered', *EHR*, cvii (1992), 663.
[51] Elton, *Studies*, ii, 52; Starkey, 'Introduction', 9–10.
[52] Bernard, 'Politics and Government', 160–3; G. W. Bernard, 'The Fall of Anne Boleyn: A Rejoinder', *EHR*, cvii (1992), 672–3; Gwyn, *King's Cardinal*, 7–12, 581–7. Cf. G. R. Elton, 'Tudor Government', *HJ*, xxi (1988), 428.
[53] Gunn, 'Structure of Politics', 59–90.

because the interest of the king's sons had become inseparable from theirs. They were managers of what has been described as 'the faction of the prince'. Richard of Gloucester could have done far more than he did in 1483 to cooperate with them, but having perceived them as rivals for power he demonstrated a ruthless determination to cripple them some time before his own claims to the throne were declared.[54]

At the very end of our period, the Boleyn family became the focus of a court faction in the period when Henry VIII's divorce from Catherine of Aragon was running into trouble. Like the Woodvilles, the Boleyns were critically dependent for their status upon the king's favour at court. Especially from January 1529, as Cardinal Wolsey's labours with the papacy were seen to be floundering, those in favour of more energetic action against the church in general, and Wolsey in particular, together with those who simply felt the way the wind was blowing, aligned themselves to Anne Boleyn's cause. By the end of July, accusations against Wolsey had been collected together into a book as a means to turn the king against him and force him out of office. Since this faction would never have had the power it did unless its goals had coincided with the king's desire to divorce Catherine of Aragon, its independent weight in determining the course of events lay in details of strategy rather than in the overall objects of policy. However, Wolsey himself never doubted that his fall was engineered by enemies at court, headed by Anne, and he was surely right in thinking that the anxious jealousies of the Boleyn faction affected the way he was handled by the king both before and after his fall.[55]

Outside these contexts the evidence for factions as long-standing alignments of interest is weaker. It attests, rather, the existence of small groups who helped each other in various ways, but which lacked the coherence that common political purpose would imply.[56] In other words, political rivalries and disagreements were probably less structured, under normal conditions, than the word 'faction' suggests. Wolsey's dominating position between 1515 and 1529 was no doubt distasteful to many, and it was one he had to work hard to maintain, but the evidence for any coordinated attempt to weaken him is thin before 1527. He

---

[54] Hicks, *False Fleeting, Perjur'd Clarence*, 146–7; Hicks, *Richard III and his Rivals*, 225; Horrox, *Richard III*, 80–1, 92–9, 113–15.

[55] Cavendish, 108, 113, 115, 136–7, 156–7, 159, 163, 165–6; Ives, 'Fall of Wolsey', 295–9.

[56] Gunn, 'Courtiers', 47–8; Gunn, 'Structure of Politics', 77–82.

was opposed by individuals and groups on particular issues all through his career, and yet both he and his politically responsible critics were anxious not to allow such disagreements to become entrenched in personal animosities.[57] They knew that on other occasions they would need to cooperate. Skelton, writing from outside the court, expressed his contempt for the willingness of noblemen to come to terms with Wolsey rather than close rank against him, but his views represent little more than a conventional prejudice that the country would be better administered by noblemen than by a butcher's son from Ipswich.[58] It is difficult to imagine, in reality, what political foundation there could have been for a factional alliance against Wolsey through most of his period in power. Political manoeuvres at court did not bring into being anything so cumbersome and precarious as a faction until the desperate circumstances of 1527–9.

---

[57] Gunn, *Charles Brandon*, 58–9.
[58] Skelton, 286; G. Walker, *John Skelton and the Politics of the 1520s*, Cambridge 1988, 139–42.

5

Country Politics

Making moral contrasts between court and country society was an old literary device. It was employed by Alexander Barclay in his *Eclogues*, written about 1513–14, which define country life as one of freedom, and court life as one of constraint and vexation.[1] Others stressed the artificiality and moral decadence of the court. 'The court', as a printed work of 1483 has it, 'is a convent of people that under fantasy of common weal assemble them together for to deceive each other.'[2] But writers of the day, like the Roman poets whom they read, knew there was more to country life than liberated shepherds. Country society constituted a sphere of political life in which courtiers were to be found, for much of their lives, in other roles. They associated there with landed families – often wealthy and well established – who had few or no court connections.

Country politics involved the cooperation, or non-cooperation, of royal servants and others in the management of the crown interest and the enforcement of law in the shires. The king had a small, but growing, number of permanent posts with which to create a network of servants of his own through the shires, and so maintain vital links between court and country. In Richard III's reign the establishment directly answerable to the king, excluding those employed in the law courts and the royal household, amounted to about 800–900 men, appointed as wardens of royal parks, castles and forests, stewards of royal manors and customs officials. Outside that establishment, local government depended on the voluntary activities of men who happened to be influential. The administration of law in the countryside depended upon the

[1] Barclay, *Eclogues*, 12.
[2] D. A. L. Morgan, 'The House of Policy: The Political Role of the Late Plantagenet Household', in D. Starkey (ed.), *The English Court from the Wars of the Roses to the Civil War*, London 1987, 69.

FIGURE 5.1   England in 1524–1525, showing county boundaries and the
leading 20 towns, ranked by taxpaying population

sheriff, who was the key figure in enforcing locally the processes
of the common-law courts, and upon a group of nominees, mostly
selected from the gentry, willing to fulfil the duties of justices of
the peace. Local government also depended upon men being willing
to undertake a variety of *ad hoc* commissions on behalf of the
crown, to conduct local inquests into the king's rights, to levy

taxes or troops, or to tackle particular local problems such as the maintenance of watercourses and prevention of floods. For these duties, local men had to commit private resources to public service; even a sheriff's staff was not directly employed by the king.[3]

This meant that the king's power to govern the shires depended partly on the private power of individuals who lived there and partly on his own capacity to secure and retain their goodwill. These constraints permitted different patterns of local power at different times and places, but looking at the period as a whole, a shift to greater royal intervention can be perceived. Kings were able to reduce their dependence upon the independent power of the nobility and to increase their reliance upon networks of servants exclusively attached to the king's interest. This was partly the result of opportunities to refashion the distribution of power through attainders, notably in 1483 and 1485, and partly the result of autonomous changes reducing the authority of noblemen in much of the kingdom. Following earlier legislation against the creation of private retinues in 1468, a statute of 1487 made it illegal for members of the nobility to retain royal servants, and so established the latter as a body of men attached uniquely to the royal interest. Increasingly, by means of more interventionist policies to be examined later, the kings were able to manipulate patterns of local authority to suit themselves. One sign of this shift was a growing capacity of the crown, apparent especially after about 1502, to use the law to enforce local obedience.[4]

The motives for which men participated in local politics varied, and the hope of extra income, or of some other material advantage, played a part. Nevertheless, because it affected the distribution of power and influence, such political activity was rarely governed solely by material rewards. A position in local government brought social status and family honour. In times of political stability there was widespread willingness to cooperate with the king in governing the realm. In general, the higher a man's income and status, the more was expected of him. It was difficult for a nobleman or knights to escape from public duties, but lesser landowners were more likely to be able to choose the extent of their public engagements.[5] Local politics was underpinned by a set of values that set bounds to what was acceptable behaviour either by noblemen or others. Most landowners, great and small, were committed to maintaining the peace, to avoiding both

---

[3] Lander, *English Justices*, 82–4; Lander, *Limitations*, 21–2.

[4] Gunn, *Early Tudor Government*, 30–1; J. Guy, 'Wolsey and the Tudor Polity', 65–75; Luckett, 'Crown Officers', 223–38.

[5] Lander, *Government and Community*, 44.

violence and litigation, and to operating within a framework of accepted conventions, both public and private, in which social etiquette was complex. When, around 1472, three of Thomas Stonor's tenants failed to deliver some barley to Robert Goldriche at Bradfield (Berkshire), Goldriche's landlord and master, Edward Langford, wrote a polite letter to Stonor asking him to put pressure on his tenants; 'my servant', he said, 'neither will nor dare take action against them unto the time that he have leave of you'.[6] Accounts of local conflict yield numerous stories of outrageous behaviour on the part of those locked in conflict, but in these cases normal principles of caution and processes of mediation had failed. There were limits to the extent that individuals could push their own interests at the expense of their neighbours without infringing unwritten codes of conduct and incurring political penalties.[7]

Noblemen were leading representatives of the crown in the provinces, taking precedence over local officers such as sheriffs if the situation required any extraordinary assertion of authority. From the early years of Edward IV's second reign, regional spheres of influence were clearly and deliberately allocated to members of the royal family and leading officers of the king's household. From the summer of 1471 the king's brother, Richard, duke of Gloucester, was allowed to construct a local ascendancy in the north. Clarence, by marriage, acquired part of the former Warwick connection in the midlands, though his control there was checked from 1474 by the rising power of the king's chamberlain, William, Lord Hastings, with a base at Tutbury Castle. The influence of Hastings was most pervasive in north Warwickshire, Staffordshire and Derbyshire. Lord Stanley, the king's steward, and his younger brother William became dominant figures in Lancashire and north-east Wales. The Welsh March was supervised in the name of the king's elder son, Edward prince of Wales, by a council of which the queen's brother, Anthony Woodville, Earl Rivers, was a prominent member. This council's authority was increased, from 1476 onwards, to encroach on the authority of the second earl of Pembroke, who had since 1471 been entrusted with a dominant executive role in south Wales. It had its headquarters in the castle at Ludlow (Shropshire), which explains why the prince and Rivers were there when Edward IV died in 1483.[8]

[6] *Stonor Letters*, 210.
[7] Carpenter, *Locality and Polity*, 622–3, 628.
[8] Carpenter, *Locality and Polity*, 518–28; Horrox, *Richard III*, 39–72; Ross, *Edward IV*, 196–8, 334–5, 424; D. A. L. Morgan, 'The King's Affinity in the Politics of Yorkist England', *TRHS*, 5th ser., xxiii (1973), 18–19; Williams, *Recovery*, 52, 209–10.

Spheres of influence were less clear-cut under Edward's successors. Henry VII's family was so much sparser than Edward IV's
that he could not have ruled in quite the same way even had he
wanted to, and being more suspicious of concentrations of noble
influence, he did nothing to find substitutes. Nevertheless elements of the same policy survived, particularly in parts of the
realm farthest from Westminster, in the north, in Wales and in
Ireland. Henry recognized the invaluable services of his uncle
Jasper by restoring him to the earldom of Pembroke and giving
him additional grants of lordship in Wales that made him the
most powerful member of the nobility. The earls of Derby, Northumberland and Oxford retained concentrations of regional authority.[9] Henry also allowed local power to his mother and her
council at Collyweston (Northamptonshire), which between 1499
and 1505 operated as an agency of royal conciliar justice in the
midlands.[10] The Tudors continued to depend upon noblemen to
serve as royal agents in moments of crisis when called upon to do
so. In 1489 the earl of Northumberland was assassinated in the
course of supervising the collection of an unpopular tax in Yorkshire. In 1525, unrest in Suffolk, occasioned by another unpopular levy, the Amicable Grant, was handled by the dukes of Norfolk
and Suffolk between them. Noblemen were able to perform such
duties not only because of their social status but also because of
the personal attachments which they characteristically formed
with subordinate families.

Dependence upon the powers of the local nobility continued to
be greatest in the border counties of England, in Wales and in the
lordship of Ireland. In these areas the government was often in
a cleft stick, in that it could neither impose a governor from the
outside with any chance of success, nor wholly trust the resident
aristocracy to cooperate in the interests of the crown. The relative weakness of the king on the margins of the kingdom increased both the incidence of corruption in local government,
and the rewards of local office, so that competition for power
remained keener than elsewhere.

The north was stable under Richard of Gloucester's personal
direction from 1471 to 1483. No subsequent king was prepared
to depend so heavily upon a single individual, and the government of the region became more of a balancing act. Richard III

---

[9] Grant, *Henry VII*, 27; T. B. Pugh, 'Henry VII and the English Nobility', in Bernard,
Tudor Nobility, 84.
[10] Jones and Underwood, *King's Mother*, 87–90.

attempted to maintain as king the personal hegemony he had achieved between 1471 and 1483, but the events of 1485 suggested that he was not very successful in holding the loyalties of the northern nobility, some of whose members were disappointed that they had not received more of his bounty. Henry VII had nothing of his predecessor's personal rapport with the region, and made no attempt to maintain the council of the north that had served Richard between 1483 and 1485, but there was no easy solution. His task was complicated first by his mistrust of Henry Percy, fourth earl of Northumberland, who had equivocated at the battle of Bosworth, and then by the earl's assassination in 1489, which left the earldom in the hands of a minor. Following that disaster, management of the north was entrusted to an outsider, Thomas Howard, recently restored to the earldom of Surrey which he had forfeited after the battle of Bosworth. He was appointed, as lieutenant, to govern in the name of the infant Prince of Wales, the titular warden of the east and middle marches, and remained there till 1501.[11]

Henry VII always mistrusted the northern elites, and his son continued to be cautious. Since the junior Percy turned out to be less useful than might be, management of the far north, throughout the period to 1529, had to be either neglected or entrusted to minor nobility, notably the Clifford family of Skipton (earls of Cumberland from 1525) and the Dacre family of Gilsland. Thomas, Lord Dacre, who was warden of all three northern marches from 1511 to 1525, was by far the most able of those available to serve the crown, though his power was weak in the eastern marches. Tudor dependence on relatively minor families implied that nobody was in very effective control in the north. However, such problems were more than compensated for by freedom from the danger of overmighty subjects. This was no minor advantage, since northerners had been the bane of the English crown from 1399 through to 1483.[12]

The English lordship of Ireland, governed from Dublin, presented comparable problems of control, made more difficult by the considerable power of local families. Though the Fitzgeralds might never present themselves as a threat to the ruling English dynasty, they were in a position to support others who did. Gerald Fitzgerald, eighth earl of Kildare, had acknowledged Lambert Simnel as king of England in 1487 and given him military support. In

[11] Pollard, *North-Eastern England*, 316–96.
[12] Ellis, *Tudor Frontiers*, 44, 146–70; Gwyn, *King's Cardinal*, 212–37.

1494, fear that Perkin Warbeck would find support in Ireland spurred Henry VII into an uncharacteristic interest in his subjects there. Sir Edward Poynings was appointed as deputy lieutenant of Ireland, governing in the name of the young Prince Henry – an arrangement parallel to the current disposition of the north of England. With the passing of such dynastic anxieties, royal interest in Ireland waned once more. In 1496 Kildare was reappointed deputy governor, and for most of the period to 1529 the Fitzgeralds were allowed to govern on behalf of the English crown. The expanding resources of the family, which placed the ninth earl amongst the top ten of the Tudor nobility by the 1520s, together with the breadth of their family connections, meant that they were the most capable of imposing authority on the lordship, representing English interests, and handling relations with Gaelic Ireland beyond the pale. Only once, in 1520–2, was the principle of local control seriously challenged. Thomas Howard, earl of Surrey since 1514, was commissioned to raise the level of royal control over the lordship and increase the king's income. The complete collapse of his mission, for want of adequate resources, political information or strategy, confirmed the necessity of leaving things in the hands of the local nobility.[13]

The undoubted usefulness of the nobility for the crown's management of local affairs does not imply, however, that country politics reduces to deferential local groupings with dominant peers at their apex. Not only does such a picture greatly oversimplify the political geography of England, where spheres of aristocratic influence were rarely predictable or stable. It also misrepresents the relationship between noblemen and men of lower rank, who were often highly experienced and knowledgeable in local affairs and capable of autonomous action. The experience of the 1450s and 1460s had taught them the art of self-preservation when dealing with irresponsible magnates like the duke of Clarence. Evidence from the midlands suggests that in the course of the later fifteenth century the gentry became less inclined to follow noblemen into local conflicts, and more inclined to rely for their security upon their less exalted friends, relatives and neighbours.[14] The weakening of the link between gentry and noble families was giving scope for the crown to interpose itself more in country politics in the course of the period. The study of country politics, therefore,

---

[13] S. G. Ellis, *Tudor Ireland: Crown, Community and the Conflict of Cultures, 1470–1603*, London 1985, 85–115; Ellis, *Tudor Frontiers*, 107–45.

[14] Carpenter, *Locality and Polity*, 521, 609–10.

has to take relationships between the crown, the nobility and those beneath them as a matter for close observation and analysis rather than as one to be settled by some foregone conclusion.

Aristocratic Patronage

Aristocratic patronage, or 'bastard feudalism', was once considered the cause of most of the ills known to the late Middle Ages. However, despite the pejorative implications of the term, bastard feudalism simply designates the normal procedure by which noblemen contracted for the services of lesser men in return for money fees, for some other contractual payment, or even merely in return for 'good lordship', rather than by giving them hereditary grants of land.[15] Undoubtedly noblemen commonly had such retainers for a range of purposes, many of a domestic or administrative nature. The third duke of Buckingham, shortly before his execution in 1521, employed a household staff of 148, of whom over a half were given liveries of cloth by his wardrobe officials. Some of these would be expected to ride with him on long journeys, but their essential duties were domestic. Retainers employed outside a noble household were likely to be family connections, lawyers, councillors or estate officers. The Plumptons held the stewardship of Spofforth in west Yorkshire from the Percies for an annuity of £20, and there was never any question of where their loyalties lay.[16] Such ties had long been a normal feature of landed society.

Permanent retinues continued to have military significance in the northern marches because of the need for rapid mobilization against the Scots in wartime. The fifth earl of Northumberland gave fees and liveries well beyond the circle of his household servants and estate officers.[17] Yet his circumstances were exceptional. Most noblemen, even if interested in the exercise of power, had few retainers by this time. George, duke of Clarence had only a handful, most of whom had taken on along with his estates; he had not even recruited them himself.[18] Quite apart from the heavy financial burden of maintaining a large retinue, the political

[15] Lander, *Limitations*, 32–3.
[16] J. W. Kirby, 'A Fifteenth-Century Family: The Plumptons of Plumpton and their Lawyers, 1461–1515', *NH*, xxv (1989), 110–11; C. Rawcliffe, *The Staffords, Earls of Stafford and Dukes of Buckingham, 1394–1521*, Cambridge 1978, 88–9, 101–2.
[17] M. James, *Society, Politics and Culture: Studies in Early Modern England*, Cambridge 1986, 52, 81.
[18] Hicks, *False, Fleeting, Perjur'd Clarence*, 183.

dangers of doing so increased significantly during the period, since kings set their faces firmly against tolerating the use of retainers as symbols and agents of aristocratic might and legislated against it.[19] For these reasons, particularly in the heartland of England, the political significance of aristocratic retinues diminished between 1470 and 1529.

Two qualifications need to be made to this argument however, one concerning the nature of aristocratic authority and one concerning the pattern of retaining. On the first of these counts, it is important to appreciate that aristocratic authority had never depended narrowly on formal retaining, even in the north. Noblemen had large numbers of tenants, employed large numbers of people, and inevitably attracted the deference of others who hoped for employment, assistance or other favours. For these reasons, a study of retaining would always vastly understate the number of a nobleman's dependants and potential supporters. In the campaign that restored Edward IV to the throne in 1471, George, duke of Clarence, was followed by 4000 men, drawn from his own tenants and servants and from those of his dependants, despite the small size of his permanent retinue.[20] At the time of his downfall in 1521 the duke of Buckingham had only twenty-seven retainers, of no military significance, outside his domestic staff. Yet only a few months before he had contemplated visiting his estates in Wales with 300 or 400 men, 'and though we shall have them of our own officers and tenants, yet many of them shall be our gentlemen's servants of small stature [i.e. of modest social status]'.[21]

The second qualification concerning the diminishing importance of retaining concerns the extent to which, in spite of legislation against retaining, some of its forms were tolerated as a technique for consolidating the local authority of the king's own servants and those whom he trusted. Under Edward IV this meant allowing considerable retaining by Richard of Gloucester in the north. When in 1474 William, Lord Hastings, was appointed steward of the honour of Tutbury, part of the duchy of Lancaster estates, he was allowed to retain at least fifty-four men from the king's duchy retinue, though his own followers were not formally retained.[22] Under Henry VII the build-up of retinues recruited by the king's servants became a striking feature of royal penetration

[19] Below, p. 171.
[20] Hicks, *False, Fleeting, Perjur'd Clarence*, 183.
[21] Rawcliffe, *Staffords*, 100–1.
[22] Carpenter, *Locality and Polity*, 520.

into country politics, but consideration of this development may conveniently be postponed to the next section of this chapter.

Though the leaders of country society were commonly noblemen, it does not follow that country politics was normally structured into separate pyramidal hierarchies. There were fifty-five temporal lords in England in 1485, forty-one in 1509 and fifty-four in 1529, and they varied greatly in their resources, in their abilities and in the distribution of their estates.[23] In some counties – like Essex, where in Henry VII's reign the king himself, the earl of Essex, the earl of Oxford, the earl of Ormond, the lord Fitzwalter and the bishop of London all had valuable properties[24] – there were too many powerful interests for a simple hierarchy of allegiance to emerge. Furthermore, some of the lesser nobility were not much wealthier than their non-noble neighbours, and they might be considerably less experienced. In some cases noblemen were mere figureheads without significant authority in a region where they had some titular responsibility. Charles Brandon, duke of Suffolk, had built up a power base in north Wales in 1512–13 based on office under the crown, and he retained it until 1525, but since he never went there power was effectively in the hands of Sir William Griffith, his subordinate.[25]

Historians analysing the complexities of country politics have found themselves, in different contexts, working with three contrasting models, whose respective characteristics are determined by the structures of regional lordship. The first of these, which might be described as the pyramid model, represents the situation in which a single member of the nobility was clearly dominant in a particular region. The local gentry looked to this lord and his council for the coordination of local political responsibilities, as well as for other purposes such as the settlement of disputes. Many relations between neighbouring gentry families, in this context, were mediated by their connection with the nobleman in question. Some regions at some periods were indeed like this, as for example when Richard, duke of Gloucester, was building up his influence in the northern counties between 1471 and 1483. He was able to establish workable demarcations of power with other leading northern magnates, Henry Percy, third earl of Northumberland, Thomas, Lord Stanley, and the bishop of Durham, in

[23] Pugh, 'Henry VII and the English Nobility', 78; S. E. Lehmberg, *The Reformation Parliament, 1529–1536*, Cambridge 1970, 37n, 47.

[24] S. J. Gunn, 'Henry Bourchier, Earl of Essex (1472–1540)', in Bernard, *Tudor Nobility*, 152–3.

[25] Gunn, 'Regime of Charles, Duke of Suffolk', 461–73.

such a way as to establish a clear territorial hegemony over an area stretching northwards from eastern Lancashire and the West Riding of Yorkshire, straddling the Pennines. The lesser nobility of the region, together with many of the gentry, clergy and borough authorities, attached themselves to his interest.[26] In general, however, this way of thinking about country politics is of declining relevance through most of England after Edward IV's reign.

The second possibility, the conflict model, is relevant to the situation where two or more lords were effectively competing for influence. In this case local families would be inclined to attach themselves to different noble affinities, and there was likely to be trouble when lawsuits, or rivalry for local offices, brought the different groups into conflict. This is the model that has given fifteenth-century local politics a bad name for violence and corruption. The classic examples belong to the 1450s, when the dukes of Suffolk and Norfolk were battling for East Anglia, when Yorkshire was disturbed by conflict between the earl of Salisbury and the earl of Northumberland, and when the earl of Devon was clashing with Lord Bonville in the south-west.[27] Examples of such rivalry are sometimes to be found even between 1471 and 1529, though they were becoming anomalous. As already suggested, by 1529 this model was most relevant to outlying parts of the realm, where government control was most dependent upon the local nobility and office was most worth having. In the marches of Scotland there was rivalry for high office and influence between the Dacre and Clifford families in the 1520s. In 1525 Henry, Lord Clifford was created earl of Cumberland and appointed warden of the West March, but he was of insufficient wealth and standing for this position, and met such opposition from the Dacre family and its supporters that law and order were in danger of breaking down. After only two years in office, he was replaced as warden by his principal rival, William, Lord Dacre. This did not put a stop to the feuding, however, which continued long after 1529.[28] Another region still riven by local rivalries in the 1520s was the lordship of Ireland, where Gerald Fitzgerald, ninth earl of Kildare, contested for power with Piers Butler, eighth earl of Ormond. In 1524 commissioners were sent from England to work out an elaborate settlement of all the disputes between the two earls, and Kildare replaced Ormond as

---

[26] Horrox, *Richard III*, 39–72; Pollard, *North-Eastern England*, 316–41.

[27] R. L. Storey, *The End of the House of Lancaster*, 2nd edn, Gloucester 1986.

[28] Gwyn, *King's Cardinal*, 215–16; R. W. Hoyle, 'The First Earl of Cumberland: A Reputation Reassessed', *NH*, xxii (1986), 91–4.

Governor of Ireland, but the ensuing peace was maintained for only a few months.[29]

The third alternative, the consensus model, is more relevant to normal circumstances than the first two. It relates to a context without either a dominant aristocratic presence or any significant attempt to assert such dominance. In such a region leadership was likely to be shared by a group of local families working with the local nobility, both formally through the institutions of royal administration and more informally through family and neighbourhood connections. Such a society has been described from Derbyshire, where there was no dominant aristocratic interest and the gentry were leaders rather than followers. In the late fifteenth century the leading county offices were shared between members of the Babington, Blount, Curzon, Kniveton, Vernon and other families, who constituted a broad political elite.[30] This pattern was becoming more normal in the course of the period, chiefly because aristocratic authority was weakening and direct royal authority increasing in parts of the kingdom, as in Warwickshire and the north-east.[31]

Not all local politics, of course, can be analysed neatly in accordance with a single one of these simplified accounts. Nor do these comments do justice to the complicated grades of deference to be observed within gentry society. However, looking at local politics with clearly-defined alternatives in mind has the advantage of drawing the focus of attention away from any simple assumptions about the implications of aristocratic patronage, which was often of subordinate importance for local politics. It is now recognized that even when a lord had high status because of his family and possessions, his relationship with his neighbours would be affected by his other interests, his ambitions, his energy, his competence, and the extent to which he was trusted by the king. Because the king never considered him reliable enough, Henry Percy, the fifth earl of Northumberland, died in 1527 without ever having exercised the sort of local authority that his family name would have warranted.[32]

The responsibilities of senior officers of the crown were often circumscribed by county boundaries, and for this reason studies of country politics often focus on the county as the unit of study.

[29] Ellis, *Tudor Ireland*, 116–17.
[30] Wright, *Derbyshire Gentry*, 121–4, 146, 251–7.
[31] R. E. Horrox, 'Local and National Politics in Fifteenth-Century England', *JMH*, xviii (1992), 396.
[32] Gwyn, *King's Cardinal*, 221–5.

The high level of interaction between the officers of each county, and the fact that counties were units by which the country was represented in parliament, mean that the notion of a county community can be given some meaningful content for some administrative operations. However, this idea of county community will not do as a generally applicable framework for political history, and its applicability to the mid-fifteenth century is especially questionable. The estates of English landlords were generally widely dispersed between several counties. Such men did not confine their private or public interests to a single shire, and their activities would be misrepresented by a model of country politics that considered each shire as an separate political arena. This may be easily demonstrated with some illustrious examples. Between 1461 and 1483 William, Lord Hastings built up a connection that ignored county boundaries right across the midlands.[33] Richard of Gloucester's hegemony of northern England between 1471 and 1483 was similarly constructed on lordships and patronage extending across many shires.[34] The waning of aristocratic influence, implying that local county families were more directly responsible to the crown for the administration of the shires, meant that the concept of a county community became more relevant in the course of the Yorkist and early Tudor period; it signifies one aspect of the cooperation between families described by the 'consensus model'. In that respect the county community meant more in 1529 than in 1471.

Even so, care needs to be taken to prevent country politics from becoming too circumscribed by county boundaries. The interests of gentry families, like the Stonors and their connections, were often widely spread.[35] By contrast, in some parts of England there were units smaller than counties with which minor gentry families identified themselves, such as Cleveland, Richmondshire, Craven and Hallamshire within the county of York.[36] The development of quarter-sessions at the expense of the older county court had probably weakened the county as a unit of law enforcement, even though justices of the peace were appointed county by county. The quarter-sessions alternated between different towns in many shires, and it is likely that, as in the late sixteenth century, some gentlemen attended only the sessions near where they lived.[37] Some

---

[33] Carpenter, *Locality and Polity*, 518, 520, 523–5.
[34] Pollard, *North-Eastern England*, 316–41.
[35] Carpenter, 'Stonor Circle', 179–80.
[36] Pollard, *North-Eastern England*, 153.
[37] Lander, *English Justices of the Peace*, 74, 158–9.

gentlemen, too, were associated with particular boroughs rather than with county politics.[38] Instead of forcing their information into stereotypes of 'bastard feudalism' and 'county community', historians are now exploring a wider variety of patterns of inter-action between local landed families. For this sort of research one of the most valuable methods is that of network analysis, using the available documentation to chart systematically different forms of cooperation, antagonism and family connection within and across county boundaries.[39]

Royal Intervention in Country Politics

Kings could not afford to take the working of country politics for granted. Two dangers, in particular, were obvious. One was the exploitation of local connections by members of the nobility and gentry to express political disaffection. Governments needed to ensure that effective local leadership was combined with loyalty to the government, and this sometimes required vigorous inter-vention when there were grounds for unease. The second dan-ger was the possibility of local disorder, when local officers were either powerless to maintain the peace, apathetic, or so corrupted by self-interest that the reputation of the crown was in jeopardy. Such a local breakdown of law and order was not immediately fatal to political stability – indeed, parts of the kingdom, like the Welsh and Scottish borders, were known to be exceptionally untamed – but past experience showed how lawlessness could weaken a king's capacity to secure cooperation. The regimes of the period 1471–1529 were alert to these dangers, and insisted on a basic level of respect for the king's courts. The declining significance of the 'lordship' and 'competition' models of country politics after the 1460s is one indication of the success of the monarchy in imposing higher standards of service to the crown upon its agents in the country. Not all crown appointments were lucrative, and some were burdensome, so that to maintain effect-ive government while deterring corruption implied retaining a reliable level of goodwill.

As we have seen, the crown had its own local officers in posi-tions of responsibility in local government as receivers of royal income, keepers of the king's estates, and so on. Sir John Fortescue

---

[38] R. Horrox, 'The Urban Gentry in the Fifteenth Century', in J. A. F. Thomson (ed.), *Towns and Townspeople in the Fifteenth Century*, Gloucester 1988, 22–44.
[39] Carpenter, 'Gentry and Community', 340–80; Carpenter, 'Stonor Circle', 175–200.

had stressed the importance of using royal officers to good advantage in resisting the encroachment of power by overmighty subjects, and the point was well taken. Edward IV had strengthened the links between court and country in this way during the 1470s. One advantage of having a network of trusted royal servants through the shires as keepers of castles, manors, forests and parks, was that its personnel operated as the government's eyes and ears in the countryside.[40] Their number grew during the late fifteenth century, with the expansion of the royal demesne, and they provided the framework for an increasingly effective royal presence in the shires. The king's servants in the shires were also increasingly attached more closely to the king's interest by being given supernumerary, mostly unsalaried, posts at court, to which they were sworn in the king's chamber of presence; about 200 men are listed as such by 1525. In the 1520s, Henry VIII had a register of all his servants in the shires, listing 184 knights, 148 esquires, 5 carvers, 13 cupbearers, 107 sewers and 138 gentlemen-ushers all over England. By 1529 royal control of local offices was a far more effective form of political control than it had been in 1471.[41]

Some positions in the provinces, like some of those in his own household, were reserved for trusted noblemen; under Henry VIII these included those of the chief justices of forests and the wardens of the northern march. There were other duties most noblemen were expected to perform, like serving in commissions of justices of the peace. In Westmorland the Cliffords were hereditary sheriffs. Some noblemen were appointed to appropriate offices on the royal estates, as when Henry Courtenay, earl of Devon, became steward of the duchy of Cornwall in 1523.[42] Most offices on the royal estates, however, were not in noble hands. Responsible officials, like constables of castles, were often household servants, and the growth of the royal lands in the later fifteenth century corresponded to an expansion of the opportunities for such men, even if their financial obligations to the crown were closely supervised.

As the monarchy clamped down on private retaining by noblemen, the position of royal servants in the shires became more distinctive. Despite legislation against retaining, Henry VII was content to allow his servants to become key figures in the royal patronage structure by licensing them to retain local followers, so

[40] *Crowland Continuations*, 146–7; Morgan, 'King's Affinity', 20–1.
[41] S. J. Gunn, 'The Act of Resumption of 1515', in D. Williams (ed.), *Early Tudor England*, Woodbridge 1989, 102; Guy, 'Wolsey and the Tudor Polity', 67–8.
[42] Miller, *Henry VIII and the English Nobility*, 187–204.

that in this way the number of the king's men throughout the country was larger than a count of royal officers would imply. Such licences, whatever their form, authorized royal officers to distribute not their own emblems but those of the king. Sir William Sandys in Hampshire and Sir Edward Darell in Berkshire are reported to have distributed red-rose badges in 1504–5. Some of the authorized retinues of this kind created by Tudor trusties were large; that created by Sir Thomas Lovell as steward of Sherwood Forest and constable of Nottingham Castle numbered over 1300. Such retinues did not imply heavy expenditure on retaining fees, but they employed one device – the livery badge – of which kings were understandably nervous when the badges were not their own.[43] Court connections were important for effective royal control over the provinces. In the north and in Wales the most striking increase in royal presence under Wolsey was the establishment of the council of the north (under the duke of Richmond) and the council in the marches of Wales (under the Princess Mary) in 1525, but a more concealed growth of influence was the increasing network of ties with Wolsey and the court. Wolsey himself cultivated an extensive connection with the north. In north Wales and Cheshire, following the withdrawal of the duke of Suffolk from office in 1525, an extensive connection was built up by Sir William Brereton, groom of the king's privy chamber.[44]

Royal intervention in country politics was not limited to the appointment and multiplication of crown officers. Royal dependence on nobility and gentry for the government of the country meant that the king had a strong incentive to redistribute property in favour of trusted men whenever possible. Euphoria and vindictiveness followed dynastic victories, as the king's friends were advanced for their loyalty and his enemies were destroyed for their treason. The biggest transformations of property ownership within the period were those following the Yorkist triumph of 1471, the defeat of the rebellion against Richard III in 1483 and the Tudor victory of 1485. There were major intervening redistributions of property following the condemnation of prominent individuals, notably the duke of Clarence in 1478 and the duke of Buckingham in 1521. The government's chief weapon on such occasions was a parliamentary act of attainder, which summarized the treasonous activities of a named individual, or

[43] Luckett, 'Crown Officers', 226–33.
[44] Gunn, 'Regime of Charles, Duke of Suffolk', 489–90; Guy, 'Wolsey and the Tudor Polity', 69–70.

individuals, and declared his goods confiscated to the crown. This procedure was particularly useful in dealing with political enemies who had fallen in battle, or who had been killed without trial in some other way.[45]

Estates confiscated from political enemies often became the means by which to reward friends, and so consolidate support for the government in the provinces. Inserting new families into confiscated estates, rather than allowing the heirs of traitors to work their way back into favour, was becoming more common in the period under discussion, particularly under Henry VII.[46] The implications of political turns of fortune for the greater families may be illustrated by a comparison between the fortunes of the Bourchiers and the de Veres. The Bourchiers had been stalwart supporters of the Yorkist dynasty ever since Henry, Viscount Bourchier fell foul of the Lancastrian court in 1456 and committed himself to the cause of Richard, duke of York in 1459. Henry had benefited from this attachment by being created earl of Essex in 1461. He was regularly in high office under Edward IV from this time; between 1471 and his death in 1483, five days before the king he had served, he was chief steward of the duchy of Lancaster south of the Trent. His grandson, who succeeded him as the second Bourchier earl of Essex, was still in his teens when he carried the spurs at the coronation of Henry VII.[47] Meanwhile the career of John de Vere, thirteenth earl of Oxford, had followed a disastrous Lancastrian tack. After the battle of Barnet, where he had commanded the left wing of Henry VI's forces, he had been forced into exile. In 1473 he was captured at St Michael's Mount (Cornwall), which he had besieged and captured, and then suffered twelve years of imprisonment in Hammes Castle, near Calais. Edward IV deprived him of his title and estates by parliamentary act of attainder in 1475. In 1485, however, the political fortunes of the two families were reversed. In November 1484, John de Vere escaped from Hames Castle, joined Henry Tudor in Paris, then accompanied his invading forces to Milford Haven and commanded the archers for him at Bosworth. Following the victory there, he was restored to his title as earl of Oxford and to extensive estates in East Anglia and Essex, including the

[45] J. G. Bellamy, *The Law of Treason in England in the Later Middle Ages*, Cambridge 1970, 123–4.

[46] Carpenter, *Locality and Polity*, 131, 634–5; Lander, *Crown and Nobility*, 142–5, 154.

[47] G. E. C., *Complete Peerage*, v, 137–8; P. A. Johnson, *Duke Richard of York, 1411–1460*, Oxford 1988, 177, 185.

manor of Wivenhoe, where Essex University now stands. He was appointed to be lord high admiral and constable of the Tower of London, and was given Henry Bourchier's former office as chief steward of the duchy of Lancaster. As a pillar of the Tudor establishment he inevitably became the government's main support in Essex, and his superior abilities and political influence prevented the young earl of Essex from ever achieving much of a role in country politics, even though the latter became firmly attached to the new dynasty. In East Anglia the earl of Oxford similarly eclipsed the Howard family after the death of John Howard, duke of Norfolk, in Richard III's service at the Battle of Bosworth.[48]

Redistributions of property did not affect only the nobility, since kings were concerned about their support amongst lesser landowners as well. After the 1483 rebellion, Richard III was no longer able to trust the local basis of support for the Yorkist regime under his brother, and was obliged to create a new one using men he could depend upon by planting new men and rewarding proven loyalty amongst existing families. The politics of such redistributions was difficult. One of the dilemmas was the reluctance of local groups to accept some outsiders intruded for political reasons. Richard III experienced this problem in reallocating estates in southern England. Inevitably, given the nature of his personal following, many beneficiaries were his northern retainers, like Robert Brackenbury from County Durham, who took over lands and local offices and administration from southern families. According to the contemporary account of the Crowland Chronicle, Richard's distribution of forfeited estates amongst his northern followers scandalized 'all the southern people'.[49] Another dilemma arising from the redistribution of estates was that even generous patronage could create resentment amongst those who failed to benefit. Many of those in Devon and Somerset who had welcomed Henry Tudor in 1485 were sadly disappointed when the rewards of victory went chiefly to friends of the king like Sir Giles Daubeney.[50]

The confiscation of estates sometimes contributed directly to an expansion of the royal estate and the absorption of a royal following into the ranks of the king's own servants. After 1478,

---

[48] Gunn, 'Henry Bourchier', 152–8; R. Virgoe, 'The Recovery of the Howards in East Anglia, 1485–1529', in E. W. Ives, R. J. Knecht and J. J. Scarisbrick (eds), *Wealth and Power in Tudor England: Essays Presented to S.T. Bindoff*, London 1978, 7–11.

[49] *Crowland Continuations*, 170–1; Horrox, *Richard III*, 180–205; Pollard, 'Tyranny of Richard III', 147–65.

[50] Luckett, 'Patronage', 155–7.

for example, Edward IV took over the duke of Clarence's estates and following in south Warwickshire, and was able to dominate that part of the county through the selective bestowal of crown patronage on local families. He used his influence to such good effect, supported by that of Lord Hastings in the north of the county, that by the end of his reign Warwickshire was more peaceful than in living memory. The strengthening of royal power by the accumulation of property and lordship in the king's hands was most strikingly exemplified in the north, following the absorption of the Neville lands and lordships accumulated by Richard of Gloucester into the royal estate in 1483. In addition, Henry VII reclaimed his earldom of Richmond in 1485, and thereby acquired a considerable estate in north-western Yorkshire. Richard III had retained his personal authority in the north through a council of the north, centred in York, in the years 1483–5. Henry VII abandoned that experiment, but in his reign the north experienced an level of direct intervention by the king's council from Westminster to which it was unaccustomed.[51] By the time Henry VIII revived the council of the north in 1525, he could reasonably claim that the region had been tamed.

The effectiveness of such expansion of the lordship of the crown depended, of course, on the king's ability to assume the associated responsibilities. Henry VII, though he expanded the area of the royal demesne, adopted a policy of neglect coupled with intermittent repression that was far removed from traditional ideals of good lordship, and there is no area of government in which his lack of political experience shows so clearly as in his clumsiness in handling local issues. The way in which disorder grew in Warwickshire between 1485 and 1502 demonstrates how necessary it was for the crown to establish a cooperative relationship with local interests; by the end of this period he was putting the loyalty of his subjects under severe strain in much of the county.[52]

The ways in which government used statutory provisions and legal institutions rather than patronage to intervene in the counties will be examined in the discussion of law in chapter 9. Kings required some direct control to suppress the worst abuses of retaining. It is pertinent here to observe, however, that if there was one period between 1485 and 1529 when government was particularly interventionist in this way, it was the reign of Henry VII. He proceeded more consistently against unauthorized retaining

---

[51] Pollard, *North-Eastern England*, 384, 390–2.
[52] Carpenter, *Locality and Polity*, 523–6, 545, 560–92.

than his predecessors, and made exceptionally oppressive use of the threat of the stick rather than the promise of the carrot in inducing noblemen to abide by legal decisions. This policy was possible partly because of the weakening of aristocratic leadership in country politics during the previous generation. It was unfortunate for Henry's reputation, however, that such a stance was accompanied by indifference to the doings of his own servants. The local influence of royal favourites and household men always carried with it the risk that these would create a complacent and corrupt interest group within county society, and so bring about the sort of local disaffection that they were supposed to prevent. Henry VII's tolerance of such corruption was blatant, and the Plumpton letters from his reign are as rife with it as the Paston letters of the 1450s and 1460s. Reynold Bray, Edmund Dudley and Richard Empson are usually remembered for the ways in which they extorted money on Henry VII's behalf, but they were equally notorious for the way in which they used their legal knowledge and influence to advance their own interests.[53] Henry VIII's government was more sensitive to the dangers of this position, which undermined the government's declared concern with law enforcement.

Henry VII has often been praised for his heavy handling of the nobility, on the assumption that he had found the only way to bring them to heel. Given the odium he incurred, and the speed with which his son dismantled much of his oppressive policy, this judgement needs to be questioned. It has been well said that if this was the criterion of 'new monarchy', then it began and ended with him.[54] Between Edward IV's dependence upon powerful regional lordships, and Henry VII's overbearing pose as the great disciplinarian, there was middle ground that depended more on political skills. Henry VIII's rule removed much of the harassment characteristic of his father's reign, though he and Wolsey continued to insist as firmly as ever that members of the nobility should know their place under the law.

[53] *Plumpton Correspondence*, cii–cxix; M. Condon, 'From Caitiff and Villain to Pater Patriae: Reynold Bray and the Profits of Office', in M. Hicks (ed.), *Profit, Piety and the Professions in Later Medieval England*, Gloucester 1990, 155; Kirby, 'Fifteenth-Century Family', 116–19; M. Hastings, *The Court of Common Pleas in Fifteenth Century England*, Ithaca 1947, 240.
[54] Pugh, 'Henry VII and the English Nobility', 91.

6

Parliamentary and
Popular Politics

Court politics and country politics were matters of everyday concern, centring essentially around the households of the king and other landlords. Meanwhile, there was another sphere of political activity, parliament, which, from time to time, brought together the worlds of court and country politics into a single forum. Since parliaments met for the equivalent of only 187 weeks in total between January 1471 and December 1529 (see table 6.1), these sessions cannot be treated as the primary focus of decision-taking. Yet parliament was an intrinsic part of the political scene. It had been developed from the late thirteenth century to give expression to the common interest of the king and his subjects. It represented a real check on the power of kings to tax their subjects, and it was so rarely summoned chiefly because kings were aware of the difficulty of getting the sums they wanted on inadequate pretexts.

Parliaments invariably met in Westminster. They opened with a general meeting of lords and commons together in a room known as the Painted Chamber, adjoining Whitehall. After that, the lords adjourned to their own meeting-place in the White Chamber, adjoining the Painted Chamber to the south, parallel to the Thames, while the commons decamped to the chapter house or refectory of Westminster Abbey.[1] The commons had no definite building of their own, but since contemporaries spoke in an institutional sense of the 'lower house' or 'common house' and the 'higher house', or 'upper house', it is legitimate as well as convenient to write of parliament as made up of two houses.[2]

The lords who attended parliament did so on personal summons from the king. They were there as powerful men in their

---

[1] Butt, *History of Parliament*, xxii–xxiii; Loach, *Parliament*, 43.
[2] Chrimes, *Henry VII*, 136–7; Graves, *Tudor Parliaments*, 19–22, 45–9.

Table 6.1   Parliaments between 1471 and 1529

Date of assembly	Date of dissolution	Number of sessions	Duration of sessions (days)
6.10.1472	14.3.1475	7	286
16.1.1478	26.2.1478	1	42
20.1.1483	18.2.1483	1	30
23.1.1484	20.2.1484	1	29
7.11.1485	about 4.3.1485	2	75
9.11.1487	about 18.12.1487	1	40
13.1.1489	27.2.1490	3	128
17.10.1491	5.3.1492	2	59
14.10.1495	21–22.12.1495	1	70
16.1.1497	13.3.1497	1	57
25.1.1504	about 1.4.1504	1	67
21.1.1510	23.2.1510	1	34
4.2.1512	4.3.1514	3	144
5.2.1515	22.12.1515	2	101
15.4.1523	13.8.1523	3	101
3.11.1529	14.4.1536	8	(44)[a]

[a] First session only.
Source: E. B. Fryde, D. E. Greenway, S. Porter and I. Roy (eds), *Handbook of British Chronology*, 3rd edn, London 1986, 571–3

own right, not as representatives of any of the component communities of the realm. Stephen Hawes, in a sombre poem published in 1509 designed to discourage swearing, called for the united support of kings, princes, dukes and lords of every degree 'over the commons having the sovereignty'.[3] There were both practical and symbolic reasons for drawing together the magnates of the realm in parliament – practical because their consent increased the likelihood that decisions taken in parliament would be enforceable, and symbolic because their presence implied unity amongst the dignitaries of the realm. It was a common rhetorical device to suppose that superior power and riches were linked to superior virtue – that the nobility were 'endued with manhood, wisdom and riches', to quote Hawes once more. As a generalization this was vulnerable to plain evidence, since it was not difficult to find incompetent mediocrities.[4] However, some more able lay peers had

[3] Hawes, 78.
[4] S. J. Gunn, 'Henry Bourchier, Earl of Essex (1472–1540)', in Bernard, *Tudor Nobility*, 169.

considerable expertise in local affairs and royal service, and the bishops and the abbots of the larger abbeys in the upper house, together with up to about a dozen leading officers of the law, could all be expected to have useful professional expertise. Lawyers played an important part in the discussion and preparation of legislation in the upper house.[5] The careerist element of clerics and lawyers was numerically predominant in the house of lords. Under Henry VII, lay peers numbered at most forty-three out of a total number that varied between eighty-eight and 101,[6] and since many of them did not attend, this enhanced yet further the significance of those closest to the everyday work of advising the king and running the country.

For some purposes kings found it convenient to summon lords alone without the commons, in which case the assembly was known as a great council rather than a parliament. This happened at least three times under Edward IV between 1476 and 1480, and five times under Henry VII between 1487 and 1502.[7] Henry VIII did not use this device between 1509 and 1529, but the idea was not dead; a grand council was called to Hampton Court in October 1530 while Henry was still thrashing around for a solution to his matrimonial problem.[8] Such occasions are poorly recorded, but they seem to correspond to moments when the king wanted quick soundings of opinion without going through the lengthy process of initiating elections by the commons. Most of the great councils called by Henry VII were to discuss the threat of war or rebellion.[9] Even when both houses met, the house of lords had considerable influence, and it retained a prominent legislative function. In some parliaments a majority of acts commenced there, though the lords alone, according to a legal judgement of 1489, could not pass a bill into law without the assent of the commons.[10]

For some royal purposes a full parliament had long been essential. The commons had the power to commit the king's subjects to obedience to new statutes, particularly those which affected the king's powers over the property of his subjects such as acts of attainder or acts of resumption. Taxes on the laity, too, required the consent of the commons. This power rested upon the principle

[5] Loach, *Parliament*, 20–1.
[6] Chrimes, *Henry VII*, 140; Graves, *Tudor Parliaments*, 45.
[7] Ross, *Edward IV*, 311; Chrimes, *Henry VII*, 135.
[8] Guy, *Tudor England*, 126–7.
[9] Chrimes, *Henry VII*, 144.
[10] Graves, *Tudor Parliaments*, 54–6, 58.

PLATE 6.1 Henry VIII in parliament, 1515, with the bishops to his right, lay lords to his left and the judges on woolsacks in the centre. Cardinal Wolsey, seated second from the king's right hand, is indicated by his cardinal's hat. The drawing illustrates the numerical superiority of legal and ecclesiastical members in the house of lords. The Speaker of the Commons is represented in the middle of the bottom edge of the picture. (*The Royal Collection © Her Majesty the Queen*)

of representation. John Catesby, serjeant-at-law, expounded in 1482 the idea that everyone was bound by parliamentary acts because the members elected from each separate 'commonalty' had the power to bind the 'commonalty' of the realm collectively.[11] Thirty-seven counties (not including Chester and Durham) were asked to send two men each, and so were each of the represented boroughs except London, which sent four. There was no sense, however, in which even the commons were supposed to be a balanced representation of English society either by rank or by location. Places in parliament were overwhelmingly allocated to southern England. Drawing an east–west line between Shrewsbury and King's Lynn, only ten counties lay wholly or predominantly to the north, and only fifteen boroughs, including these two. This meant that in 1471 only fifty out of 295 members of the commons were elected from the northern parts of England, so defined.[12] By 1529 the number of northern seats had grown to fifty-six as a result of the enfranchisement of Berwick (by 1512), Lancaster (by 1523) and Preston (by 1529), but as the total number of places in the house of commons had risen to 310 the overall balance between north and south was not improved.[13]

The commons were elected only in the sense that they were not nominated by the crown, for very few elections were contested. In none of those to the Reformation Parliament of 1529 are the electors known to have had any choice.[14] County members were locally well-connected landowners, often active in the king's service, and because they were of higher status in the house than the more numerous borough members, speakers of the house of commons were invariably elected from their ranks. Yet county members were usually chosen in advance of the election in the course of discussions or conflicts amongst major interest groups. In the boroughs, too, election was usually a formality. Only about thirty of the 110 boroughs represented in parliament showed even a strong preference for being represented by their own burgesses; these included York, Newcastle upon Tyne and Hull in northern England, London, Bristol, Winchester, Exeter and Colchester in southern England.[15] The remaining eighty boroughs either often bargained to make their seats available to some patron who would

[11] Chrimes, *English Constitutional Ideas*, 79.
[12] Wedgwood, *History of Parliament*, i, pp. vi–viii.
[13] Bindoff, *House of Commons*, i, 5, 121, 125, 162.
[14] Lehmberg, *Reformation Parliament*, 10–11.
[15] Wedgwood, *History of Parliament*, ii, 631, 643, 645, 659–60, 667, 681, 719, 721; Bindoff, *House of Commons*, i, 70, 89, 93, 102, 140, 164, 245, 253.

bear the costs of maintaining their members, or were so subordinate to a particular lord that they had no choice in the matter. An extreme example in the second category – pocket boroughs, as they were later known – is Gatton (Surrey), where the lord of the manor was the sole burgess and elector.[16] Parliamentary representatives were so frequently seigniorial nominees that the social origins of their MPs were not clearly distinct from those of county MPs.[17]

Most parliamentary debates related to subjects like taxation that had little or nothing to do with the issues of county politics. The debate in 1515 concerning clerical privilege is another case in point. It is unlikely that many members of the lower house were constrained by external obligations to noble patrons in discussing such matters. The fact that a member of parliament owed his election to a particular lord might restrict his independence on some specific issue, but it did not commit him on most of the matters that would arise. The commons, especially knights of the shire, were men used to independent action. Other constraints on the activities of MPs were far more significant than noble patronage. In 1523, upon his election as speaker, Thomas More asked the king to allow freedom of speech in the lower house as a condition of genuine debate, but he did not step beyond the bounds of prudence and he was not in fact asking very much.[18] In practice any freedom of debate was constrained by the limits set to parliamentary agenda. Control over what is discussed is, in any institution, a critical aspect of the exercise of power, and in this respect More was duty-bound. The speaker was an agent of the crown, chosen well in advance of the meeting of parliament and made responsible for running an orderly house. It was his duty to see that the king's official agenda was effectively handled, as well as to control the passage of private bills through the commons. Under Edward IV speakers began to be paid a handsome amount of cash for performing this service.[19]

'Ideally,' it has been observed, 'a parliament was a demonstration of community of interests between the government and the governed.'[20] Such community of interests is best observed in parliament's handling of matters relating to dynastic security. In the interests of buttressing the status quo, the dynastic interest of the

[16] Bindoff, House of Commons, i, 194–5.
[17] Wedgwood, History of Parliament, ii, p. lxxxviii.
[18] Loach, Parliament, 60–1.
[19] Roskell, Commons, 76–103.
[20] Roskell, Commons, 98.

current monarch and his vendettas against his personal enemies were generally supported, even if reluctantly. The acts of attainder by which kings laid hands on the properties of their defeated enemies were standard expressions of propaganda, whose statements bore little relationship to any known facts. Edward IV was generous with pardons after his victory of 1471, but the parliament of October 1472 authorized all the sentences of attainder that he required. More strikingly, that same parliament, at its fifth session in May 1474, accepted without demur the sordid deal in favour of the king's brothers, overturning the legal rights of the widowed countess of Warwick.[21] A few years later, in the parliament of January 1478, the duke of Clarence was condemned for treason on the strength of the king's own word, and an act of attainder was passed against him without dissent even from his known friends.[22] Another remarkable instance of this is the way in which the parliament of January 1484 ratified the usurpation of Richard III and accepted the attainder of those who had rebelled the previous summer. The Crowland chronicler particularly comments on the absence of any token of resistance.[23]

In view of these examples, it is hardly surprising that Henry VII had it all his own way when he acceded to the throne by force of arms. The first parliament of his reign reversed attainders authorized on Richard III's behalf only the previous year, and then attainted twenty-eight of Richard's supporters. The legal implications here should have been a matter of concern, since Richard III had been the crowned king of England at the time of the battle of Bosworth. On this occasion there were expressions of disapproval in the commons, and a private letter records that 'there was many gentlemen against it'.[24] Yet because they related to the security of the reigning king, parliament swallowed both the proposed attainders and the verbiage that accompanied them.[25] These examples illustrate the complicity of parliaments in the cleaning-up operations incident to dynastic crises and rebellion, and show the extent to which parliaments were the loyal instruments of the current monarch.

The normal level of government patronage was enough to ensure a working royal interest in the commons without rigging elections. It is true that of the 291 members of the commons in the

[21] Ross, *Edward IV*, 183–4, 190.
[22] Hicks, *False, Fleeting, Perjur'd Clarence*, 141, 153.
[23] Ross, *Richard III*, 184–5.
[24] *Crowland Continuations*, 194–5; *Plumpton Correspondence*, 49.
[25] Chrimes, *Henry VII*, 62–3.

highly-charged parliament of 1478 whose names are known, about a fifth were royal servants. Friends of the government tampered with election returns in Cornwall, whose elected members were nominees of the Lord Hastings, the receiver-general of the duchy of Cornwall, and his associate Sir John Fogge. Yet the king could not effectively pack the house by such means, and it is improbable that he tried to do so. The pressure on seats in 1478 is likely to have come from royal servants themselves, wanting to be present at the trial of Clarence. Many of those concerned would also have liked to be in Westminster on 15 January 1478 for the exceptionally extravagant wedding of the king's second son, Richard, duke of York and of Norfolk, earl of Nottingham and Warenne (aged four), to the heiress Anne Mowbray (aged five).[26] At the very end of our period Henry VIII and his councillors were alleged to have intervened to ensure a strong royalist element in the Reformation Parliament of 1529. Yet analysis of the membership of this parliament has failed to establish that there was in fact anything unusual about it.[27]

Members of parliament made a clear distinction between issues requiring their support for the crown, even if critical, and those on which they might strenuously manoeuvre for position. Grants of taxation fell unambiguously into this latter category, and the commons were not expected to give what the king asked. Taxation was usually debated in the commons before going to the lords, and until 1492 a written indenture with full details of the agreed grant was ceremonially presented to the king by the speaker of the commons. (From 1492 grants of taxation came to be treated in the same way as other acts of parliament.)[28] In reaching agreement the king was normally challenged to moderate his requests for cash, and even the speaker of the commons was not bound to argue the king's case. These being the expectations, there was inevitably an element of gamesmanship in all such debates, and the declared intentions of the opposing sides must be interpreted as bargaining ploys. So when, for example, Archbishop Warham, as chancellor, asked for a grant of £600,000 in 1512, or when Cardinal Wolsey asked for £800,000 in 1523, it was never supposed that the commons would agree to such figures. Warham obtained a grant equivalent to about £127,000. Wolsey, in the end, secured a promise equivalent to no more than £152,000,

---

[26] Hicks, *False, Fleeting, Perjur'd Clarence*, 143–4; Ross, *Edward IV*, 248.
[27] Lehmberg, *Reformation Parliament*, 8–18.
[28] R. S. Schofield, 'Parliamentary Lay Taxation, 1485–1547', unpublished Ph.D. thesis, Cambridge 1963, 51–5.

collectable over four years.[29] Yet in the latter case Thomas Cromwell described the final outcome as 'a right large subsidy, the like whereof was never granted in this realm', and on 24 August Wolsey petitioned the king for More to be allowed twice the normal speaker's fee because of the exceptionally diligent way in which he had performed his duties.[30]

From the list of parliamentary grants between 1471 and 1529 shown in table 6.2 it can instantly be seen that the taxation of lay wealth followed no regular course. Taxes were collected only in twenty-two years during the period (in 1472–5, 1483, 1488–92, 1497, 1504, 1512–17 and 1524–7), and there was marked bunching of these years into particular periods of financial strain. This is chiefly explained by parliament's acceptance of decisions to go to war. It had long been recognized that military expenditure could not be funded out of the ordinary revenues of the crown, and that parliament was under some obligation to grant supplies. The large grants made by the parliament of 1472–5 in the course of its seven sessions were founded on Edward IV's declared intent to go to war with France, and their nearest precedent was Henry V's wartime taxation of 1413–17. They went some way to funding Edward's French campaign of 1475. The high taxation of the years 1488–92 was similarly related to military preparations against France that, despite their limited scale, cost £108,000. Warfare between the spring of 1511 and the spring of 1514 is estimated to have added at least £892,000 to the normal level of government spending. Warfare in 1522 and 1523 cost something around £400,000.[31] The king's dependence on taxation for sums such as these meant that parliamentary politics revived in periods of aggressive foreign policy, but then died down again in periods of international harmony. Parliament debated only the taxation of the laity, since clerical taxation was negotiated separately in the convocations of Canterbury and York.[32]

There were two different ways in which lay wealth was taxed in this period (see table 6.2). The older, known as a fifteenth and tenth, was a fixed levy on every village and town in the kingdom, except in Cheshire and the palatinate of Durham. A single fifteenth

---

[29] Bernard, *War, Taxation and Rebellion*, 120–2; Gwyn, *King's Cardinal*, 370.

[30] *SP*, i, 124, 127. For a critical assessment of Wolsey's handling of the negotiations in parliament, see Guy, 'Wolsey and the Parliament of 1523'.

[31] Bernard, *War, Taxation and Rebellion*, 53; S. J. Gunn, 'The Act of Resumption of 1515', in D. Williams (ed.), *Early Tudor England*, Woodbridge 1989, 92; R. Hoyle, 'War and Public Finance', in MacCulloch, *Reign of Henry VIII*, 87–8.

[32] Below, p. 156.

and tenth could be expected to raise just over £29,000 after the deduction of the costs of collection and exemptions.[33] This tax has been described as 'the most underdeveloped in Western Europe', and its survival testifies to the power of parliament to inhibit fiscal innovation in the fifteenth century. The way in which individual places raised the sum that they owed varied greatly, but the fact that the sum was fixed meant that little government supervision was necessary; if the collectors nominated for each shire and borough returned the correct sum, no questions needed to be asked. The disadvantage of this form of taxation, however, was that the sums owed by each tax centre corresponded to a very ancient assessment of their relative ability to pay; it dated, in fact, from 1334, though there had been a few *ad hoc* modifications in the fifteenth century. There had been changes in the geographical distribution of wealth during the late Middle Ages, which meant that contributions to a fifteenth and tenth bore little relationship to the real taxable wealth of different towns and villages.[34]

Parliament had permitted a few tentative experiments with new assessed taxes under the Lancastrian kings, but in the late fifteenth century there were still no regular principles by which this could best be done. The subsidy of 1472, whose transfer into the king's hands was cautiously made dependent on his actually going to war, was assessed as a tenth of incomes from land, fees and wages. The more ambitious subsidy of 1489 was based on a new assessment of both incomes and movable wealth. It was approved specifically on the understanding that it would not constitute a precedent, and because its yield was far less than expected it was viewed at the time as a failure. It also met with violent resistance in Yorkshire. The subsidies of 1497 and 1504 were levied according to the existing fixed county assessments for fifteenths and tenths, but the distribution of the burden between villages and individual households within each county was reassessed by local commissioners. The eventual emergence of a reliable new form of assessed subsidy, untrammelled by the past 200 years of tradition, can be dated to the war years between 1513 and 1515. The subsidies levied in those and subsequent years were wholly based on the assessment of individual taxpayers, and the sum to be

---

[33] Schofield, 'Parliamentary Lay Taxation', 156.
[34] Bush, 'Tax Reform', 380; C. Dyer, 'Taxation and Communities in Late Medieval England', in R. H. Britnell and J. Hatcher (eds), *Progress and Problems in Medieval England: Essays in Honour of Edward Miller*, Cambridge 1996, 168–90; Schofield, 'Taxation', 230.

collected was not fixed in advance. Taxpayers could be assessed either on their income from land, or on their income from wages, or on the value of their movable possessions, whichever was most advantageous to the crown.[35]

The origins of these new developments are unrecorded in detail. The form of the new subsidies was established by the innovatory planning of royal servants, rather than in commons debate. The new developments coincide with the years of Wolsey's rise to power, but there is nothing to connect him directly with them. The fact that John Hales of Gray's Inn drew up the subsidy acts for both 1513 and 1514 may mean that he was one of the government's consultants. In any event, the commons in these years accepted not only an exceptionally steep level of taxation for the purpose of fighting in France and Scotland, but also a new principle of taxation that was more open-ended in its implications than the old fifteenths and tenths with their fixed yields. In effect, Henry VIII's parliaments displayed a more cooperative attitude to the crown in this respect than earlier ones. There was less hostility to granting taxes to the crown, and less restriction was placed on the use of the sums so raised. Henry VIII had little trouble, too, in actually levying the sums that parliament had granted.[36]

The greater complacency of parliaments in approving financial bills is also demonstrated in this period in the history of revenue from customs duties on overseas trade. This was the other principal form of taxation, and like taxes on incomes and wealth, it required the consent of parliament. The principle customs duties were the subsidies on wool and cloth exports, tunnage on wine imports, and poundage on all other imports and exports. Although customs revenues had long been a normal and necessary part of the king's income, it had been usual for parliament to retain some control over them by making temporary grants for short, fixed periods. Edward IV was granted all the customs dues for life in 1465, but the first king to be given a life grant at his first parliament was Richard III in 1484. From that time the need for a lifetime grant of customs was accepted; Henry VII received such a grant in 1485 and Henry VIII in 1510.[37]

Another feature of parliamentary assemblies was the bringing of private or local interests before the king. Very little of this

[35] Bush, 'Tax Reform', 383–4; Schofield, 'Parliamentary Lay Taxation', 160–205; Schofield, 'Taxation', 231–3.

[36] Schofield, 'Taxation', 233, 237–8.

[37] Chrimes, *Henry VII*, 195; F. C. Dietz, *English Government Finance, 1485–1641*, 2nd edn, 2 vols, Urbana 1964, i, 88; Ross, *Richard III*, 178.

Table 6.2 Net yield of taxes on lay wealth levied between 1471 and 1529 (excluding taxes on aliens)

Year granted	Year due	Nature of tax	Sum raised (£)
1472	1473	tenth of landed revenues	36,794
1474	1474	fifteenth and tenth	(29,000)
1475	1475	fifteenth and tenth	(29,000)
1475	1475	³/₄ fifteenth and tenth	(21,750)
1483	1483	fifteenth and tenth	(29,000)
1487	1488	fifteenth and tenth	29,072
1487	1489	fifteenth and tenth	29,405
1489	1489	subsidy	18,300
1490	1490	½ fifteenth and tenth	14,431
1490	1491	½ fifteenth and tenth	14,430
1490	1492 (i)	fifteenth and tenth	29,300
1490	1492 (ii)	fifteenth and tenth	27,011
1497	1497 (i)	fifteenth and tenth	29,266
1497	1497 (ii)	fifteenth and tenth	29,252
1497	1497	subsidy	30,088
1504	1504	subsidy	30,873
1512	1512	fifteenth and tenth	29,501
1512	1513	fifteenth and tenth	29,563
1512	1513	subsidy	32,563
1512	1514	fifteenth and tenth	29,319
1514	1514	subsidy	49,422
1515	1515	subsidy	44,819
1515	1516	subsidy	44,074
1515	1517	fifteenth and tenth	29,553
1523	1524	subsidy	72,061
1523	1525	subsidy	64,517
1523	1526	subsidy	5521
1523	1527	subsidy	9116

The figures for 1490–1 distribute Dr Schofield's figure of £28,861, for a fifteenth and tenth of which half was payable by 11 November 1490 and the other half by 11 November 1491.

Sources: R. H. Britnell, 'The Economic Context', in A. J. Pollard, *The Wars of the Roses*, London 1995, 61 (for figures to 1483); R. S. Schofield, 'Parliamentary Lay Taxation, 1485–1547', unpublished Ph.D. thesis, Cambridge 1963, 473 (all figures after 1485)

parliamentary business can be considered as a continuation of county politics, except in so far as individuals or borough communities sought help in presenting their petitions to the king. The greater issues of local power were not on the agenda; the commons did not discuss the private affairs of noblemen. Indeed, in one respect the business of the commons sometimes appeared to undermine county politics to the extent that, in very general terms, petitioners sought to introduce limitations on excessive or oppressive retaining. It was through petitions that parliament was able to represent the independent views of the king's subjects on matters thought to need action or redress. Petitions in parliament often touched on criticisms of current institutions or those who managed them. In this context, however, it is noteworthy that parliaments of the period 1471–1529 were more cautious than their predecessors had been. At no point in this period was there any attempt in parliament to criticize the king's choice of ministers or councillors. This cannot be because there were no grievances. Henry VII's servants, Richard Empson and Edmund Dudley, were so widely disliked that Henry VIII inaugurated his reign and established his virtue by having them arrested. Another issue on which parliaments were silent was the level of expenditure on the king's household, which had been a major source of conflict several times in the preceding 100 years. Again, it was not that king's were living cheaply or that their household expenditure did not need to be checked.[38] Certain forms of criticism and opposition, it would seem, had been rejected from the parliamentary agenda. This is unlikely to be because parliamentarians of the period 1471–1529 were more easily intimidated than their forefathers, or because kings were more intimidating.

From this analysis it would seem that parliament was in fact of little significance either for the continuation of court politics (except in the extreme case of ratifying attainders or the repeal of attainders) or for the continuation of country politics. Parliamentary issues were too particular for there to be great overlap with these other spheres. One motive that took men to parliament was surely an active interest in the public affairs of the realm and the doings of the great. It is probably a relevant consideration, too, that in the course of the period men could be increasingly confident that if they attended parliament they might see what went on without risking involvement in embarrassing political antagonisms. The adverse side of this sophisticated political culture

[38] Above, p. 59.

is not difficult to define. Members of parliament came from a restricted range of social and educational backgrounds. Their political ideals were strongly hierarchical, and their sympathies were restricted. Some of the implications of these limitations – which long outlived the Middle Ages – are to be seen most clearly in the common cause made by the king and the parliamentary classes in the face of popular opposition to their decisions.

Popular Politics

Popular politics, the fourth and final dimension of political activity to be analysed here, leaves less evidence in the archives than the others. Like parliamentary politics, it was discontinuous. This type of political action was led by those excluded from participation in the politics of court, country and parliament, but who nevertheless felt the effects of government on their welfare. By this definition, popular politics excludes episodes in which tenants and townsmen got caught up in the politics of court and country through following aristocratic leaders who were powerful in the area where they lived. Popular politics was characteristically a form of protest about issues of social justice, with varying degrees of militancy, rather than any sort of bid for power.[39]

There were no formal institutions for representing the views of most people outside the confines of local courts or guild meetings. There are therefore no records of formal debate, no official narratives, and usually little biographical information relating to participants in popular politics. Virtually the only relevant narratives are those of infrequent uprisings, and the only information about the leaders of popular politics is the one-sided evidence of those prosecuted as traitors, which serves to identify them by name, occupation and place of residence. As this implies, a historian can know popular politics only in the form of tales of serious trouble stirred up by malefactors. The intentions of rebels and their leaders are masked by official propaganda in all the records, and it is up to the historian to understand that in this period governments made no distinction between rebellions and protest movements. The use of force to put down a popular movement does not prove that its leaders had violent intentions, though this is an assumption that historians make surprisingly often. Even the use of terms such as 'rebellion' is tendentious, since in none of the

[39] Harvey, 'Was There Popular Politics?', 155–74.

popular uprisings of the period 1471–1529 was there any intention of overthrowing the government. The most that can be hoped for from the available evidence is some analysis of what sort of actions by people in power put a strain on popular loyalties, what sort of people were most likely to protest actively, how they actually behaved, and how the government responded.

In the major episodes of unrest, resistance to novel forms of taxation was unambiguously the main concern. To that extent, popular rebellions were the mirror-image of the commons' compliance in authorizing fiscal innovation. The first example of this was resistance to the subsidy of 1489. It provoked an uprising in Yorkshire that involved perhaps 5000 or more people at its peak, following unsuccessful attempts at lobbying the king to gain some remission. On the king's instructions, Henry Percy, earl of Northumberland, the leading nobleman in the north, insisted that the tax would have be levied 'to the uttermost farthing'. On 24 April, at an early stage in the build-up of organized opposition, the earl summoned his followers to meet at Thirsk with a view to intercepting a march of the insurgents. However, four days later an armed band surrounded and assassinated him at Cocklodge near Thirsk; he was the only person to be killed in the course of the rising. Temporarily unopposed, supporters of the rising came together in the first week of May from the East and North Riding, and they managed to enter York on 15 May, with the help of friends in the city. Though resistance to taxation was the principal issue, the revolt gave vent to old Yorkshire loyalties to Richard III. The rebels scattered, however, at the approach of a large army led by the king, who made a triumphal entry into York on 23 May. The judicial retaliation for the uprising was prompt but moderate. At least six rebels were executed following trials before the king at Pontefract on 21 May, and there was a similar number of executions at York soon afterwards; the exact toll is obscured by inconsistencies in the sources. To judge from those indicted at York, most of whom were pardoned, the leaders of the rebellion had almost all been men of very modest property – husbandmen, yeomen and craftsmen.[40]

In June 1497 there was another major protest over taxation, often called the Cornish Rising or Cornish Revolt, this time centred in the south-west, but with support from other southern counties. This was a bigger affair than the Yorkshire revolt of eight years

---

[40] Bennett, 'Henry VII and the Northern Rising', 34–59; Hicks, *Richard III and his Rivals*, 395–418; Pollard, *North-Eastern England*, 379–82.

before, and had a broader geographical and social base. It also had a more disastrous outcome. Although the movement attracted the support of some gentlemen from the west country, and of James Lord Audley from amongst the peers of the realm, it was neither a struggle for local power nor a challenge to the dynastic right of the Tudors, even if it drew upon residual Yorkist nostalgia. Its declared aim was to petition the king to reduce his high wartime demands for taxation, and in particular the imposition of two fifteenths and tenths to be collected in the same year. Its captain was Michael Joseph An Gof, a blacksmith from Bodmin. Like a number of earlier popular movements in southern England, this one had a march on London as its central feature. Some at least of its open supporters were women, though it is not known whether they went on the march. The journey towards London, which was disciplined and non-violent, met little opposition because the local military leaders were engaged in a campaign in Scotland, and because many of the gentry families that remained were either apathetic or sympathetic to the rising. About 15,000 insurgents reached Blackheath and camped there on 16 June. As in 1489, the king responded with massive force, hastily assembling 25,000 men under the command of Giles Daubeney. The government was concerned that, as in past uprisings, armed men might enter London and create havoc there at the expense of the citizens in general and the king's ministers in particular. Government troops first barred the approach to London, and then, with far less justification, assaulted the insurgents in pitched battle on 17 June. The result was inevitably brutal. Hundreds were killed, mostly on the rebels' side. This carnage was considered sufficient, except for the executions of three men deemed to be rebel leaders; Michael Joseph An Gof and a lawyer called Thomas Flamank were hanged at Tyburn on 27 June, and Lord Audley was beheaded on Tower Hill the following day. The king followed up the rising by imposing heavy fines on people in the West Country who were judged to be implicated in various ways. The seriousness of this rising has been variously estimated. One reading of it is that the government grossly over-reacted, and then used the judicial system to recover its financial costs.[41]

In the summer of 1513, parts of Yorkshire again resisted heavy wartime taxation when the principle of assessment that had caused

---

[41] Arthurson, 'Rising of 1497', 1–18; Chrimes, *Henry VII*, 90; Guy, *Tudor England*, 58. Estimates of the number of rebels killed at Blackheath range from 200 (*Great Chronicle*, 277) to over 2000 (Hall, 479).

trouble in 1489 was revived.[42] The trouble this time started in Richmondshire in the North Riding and spread to Craven in the West. People refused to cooperate with the commissioners appointed to assess them. Most of the recalcitrant taxpayers were persuaded over the next eighteen months to comply with the parliamentary grant, but at least eighteen townships in Bolland Forest and the wapentake of Ewcross, in the far west by the Lancashire border, never paid. In 1516, commissioners appointed to assess a new subsidy tactfully declined to assess Ewcross because, they said, of pestilence there. On this occasion the government chose to handle the revolt by peaceful means, either because there was no violence from the villagers, or because their resistance was so localized, or because the government accepted the argument reported by Polydore Vergil that they were too poor to pay.[43]

The troubles of 1525 came at the end of a long period of contention over government funding. Loans raised in 1522–3 for the war with France were still unpaid, the subsidy of 1523 was still being collected, and there were more subsidies in store for the years 1524, 1525 and 1526. It was in this context that the defeat of Francis I at Pavia on 24 February 1525, and the consequent turmoil into which England's foreign policy was thrown, encouraged Wolsey to raise additional funds against a possible invasion of France. The only idea he could produce that would work in the available time was a non-parliamentary income tax, the Amicable Grant, to be levied on the evidence of the assessments made in 1522 (the General Proscription). Commissioners for each county were appointed, probably on 21 March, to collect the grant within three months.[44] Much of the protest against this tax took the form of non-violent representations and remonstrances, and after the first month the government was already modifying its demands to meet the particular interests of the city of London. This initiated an untidy climb-down as different regions of the country made their dissatisfaction known. Disturbances of the king's peace were restricted to the textile region of Suffolk, where many feared that by taking so much money out of circulation the government would cause unemployment. A number of large assemblies of over 1000 people around Lavenham, Sudbury and Hadleigh are reported to have occurred in the early weeks of May. Some of those who assembled were more armed than usual,

[42] Bush, 'Tax Reform', 380, 397.
[43] R. B. Smith, *Land and Politics in the England of Henry VIII*, Oxford 1970, 198–9.
[44] Bernard, *War, Taxation and Rebellion*, 54–6.

and some blustering things were said. Some of those who were prepared to pay were reported to have been intimidated by some of those who were not. The government responded by raising troops. As rebellions go, however, this was rather tame. Its high spot was a series of negotiations between representatives of the local people and the dukes of Suffolk and Norfolk, which brought about the submission of the former on 11 May. The trouble had lasted less than a fortnight, and there had been no violence. A special commission for the peace met at Lavenham a week later and 525 men from the region were indicted for riot and unlawful assembly. In the event a few ringleaders were reprimanded in the court of star chamber,[45] and the government avoided the use of retaliatory violence.

In the suppression of popular risings the government used language implying that the goals of the rebels were treasonous and revolutionary. A royal proclamation of 10 May 1489 fulminated against Yorkshire rebels, who 'intend not only the destruction of the king's most noble person and of all the nobles and lords of this realm, but also the subversion of the politic weal of the same, and to rob, despoil and destroy all the south parts of this his realm, and to subdue and bring to captivity all the people of the same'.[46] The main problem of popular politics, in the absence of any institutional structure, was to determine what to do to focus an expression of discontent for maximum effect; the risings of 1489, 1497 and 1525 show three different solutions to this problem. In each case the rebels' use of violence was slight.

From the history of the known events, and the analysis of their causes, habits of thought in popular politics would seem to have been very close to those in parliamentary politics.[47] Popular leaders shared a hierarchical notion of the commonwealth, and did not challenge the institutions of property and law that underlay it. They thought of themselves as 'the commons' in a society that included crown and nobility. They did not seek to undermine the authority of the government or to overthrow the established structure of politics. Expressions of Yorkist sympathy were on the fringes of the rebellions of 1489 and 1497 rather than at their core. Rebels commonly accepted the principle that they were bound to support the crown with money in times of need: resistance to the Amicable Grant was justified on grounds of poverty

---

[45] Pollard, *Wolsey*, 148.
[46] *Tudor Royal Proclamations*, i, 20–1.
[47] Harvey, 'Was There Popular Politics?', 155–6.

rather than principle, even though the tax had no parliamentary authorization.[48] The main concern, where it surfaced to the level of definite political action, was to remedy what was seen as injustice, and particularly to halt the collection of taxes people felt too poor to pay. The differences between rebels and those responsible for suppressing them were points of interpretation concerning the obligations of the different ranks of the king's subjects. Wolsey told the Londoners in 1525 that 'it were better that some should suffer indigence than the king at this time should lack'.[49] But how much indigence? It is just at this practical level, of course, that differences of wealth and status might be expected to induce strong differences of opinion. By implication, those who rebelled against taxes authorized by parliament rejected the authority and wisdom of the commons as representatives of the interests of the commonwealth and considered their own leaders to be better advisers of the king. It was in this spirit that the Yorkshire rebels of 1489 called for military aid against those they supposed were about to destroy 'our sovereign lord the king and the commons of England'.[50]

The forceful suppression of all these protests against high taxes encourages the view that popular politics was a forlorn hope, an empty expression of powerlessness from those outside the system. This conclusion, however, would be unnecessarily negative. Only the rising of 1497 led to any considerable bloodshed, and that was because it seemed to threaten the security of London. In all cases, even this one, the number of rebels punished through the judicial system was tiny, which implies that the government recognized the folly of identifying popular unrest with treasonable activity. In addition, it should be noted that popular protest had direct effects on government policy, sometimes only to the benefit of those who had caused the disturbance but sometimes to a more general advantage. The protest of 1489 led to an abandonment of subsidies of that type for over twenty years, so that governments had to experiment with less satisfactory solutions to tax reform in 1497 and 1504. Yorkshire, the seat of the trouble in 1489, was excused from having to contribute to the fifteenths and tenths of 1491 and 1497; it is difficult to imagine clearer evidence for the effectiveness of popular resistance. The western rising of 1497 encouraged Henry VII to come to terms with James IV

---

[48] Bernard, *War, Taxation and Rebellion*, 111–12.
[49] Hall, 696.
[50] *Paston Letters*, i, 659.

of Scotland, and to that extent helped to curb an expensive conflict with England's northern neighbour. The Yorkshire protests of 1513 caused the postponement of both the subsidy and the fifteenth and tenth of that year in Richmondshire and Craven and its abandonment in some parts.[51] In 1525 the government first made numerous concessions to those who were protesting against the Amicable Grant and then abandoned it altogether. From this evidence the proper conclusion must surely be that popular politics was, in fact, a real and effective element in the late medieval political structure even though it was politics without institutional recognition. It posed a threat of which government had continually to take account. Governments, their advisers, and members of parliament all knew that there were limits to what burdens they could impose on the king's subjects without causing unrest, and they knew that such unrest was something to be avoided.

[51] Bush, 'Tax Reform', 396–7; Chrimes, *Henry VII*, 90.

Part III

Nation, Church, Law

7

Nationhood

Although it is often said that dynastic traditions of government precluded the development of nationalism, that idea is difficult to square with the characteristics of the late medieval English monarchy. It is true that English claims to the crown of France were dynastic, based upon the supposed legal right of Edward III's mother, Isabella of France. Yet amongst the emotions that warfare in France was capable of inspiring in parliament, and amongst those who went on campaign, nationalist aggression was prominent.

The importance of war and wartime propaganda in the construction of English national identity over the last two centuries was reflected in the choice of England's patron saint, as William Caxton realized: 'this holy and blessed martyr Saint George is patron of this realm of England, and the cry of men of war'.[1] The association between England and St George, institutionalized in 1348 when Edward III founded the order of St George (later known as the order of the garter), had been strengthened in 1415, following the battle of Agincourt, when 23 April, St George's Day, was elevated as one of the principal feasts of the year. The revival of the order of the garter as England's principal order of chivalry was a feature of Edward IV's strengthening of the monarchy. The rebuilding of St George's chapel in Windsor Castle was planned by 1474–5 and under construction by 1478.[2] The Tudors continued to celebrate St George's Day each year at Windsor. The event had added significance for Henry VIII because he dated the beginning of his reign from 22 April, the eve of the feast. Alexander Barclay's lengthy metrical 'life of the glorious martyr Saint George, patron of the realm of England', published

---

[1] Barclay, *St George*, 118.
[2] Harvey, *Perpendicular Style*, 210.

in 1515, was allegedly written at the request of Thomas Howard, duke of Norfolk.[3]

The chivalric nationalism associated with the order of the garter cannot be supposed to have stretched much beyond the nobility and its immediate adherents. Yet foreign wars drew in men from all over the kingdom, and from all ranks of society. This was politically significant because the sort of nationalism developed by war focused the loyalty of its adherents on the crown, enabling the king to be presented as the head of a nation rather than a mere ruler of men. Writers of the period were more likely to think of England from the top down, and write about the 'realm of England', than to think of it as the English nation from the bottom up.

England's military tradition accounts for the particular hostility to the French and the Scots that surfaces in the sources of the period. A sense of strong national contrast with the French, which might easily switch into jest, scorn or hostility, was to be found in all ranks of society, from pedlar to prince. The French ambassador to England in 1477–9 probably knew little English, but he was able to pick out 'French dogs' shouted after him and his companions in the streets of London.[4] An epidemic of sweating sickness in 1485 was named the French pox, because people said it had been brought from France by whores accompanying Henry VII's invading force.[5] Attitudes to the French hardened into national stereotypes and routine insults of cowardice.[6] The inflexibility of national prejudices, even amongst politically significant social groups, could inconvenience a king who wanted to chose his own path through the fashions of the day, and to choose for himself how he related to his neighbours. In 1519 the frivolity of the 'minions' in Henry VIII's court was blamed on French influence, and their supposedly French manners caused sufficiently serious discontent for the king's council to feel obliged to intervene.[7] In 1525–7 England's rapprochement with France following the battle of Pavia was a source of hostility to the government, particularly in London, and Cardinal Wolsey was criticized as a Francophile.

On the northern frontier the Scots were other ancient enemies

---

[3] Barclay, *St George*, 1.
[4] Russell, 'Language', 38.
[5] Griffiths, *King and Country*, 116.
[6] E.g. Skelton, 282–3.
[7] G. Walker, 'The "Expulsion of the Minions" of 1519 Reconsidered', *HJ*, xxxii (1989), 1–16.

of the English crown. On the very frontier national sense was blurred amongst families whose connections straddled the border. Yet outside the militarized zone, the northern counties, whose inhabitants were the first to be drawn into any military engagement against the Scots, stretched 100 miles to the south of Berwick, and through this region families were aggressively aware of their Englishness. Though the northern counties were barely affected by war, the fear of the Scots remained. The regulations of the northern towns discriminated against Scots, as in Newcastle upon Tyne, where men born in Scotland were prohibited from becoming apprentices in the craft guilds of the glovers, smiths, skinners, saddlers, fullers and dyers. It was a serious matter to be charged with Scottish birth, and one that men contested through the law courts in the interests of preserving their right to trade.[8] It was presumably as a result of prompting by his northern subjects that Henry VII in 1490 ordered the expulsion of suspect and idle Scots from northern counties on the grounds that they were hurting, disturbing and probably impoverishing the king's poor, true and honest subjects.[9] The English were capable of producing the same sort of crude caricatures of the Scots as they did of the French. John Skelton wrote four virulently anti-Scottish poems, two to celebrate the English victory at Flodden in 1513, one in about 1515 to disparage a Scot who said that Englishmen had tails, and one to describe 'how the doughty duke of Albany, like a coward knight, ran away shamefully with a hundred thousand tratland [= prattling] Scots and faint-hearted Frenchmen beside the water of Tweed' in 1523.[10]

Nationalism was in evidence not only in wartime and not only towards England's ancient enemies. A Silesian knight who came to England in 1484 reported that for the people he met there 'the world did not exist apart from England'. An Italian writer describing England around 1500 similarly commented on the English dislike of foreigners and their high estimation of themselves, implying again that they suffered in this respect from insularity: 'they think that there are no other men than themselves, and no other world but England'.[11] In 1527 Erasmus similarly warned a correspondent about to visit England not to find fault with anything he found

---

[8] Pollard, *North-Eastern England*, 17–18.
[9] *Tudor Royal Proclamations*, i, 23.
[10] Skelton, 113–21, 134–6, 359–72.
[11] *Relation*, 20–1; K. Dockray, 'Patriotism, Pride and Paranoia: England and the English in the Fifteenth Century', *The Ricardian*, viii (1990), 434.

there, the English being so patriotic.[12] Foreign visitors, long-term residents and immigrants had reason to feel insecure, and were sometimes threatened with violence.[13]

There were legally institutionalized differences between subjects of the English crown, especially relating to tax liability, which for the most part weighed more heavily on foreigners. Customs regulations distinguished between four categories of merchant – subjects of the English crown (denizens), Spaniards, those of the German Hanse, and all the rest (aliens) – and imposed different rates of duty on their imports and exports. The Spaniards and Germans were privileged in this respect – indeed, in accordance with the treaty of Utrecht of 1474 the Germans paid less duty than denizens – but alien merchants paid appreciably more. Around 1500, for example, for exporting ordinary dyed broadcloth, 'the king's subjects pay for custom of a cloth 14d., the Spaniards pay for custom of a cloth 14d., the Hanse payeth 12d, and aliens pay for a cloth 2s. 9d.'.[14] Within England only aliens had to pay the poll taxes imposed on them in 1482 and 1487.[15] Foreigners were handicapped in other ways under English law. A statute of 1484 placed severe restriction on alien merchants and craftsmen, limiting their freedom to trade and excluding them from the textile industry. A further statute of 1523, re-enacted in 1529, required alien artisans in future to take only English apprentices, and limited them to two alien servants.[16]

Away from the context of external aggression, antagonism to aliens was usually moderated. There were quite a lot of them, especially in seaports. Aliens, including several teams of French ironworkers with specialized skills, made up about 3 per cent of the taxpayers of Sussex in the 1520s.[17] London had a large transient population of foreign merchants, and some visiting craftsmen and artists were commissioned for particular projects, but there were also many permanently resident aliens, and all told they numbered over 4 per cent of the city population. They tended

[12] Erasmus, *Op. Ep.*, vii, 80.

[13] *EHD, 1485–1558*, 190.

[14] *Tudor Economic Documents*, ii, 204.

[15] Ross, *Edward IV*, 197.

[16] 1 Richard III, c. 9; 14 and 15 Henry VIII, cc. 1, 2, 7; 21 Henry VIII, c. 16: *SR*, ii, 489–93, iii, 208–9, 297–301. The legislation approved by the king after each parliament was compiled into a statute, subdivided into chapters. Legislation is referred to by (a) the regnal year in which a particular statute was approved, and (b) the particular chapter of the statute in question. For example, the first reference here is to the ninth chapter of the statute approved in Richard III's first year as king, which ran from 26 June 1483 to 25 June 1484.

[17] Cornwall, *Wealth and Society*, 48–9, 84.

to live together in the same parts of town, to work together, and to marry each other. The presence of such a minority is, of course, only a very minimal sign of tolerance. Nevertheless, social and economic links were generally sufficient to maintain a stable if precarious working relationship between English families and immigrants. In some context there was even a chance of cooperation. There were no separate parish churches for aliens, for example, and in the parish of St Margaret, Southwark, Dutch residents can be found actively involved in the life of their parishes as collectors, churchwardens and gild members. The gild of St Cornelius in Westminster may have been created by the Flemish community there, but it nevertheless took its share of responsibility for rebuilding St Margaret's parish church, and by the 1520s it maintained a small hospital for epileptics.[18]

Overt antagonism towards resident foreigners was most characteristic of economic jealousies amongst urban groups worried about their livelihood. One such eruption, in October 1494, was an early-morning onslaught directed against the German merchants who occupied premises known as the Steelyard. The attackers were led by servants of the London mercers, motivated by jealousy of the Germans' commercial success at a time of unemployment in the city. On this occasion the German merchants were able to barricade themselves in for three hours until the city authorities were able to suppress the disturbance.[19] Even those who might have known better sometimes contributed to fanning the flames of xenophobia. On 14 April 1517, for example, Dr Bele preached publicly at St Mary Spital in London 'that this land was given to Englishmen, and as birds would defend their nest, so ought Englishmen to cherish and defend themselves, and to hurt and grieve aliens for the common weal'. The sermon is on record because Dr Bele was investigated following subsequent disturbances. On 28 April various young men assaulted aliens in the streets. Though the city authorities tried to clamp down on this violence, a rumour spread that all aliens in London were going to be killed in an uprising on 1 May. On the evening of 30 April there was a rioting that involved rifling the house of a wealthy Frenchman with connections at court, as well as breaking into the houses of foreign shoemakers and throwing their wares into the street. The disturbances on 30 April were greatly exacerbated,

[18] S. Brigden, *London and the Reformation*, Oxford 1989, 136; M. Carlin, *Medieval Southwark*, London 1996, 154–6; G. Rosser, *Medieval Westminster, 1200–1540*, Oxford 1989, 194–5, 282, 284–5, 320.
[19] Carlin, *Medieval Southwark*, 161.

if not actually caused, by the London authorities. Under last-minute pressure from Cardinal Wolsey, they had imposed a curfew on the whole city at half an hour's notice, and could not cope with the predictable consequences of their own unreasonableness.[20]

Englishness

Englishness was more than a negative suspicion of foreigners. Because the English monarchy had ruled a relatively unified kingdom for so many centuries, a number of institutions effectively strengthened the association between loyalty to the crown and Englishness, contributing to a positive awareness of cultural identity. A broad swathe of the population would have been influenced by the existence of parliament and the common law as guarantors of distinctive English freedoms.[21] In this respect the construction of a sense of nationhood had been intrinsic to the development of royal government.

In this more positive sense, Englishness was inevitably a more complex phenomenon than the mere antipathy to outsiders would suggest, since many groups of English people had strong antipathies to each other. The high profile of northerners in domestic conflict between 1460 and 1471, their association with Richard III's 'tyranny' of 1483–5, and their violent resistance to taxation in 1489, had hardened antagonism towards them amongst many southerners. The Crowland chronicler described the north as the source of all evil.[22] Regional differences in spoken English were much greater than today. About 1490, William Caxton observed that 'common English that is spoken in one shire varieth from another', and illustrated his point with the story of a northern mercer who asked a southern housewife for 'eggs' only to be told that she did not speak French; her word for an egg was 'ey' (plural 'eyren').[23]

However, there were many different contexts in which people from different parts of the kingdom needed to understand each other. At government level there was a need for regular communication, written and spoken, between different regions. There

[20] Hall, 588–91; Brigden, *London*, 130–1.
[21] See chapters 6 and 9.
[22] Pollard, *North-Eastern England*, 25–7; A. J. Pollard, 'North, South and Richard III', in J. Petre (ed.), *Richard III, Crown and People*, Gloucester 1985, 349–51.
[23] Caxton, 79–80.

was considerable interchange between north and south in the normal course of trade – Newcastle upon Tyne and York being amongst the leading towns of the country – and many northerners had migrated south in search of new opportunities. One of Colchester's leading burgesses in Henry VII's reign was Thomas Jopson of Yorkshire.[24] One of the long-term effects of a politically constructed sense of national identity, coupled with administrative and commercial networks that spanned the kingdom, was to encourage linguistic differences to diminish, particularly amongst the more educated and itinerant social groups.

The immediate context of Caxton's comment is worth observing, since it represents a comparatively recent concern to define what English was, encouraged by the growth of printing. He, like other authors, wanted to be intelligible to the broad English readership that might want to buy his books. A standard written English, based on that of the London region, was already widely used, and he adopted it, though in practice he was not a great standardizer of spelling, vocabulary or style. Because of this new concern for standard forms, historians of the English language often place the divide between medieval and modern English somewhere about the 1470s, when English printing started. The relevance of national allegiance to these developments is demonstrable from the fact that the Scots continued to use and standardize their own independent linguistic forms.[25]

In its increasing use of standard English for royal documents, the crown identified itself with this linguistic development. Latin remained the usual language of legal documents such as title deeds, indentures and contracts, and was still the principle administrative language for accountancy and legal recording, so government departments needed to be manned by men with a good grounding in it. Latin was also the normal language of English diplomacy, and since the upper clergy were trained in Latin as a spoken language the leadership of embassies often fell to them.[26] The speaking of French, however, had greatly declined in England by the late Middle Ages. It survived in a debased form as a professional argot amongst professional lawyers in the central courts of common law. It is unlikely, though, that a lawyer could have made himself understood in France, and few other Englishmen at this time spoke French. When Cardinal Wolsey headed an embassy to Amiens in

---

[24] R. H. Britnell, *Growth and Decline in Colchester, 1300–1525*, Cambridge 1986, 209, 228.
[25] Davis, 'Notes', 493, 505–8.
[26] D. Potter, 'Foreign Policy', in MacCulloch, *Reign of Henry VIII*, 102–4.

1527 he called the noblemen and gentlemen accompanying him together in Calais and briefed them on how to handle foreigners:

'If they speak to you in the French tongue, speak you to them in the English tongue, for if you understand not them, they shall no more understand you.' And my lord, speaking to one of the gentlemen there (being a Welshman) said, 'Rhys,' quod he, 'speak thou Welsh to him, and I am well assured that thy Welsh shall be more defuse [= obscure] to him than his French shall be to thee'.[27]

English and Welsh

The subjects of the English crown included all Weshmen. It was not so long since Owain Glyndwr had led a long and destructive revolt to separate Wales from England as an independent principality (1400–8), and the consequence of his failure had been disastrous for his cause. Not only had it drawn attention to the need to tighten the control of England over Welsh local government, but it had provoked from Westminster a barrage of racist legislation that was still supposed to be in operation at the end of the fifteenth century. According to the law no Welshman was entitled to bear arms in public places, or to form part of any town or castle garrison. No Welshman was to hold any major office in Wales. No Welshman was to buy land in England, or in the English boroughs within Wales, nor might a Welshman be admitted as a freeman in an English borough. No Welshman might prosecute an Englishman in any court in Wales.[28] This appalling start to the century had left a legacy of resentment and fear on both sides of the border.

Glyndwr's defeat had been decisive, and there had been no further question of political independence for Wales since his day. This placed Welsh national feeling in a very different situation from that of England, since it had nothing equivalent to the military stimulus that had fanned English nationalism through the later stages of the Hundred Years War, nor any royal head on which to focus. If English nationalist fervour was generally perceived from the top down – with the kingdom as its most essential

---

[27] Cavendish, 47–8.

[28] R. R. Davies, *Conquest, Coexistence and Change: Wales, 1063–1415*, Oxford 1987, 458.

foundation – Welsh nationalism could only be from the bottom up. It was something that belonged to the people, their way of life, and their language. After the defeat of 1408 its most poignant expressions were in Welsh poetry, and it is noteworthy that Wales, with fewer than 250,000 people in the later fifteenth century, nevertheless maintained a more robust poetic tradition than England. The numerous Welsh poets of this period were 'as great as any who have written in the language'. Much of what survives is in the form of praise poems and elegies written for the Welsh nobility, a tradition that reached its peak in Tudur Aled of Llansannan in Denbighshire (c.1467–1527).[29]

Lacking an independent national political structure, the leaders of Welsh society had no alternatives between either disengagement from politics altogether or participation under the English crown. Wales, in other words, had no national politics distinct from the country politics that characterized the English provinces. In the 1460s, Edward IV had built up loyalty to his government throughout Wales, relying heavily on the leadership of Sir William Herbert, who was created Lord Herbert in 1461 and earl of Pembroke in 1468. Amongst his other responsibilities was that of bringing up the young Henry Tudor. The growing commitment of the Welsh elite to the English crown was demonstrated at the battle of Edgecote in 1469, when an army raised in Wales, and led by the earl of Pembroke in the name of Edward IV, was defeated by a rebel army under the earl of Warwick. There were 168 Welsh gentlemen among the dead, and Pembroke and his brother were beheaded after the battle.[30] Between 1471 and 1483, even without a leader equivalent to Pembroke, Wales accepted Yorkist rule as a matter of course, and southern Wales and the March experienced more direct influence from England as a result of the creation and enhancement of the resident council at Ludlow, nominally under the Prince of Wales from 1473. This allowed the power of the Woodvilles to expand at the expense of other lordships in Wales, especially the earldom of Pembroke.[31] The political allegiance of the leaders of Welsh society to the English crown was well established by 1485, and did not depend upon the coming of the Tudors.

Henry Tudor's decision to invade from Milford Haven in 1485 was not a device for exploiting Welsh nationalism, though he

---

[29] Williams, *Recovery*, 90. H. I. Bell, *A History of Welsh Literature*, Oxford 1955, 150–4, 161; E. Rowlands, 'Tudur Aled', in H. O. Jarman and G. R. Hughes, *A Guide to Welsh Literature*, 2 vols, Swansea 1976–9, ii, 322–4.

[30] Williams, *Recovery*, 204–6.

[31] Hicks, *Richard III and his Rivals*, 222–7.

was able to draw upon old loyalties to Jasper Tudor, who had been earl of Pembroke under the Lancastrians. The prime object of Henry's strategy was to avoid Richard III's agents and their troops, and the route along Cardigan Bay to Machynlleth, and then through the Cambrian Mountains to Welshpool, met this requirement. Henry's chief hopes of support probably rested on old family loyalties, especially from Sir William Stanley in North Wales and his brother, Lord Stanley, in Cheshire and Lancashire. Some of Henry's Welsh supporters – notably, Rhys ap Thomas – were more interested in bargaining for private advantage than in any wider concerns. However, the letters Henry sent to potential supporters did raise Welsh national issues. The letter written (in English) to John ap Maredudd undertook to restore the principality of Wales and its people 'to their erst [= original] liberties, delivering them of such miserable servitudes as they have piteously long stand in'.[32]

Throughout the period 1471–1529, political relations between the Welsh political elite and the English crown were eased by the facility with which, at a superficial level, dynastic histories could be merged. Despite centuries of intermittent conflict, English and Welsh were able to share the mythology of a common past. Both literatures recognized the legendary Trojan Brutus, who fled from Troy after it had fallen to the Greeks, and founded a British kingdom at the same time as his compatriot Aeneas was laying the foundations of Latin greatness.[33] Both, too, recognized the mythical King Arthur as a national hero. Edward IV gave the name Arthur to an illegitimate son, Arthur Plantagenet, whom Henry VIII created Viscount Lisle in 1523,[34] and Henry VII gave the name to his elder son, the prince of Wales. The Welsh were able, too, to acknowledge some element of Welsh descent in both Yorkist and Tudor dynasties. The fact that Edward IV's ancestors included a Welsh princess, Gwladus Ddu,[35] conveniently enabled the poets to adopt him as an honorary Welshman when it suited them. Henry Tudor's Welsh ancestry, on his father's side, was significantly more convincing, since the Tudors had been a major Welsh family. The red dragon was in evidence on Henry's standards at the battle of Bosworth and in subsequent royal pageantry.[36]

---

[32] Griffiths and Thomas, *Making*, 135–43, 148.
[33] Williams, *Recovery*, 97; S. Anglo, *Images of Tudor Kingship*, London 1992, 41–4, 57, 115.
[34] G. E. C., *Complete Peerage*, viii, 63.
[35] Williams, *Recovery*, 211, 238.
[36] Griffiths and Thomas, *Making*, 187–8, 197–8.

Besides bringing together Lancastrians and Yorkists, Henry VII's marriage to Elizabeth of York also united a descendant of Cadwaladr to a descendant of Llewelyn the Great. The poet Lewys Glyn Cothi described Henry's accession as the restoration of a truly British monarchy, restoring the dignity of Wales, and many writers – not only Welsh ones – found it appropriate to proclaim his victory as the fulfilment of ancient Welsh prophecy.[37]

Considerations of property and neighbourliness had already led to intermarriage between the English and the Welsh at the highest social levels, so that by the Tudor period marriages connecting Welsh knights to English families from adjacent counties were considerably more common than marriages linking knightly families in north and south Wales. Tudur Aled had to vary what he said about the virtues of Welsh blood from one praise poem to the next.[38] In practice Anglo-Welsh relations grew easier over the years at many levels, and already by 1471 much of the ferocity of the anti-Welsh laws was disregarded. For example, the Welsh were supposedly barred from owning property in English boroughs in Wales, yet some boroughs had been becoming increasingly Welsh since the later fourteenth century. From the mid- fifteenth century a predominant share of property in Cardigan was owned by the town's Welsh inhabitants. In 1476–7 John ap Ieuan, one of the borough reeves, was able to endow a chantry with land he held in the town. So far from the Welsh being banned from positions of military responsibility, in 1500 Sir Rhys ap Thomas was constable of Cardigan Castle and Rhydderch ap Rhys ap Maredudd was his deputy.[39] The Welsh were meanwhile increasing their importance in long-distance trade, and taking a dominant role in coastal trade.[40] Between 1504 and 1508 Henry VII granted a series of charters to Welsh shire communities by which their disabilities were formally removed, and though their legality was challenged by some hard-line English interests in the towns, in practice they seem to have been regarded as having been effective.[41]

Welsh migrants came to England in increasing numbers from the later fifteenth century. Henry VII did not make a great deal

---

[37] Hall, 423; Williams, *Recovery*, 237–8.

[38] W. R. B. Robinson, 'The Marriages of Knighted Welsh Landowners, 1485–1558', *National Library of Wales Journal*, xxv (1987–8), 388; Rowlands, 'Tudur Aled', 333.

[39] Griffiths, *Conquerors and Conquered*, 294–6.

[40] J. Kermode, 'The Trade of Late Medieval Chester, 1500–1550', in R. H. Britnell and J. Hatcher (eds), *Progress and Problems in Medieval England*, Cambridge 1996, 287, 289, 305.

[41] J. B. Smith, 'Crown and Community in the Principality of North Wales in the Reign of Henry Tudor', *Welsh History Review*, iii (1966–7), 145, 169–71.

of his Welsh ancestors once he was king, and knew little of the
Welsh language, but he was nevertheless comfortable in the company of Welsh speakers and drew a number of them to court.
One of these, Richard Williams, adopted the name Cromwell and
founded the fortunes of the family from whom Oliver Cromwell
derived. Another, David Seisyllt of Alltyrynys, a sergeant of the
guard, became the founder of the fortune of the Cecil family.[42]
Welsh migration to London, Westminster and Southwark also
stepped up noticeably in the early Tudor period. Some fortune-
seekers finished up swelling the dimensions of London's under-
world, but other thrived as tradesmen, like Morgan ap Howell,
who from 1520 ran the Wool Sack bakery in King Street, Westminster. Migrant Welshmen seem to have intermarried relatively
easily with English women in their new environment.[43] By the
end of the fifteenth century some men of recent Welsh extraction
were being put in positions of authority in English towns. In
Southampton, Thomas Thomas was controller of the customs in
1486 and a member of parliament for the borough in 1495.[44]

On balance, the status of Welsh nationality and Welsh culture
improved during the period 1471–1529, especially under Henry
VII, and relations between English and Welsh people became easier, except perhaps on the borders. Yet the terms of this improvement were quite clearly against the Welsh enjoying nationhood
in the same way that the English could. For them, there was no
political confrontation with outsiders other than the enemies of
England, no political structure other than the English, no royal
figurehead other than the king of England, and no royal administration motivated to use the Welsh language. It was difficult for
Welsh speakers not to resent the dominant influence of English
politics on their leading families; according to Tudur Aled, 'England thrives on corrupting us.'[45]

Technology from Abroad

Sir Thomas More praises the inhabitants of his imaginary island
of Utopia for their willingness to learn from foreigners. When
some Romans and Egyptians were shipwrecked there 'some twelve

---

[42] Elton, *Studies*, iv, 90; Williams, *Recovery*, 239.
[43] Carlin, *Medieval Southwark*, 156; Rosser, *Medieval Westminster*, 190, 220.
[44] C. Platt, *Medieval Southampton: The Port and Trading Community*, A.D. 1000–
1600, London and Boston 1973, 259.
[45] G. Williams, *An Introduction to Welsh Poetry*, London 1954, 171.

hundred years ago', the Utopians had taken the opportunity to learn every useful art of the Romans.[46] How did More's English contemporaries compare with them? The number of skilled craftsmen, artisans, sculptors, painters and scholars called over from the continent for various purposes in the course of the period would imply that there was a lot to be learned, at least amongst the arts and crafts that appealed to the wealthy.

It would be difficult to name any developments in agriculture that depended upon information from abroad. In manufacturing industry, however, there is good evidence of English receptivity to new ideas. One industry developing with a high input of expertise from abroad was brewing. The making of beer, using hops – rather than ale, without hops – had been introduced into England around 1400, though in the early fifteenth century beer had been a minor concern, much of it for foreign visitors. But beer was increasing its share of the brewing industry in the late fifteenth and early sixteenth centuries. The skills required for brewing beer remained concentrated in the hands of immigrant groups, so that throughout the period much of the growth of the industry was in the hands of Flemish or German brewers. In Colchester immigrant beer-brewers, Edmund Hermanson of Brabant (in the period 1466–85) and James Godfrey of Gelderland (in the period 1515–25), were among the wealthiest men in the town of their day.[47]

Another example of learning from abroad, and one that More could hardly have quarrelled with, was the printing of books. William Caxton was a well-established merchant who, in 1471–2, at about the age of fifty, learned how to print books in Cologne and brought the art back to Bruges in the Low Countries. Having worked there for about three years, he pioneered the printing press in England in 1476 at Westminster, where he continued to operate till 1491. One of his earliest publications, in 1477, was the *Canterbury Tales* of Geoffrey Chaucer, whom he regarded as 'the worshipful father and first founder and embellisher of ornate eloquence in our English'.[48] Apart from Caxton, the printers of any significance in England during the late fifteenth and early sixteenth centuries were immigrants. Those of the 1480s included William de Machlinia, from Brabant, and John Lettou, who is presumed from his name to have been Lithuanian. The

---

[46] More, *Utopia*, 40–1.
[47] D. Keene, *Survey of Medieval Winchester*, 2 vols, Winchester Studies 2, Oxford 1985, i, 269; Britnell, *Growth and Decline*, 197.
[48] Caxton, 59, 61; Blake, *Caxton*, 25, 55–63, 79, 99; L. Hellinga, *Caxton in Focus: The Beginnings of Printing in England*, London 1982, 14, 47–51.

major printers of the 1490s, when the industry was expanding rapidly, were Richard Pynson from Normandy, who printed between 1490 and 1529, and Wynkyn de Worde, probably from Holland, who printed from 1492 to 1535. Printers in England continued to depend on continental printers for fonts, woodcuts, and for bookbinding tools and techniques. Much of the paper they used was also imported; no paper mill in England is known before 1495. The technical and commercial advantages enjoyed by continental printers meant that many books for the English market were printed abroad throughout the period.[49]

A third example of technological indebtedness to neighbouring countries was the development of a new iron industry in the Weald of Sussex, though its relevance in this period was narrowly confined to munitions. At the start of Henry VII's reign iron was still being made solely in forges, in which ore was smelted first by reducing it to a spongy 'bloom' and then by repeated heating and hammering. Then, in the 1490s, French ironmasters, under royal patronage, innovated a new technique of long-term importance for the iron industry. This was the indirect process in which iron ore was smelted in a blast furnace. It could then be poured while molten into moulds to make cast-iron objects such as cannon-balls and cannon. Alternatively the molten iron could be cast into ingots ('pigs'); these could then be further refined for the manufacture of wrought-iron objects such as horseshoes and nails. The earliest evidence for a blast furnace in England is from 1496, when a new plant was in operation on crown property at Newbridge in the parish of Hartfield (Kent). The new development included a water-driven power hammer, another innovation, constructed by Lambert Symart, a hammersmith from Normandy. The earliest blast furnace, it seems, made bullets and cannon-balls. From 1509, Pauncelet Symart at Newbridge was making cast-iron guns for the navy. By the time of Henry VIII's French campaigns of 1512–13 there were several other centres of armaments manufacture round Newbridge, and by 1525 new sites had been developed a few miles to the east in the parish of Frant.[50]

[49] A. S. G. Edwards, 'Continental Influences on London Printing and Reading in the Fifteenth and Early Sixteenth Centuries', in J. Boffey and P. King (eds), *London and Europe in the Later Middle Ages*, London 1995, 229–56; L. Hellinga, 'Wynkyn de Worde's Native Land', in R. Beadle and A. J. Piper (eds), *New Science in Old Books: Studies in Honour of A. I. Doyle*, Aldershot 1995, 342–59; A. W. Pollard, G. R. Redgrave *et al.*, *A Short-Title Catalogue of Books Printed in England, Scotland and Ireland and of English Books Printed Abroad, 1475–1640*, 3 vols, London 1976–91, iii, 107, 111, 187–9.
[50] Schubert, *History*, 147–8, 157–67.

The Fine Arts

England had distinctive native traditions in the fine arts that long proved resistant to external influence. This was less true of literature – where the English were excessively aware of foreign achievements – than of architecture and music. The 'perpendicular' style of architecture retained a strong hold on the affections of those who funded large buildings for some two centuries from its invention in the early fourteenth century. Two fine examples from the period, one ecclesiastical and one secular, are St George's chapel, Windsor, and the great hall at Eltham Palace (Kent). During the last decades of the fifteenth century architects continued to develop the style technically and artistically in ways that owed nothing to Renaissance models from abroad. This can be illustrated from the chapel of King's College, Cambridge, which was completed in 1515 after having been under intermittent construction for nearly seventy years. The impressive wide fan-vaulting erected in 1512–15 could not have been contemplated at the time the chapel was planned, and was incorporated into the design only about 1480.[51] Between 1471 and 1529 the design of English palaces, the major constructions of the period, owed nothing to Italy. Henry VII's reconstruction of the palace at Richmond preserved earlier fifteenth-century work for the royal lodgings, and was fundamentally conservative.[52]

English attachment to the perpendicular style in architecture may be compared to the similar commitment to native styles of musical composition, which are best represented for the earlier part of the period by the Eton choirbook, compiled about 1490–1502. Other important collections are the Lambeth choirbook of c.1510 and the Caius College choirbook of c.1520. The most highly considered composers of the period were John Browne (flourished c.1490), Robert Fayrfax (1464–1521) and William Cornysh (died 1523), but a good indication of the maturity of English tradition is the number of excellent lesser composers. The whole school has recently begun to be appreciated and recorded as never before. Their vigorous compositions, supported by the excellence of major chapel choirs, were capable of both impressive achievements and stylistic development. In addition to elaborate liturgical church music, there survives a fair amount of smaller

[51] Harvey, *Perpendicular Style*, 205–8, 210; N. Pevsner, *The Englishness of English Art*, Harmondsworth 1964, 94.
[52] Thurley, *Royal Palaces*, 29–31.

PLATE 7.1   St George's Chapel, Windsor, south side. The work in the right-hand half of the picture, beyond the south transept and as far as the protruding chapel towards the far right, is part of Edward IV's construction from the years 1475–83. The work in the left-hand half of the picture, including the south transept, is from 1500–6 (*The Conway Library, the Courtauld Institute of Art*)

choral works such as carols and secular songs, as, for example, in the Ritson Manuscript of *c*.1470–1510.[53]

Yet the arts in England were nevertheless being moulded in part by influence from abroad in these years. Although many of these changes can be described as belonging to the Renaissance, they were not predominantly derived from Italy and many of them owed little to the classical world. Attention will be given here to three ways in which influence from abroad was enriching areas of English cultural tradition before 1529 – relating firstly to the characteristics of changing taste in architectural ornament and sculpture, secondly to the character of formal education, and thirdly to the range of reading matter available in English.

In Florence, one of the drives behind the return to Roman

[53] J. Caldwell, *The Oxford History of English Music, i: From the Beginnings to c.1715*, Oxford 1991, 174–206; F. L. Harrison, 'English Polyphony (*c*.1470–1540)', in A. Hughes and G. Abraham (eds), *The New Oxford History of Music, iii: Ars Nova and the Renaissance*, London 1960, 303–48.

forms in the earlier fifteenth century had been the desire to establish a native tradition free of French influence. Outside Italy the meaning of the new Renaissance styles was quite different, since they were a foreign intrusion rather than a return to native cultural roots. Nevertheless, the artistic value of Italian work, and its antique associations, had widespread appeal amongst the wealthy, particularly in secular contexts. Portable objects of Italian art, manuscripts, printed books and other works, had already begun to come into England as gifts or as objects of trade before 1500, so it was not surprising that some patrons should want to adopt a similar style for more fixed sculpture and ornamentation. Pietro Torrigiani, the Florentine sculptor, was commissioned to make the tomb of Henry VII's mother, Margaret Beaufort, in 1511 and that of Henry VII and Elizabeth of York in 1512; they are still to be seen in the very un-Italian context of Henry VII's chapel at Westminster Abbey. Cardinal Wolsey planned Italian tombs for himself and for Henry VIII by the Florentine sculptor Benedetto da Rovezzano, though neither was ever completed. By the end of the period the decorating of buildings with Italianate roundels containing sculptured heads was also known in England, though the fashion may not have spread very far. Probably the earliest examples are the surviving terracotta Roman busts by Giovanni da Maiano, made about 1521, which Cardinal Wolsey commissioned to ornament the outside of his new palace of Hampton Court. Italianate ornamentation is strongly in evidence in contemporary representations of the temporary buildings commissioned by Wolsey for the Field of the Cloth of Gold in 1520.[54] Meanwhile English buyers derived a great deal of their taste for new styles in art and design from French and Burgundian models, which were more familiar through commercial and diplomatic exchanges than those of Italy. Paintings were often imported from Flanders, and so were tapestries from centres such as Bruges, Tournai or Brussels, some of which portrayed subject matter in current classical taste. Skelton mocks Cardinal Wolsey's tapestries, almost certainly Flemish, which showed 'Naked boys striding, / With wanton wenches winking.'[55]

Forms of education, too, were being modified between 1471

---

[54] S. J. Gunn and P. J. Lindley, 'Introduction', and P. G. Lindley, 'Playing Check-Mate with Royal Majesty? Wolsey's Patronage of Italian Renaissance Sculpture', in Gunn and Lindley, *Cardinal Wolsey*, 32–3, 261–8, 280–1; Thurley, *Royal Palaces*, 46–8.

[55] Skelton, 270; Gunn and Lindley, 'Introduction', 45–6; C. Richmond, 'The Visual Culture of Fifteenth-Century England', in A. J. Pollard (ed.), *The Wars of the Roses*, London 1995, 188–91.

PLATE 7.2 The tomb of Henry VII and Elizabeth of York by Pietro Torrigiano (1512–18): fine Italian renaissance sculpture with English armorials (and an imperial crown) in a late Gothic architectural setting (*The Conway Library, the Courtauld Institute of Art*)

and 1529, though the shift towards new principles of classical education had affected very few people even by the end of the period. Despite the distinguished collection of classical texts given to the university of Oxford by Humphrey, duke of Gloucester, in 1444, humanism had made little impact on either English university by 1471. Humanism, in this context, has nothing to do with atheism – an association the word has acquired only in the twentieth century – but signifies the scholarly study of Greek and Roman culture, including the early history of Christianity and its sacred texts. Some instruction in Greek was already available in Oxford by the mid-1470s, but for some time acquisition of the highest levels of humanist skill in either Latin or Greek depended upon travel abroad. A set of exercises for translation into Latin from an Oxford schoolbook of about 1500 contains the sentence, 'I am purposed to leave my country and go into Italy, and that only for the desire of Latin and Greek, for though I can find here in England that can teach me, yet because I think I can learn better there than here I have a great desire to go thither.'[56]

The period 1471–1529 nevertheless saw considerable development in English humanism and humanist education. Progress in the first generation was led at the highest level by the three distinguished scholars William Grocyn, Thomas Linacre and John Colet, who all studied in Italy within the period 1488–96, and all spent some time teaching at Oxford on their return. Linacre was chiefly interested in medicine; Grocyn and Colet in early Christian and neoplatonic texts. There was enough Greek scholarship at Oxford in 1499 to attract Erasmus. Learning the Greek language still posed problems, however, since it was not taught in grammar schools and had no regular place in university syllabuses. Sir Thomas More learned his Greek from William Grocyn around 1501, some years after he had left Oxford. The move towards more formal linguistic instruction in the universities came towards the end of the period. When Richard Fox, bishop of Winchester, founded Corpus Christi College in 1517 he attached to it a lecturer to teach Greek. The next year Richard Croke, who had studied in Paris, Louvain and Cologne, was appointed professor of Greek in Cambridge.[57]

Meanwhile new learning was also having a widespread effect on the teaching of Latin grammar and the choice of study-texts in schools. The first moves towards greater classical correctness in the elementary teaching of Latin were those of John Anwykyll at Magdalen College School, Oxford, around 1481–8, where he was paid a fixed annual salary of £10 to teach grammar without fees to any students who might present themselves. He wrote his

---

[56] Orme, *Education and Society*, 147; R. Weiss, *Humanism in England during the Fifteenth Century*, Oxford 1941, 173–4.
[57] J. Newman, 'Cardinal Wolsey's Collegiate Foundations', in Gunn and Lindley, *Cardinal Wolsey*, 113; D. R. Leader, *A History of the University of Cambridge, i: The University to 1546*, Cambridge 1988, 297–8.

own compendium of Latin grammar for the purpose. It was at this school that Thomas Wolsey taught in 1500–1, at the outset of his career.[58] By 1529 the humanistic teaching programme had become generally adopted in grammar schools throughout the country, and there had been a considerable rewriting of the teaching material, some of which was imported. The new teaching of Latin included a change in the manner of speaking it, inclining to the Italian manner. Towards the end of the period new standards of schooling in classical studies were being set by St Paul's School in London, refounded in 1508–10 by John Colet as dean of St Paul's Cathedral. This school was very unusual in its day in including Greek in its programme.[59]

A final observation, that affected more people than either of the other two, was the way in which foreign models contributed to the broadening of reading matter available to the reading public. This was encouraged both by the importation of books from abroad, and by the increasing number of works translated into English from other languages. Between 1476 and 1500 about three-fifths of all printing in England was of material in English, but this was not predominantly in older English texts. A few well-known English authors were printed, like Chaucer, but Caxton and his readers preferred new translations or adaptations of classical texts or of foreign authors in modern European languages, and many of the finest writers in English of the day were engaged in supplying them.[60] There is little English literary prose of the period except in the form of translations; Sir Thomas More's *Utopia* was written in Latin. This was not a great age of English poetry, and it is noteworthy that the most important poet of the period, John Skelton, was also the most open to influence from abroad. His relationship to the current French *rhétoriqueur* tradition still awaits detailed exploration, but he owes to the French renaissance two of his most striking characteristics, his concept of poetic inspiration and his use of poetic fiction to create ambiguities of meaning more complex than straight allegory permitted.[61]

The development of English national tradition on the eve of the sixteenth-century Golden Age is therefore a complex story, and in its most innovative developments it cannot be told in

[58] Cavendish, 5; Gwyn, *King's Cardinal*, 2.

[59] Guy, *Tudor England*, 18; Newman, 'Cardinal Wolsey's Collegiate Foundations', 113; Orme, *Education and Society*, 16, 125.

[60] Blake, *Caxton*, 67–72, 171–93.

[61] A. C. Spearing, *Medieval to Renaissance in English Poetry*, Cambridge 1985, 245–7, 260–1.

terms of English isolation. Cardinal Wolsey was anxious for his international status as a cardinal to be reflected in the sort of art that was produced in Rome. With English kings and their ministers fighting for status in an international arena rather than a narrowly English one, it is not surprising that they adopted status symbols from outside national tradition. The same kings who represented most perfectly the nationhood of their subjects were amongst the most open to being influenced by foreign traditions.

8

The Church

Many of the most distinctive forms of late medieval religion were occasioned and facilitated by the liturgical calendar. To those caught up in the holiday customs of their local communities, the idea that faith and works could be neatly distinguished would not have seemed plausible, though participation in many such events was optional. The villagers of Long Melford (Suffolk) organized outdoor processions at the feasts of Corpus Christi (the Thursday after Trinity Sunday) and St Mark (25 April). On the three Rogation days (the Monday, Tuesday and Wednesday before Ascension Day) there were further processions to beat the bounds of the parish, and these were associated with some modest socializing for those participating. There were four annual bonfire nights, when poorer villagers could expect to get their ale free. And all these feasts were additional to the major festivities of the Christian year.[1] There was another strong relationship between devotion and entertainment in forms of religious instruction. Some preachers were famous for their sermons, like Rowland Philips, the outspoken vicar of Croydon, early in Henry VIII's reign.[2] Plays, too, were devised to be both instructive and entertaining, and 'a play were better than a sermon to some folk'.[3]

The chief role of the secular clergy was to administer the seven sacraments of the church (baptism, confirmation, marriage, last unction, the Eucharist, penance, ordination). All of these, except the last, were part of the everyday lives of the people as rites of passage (baptism, confirmation, marriage, last unction) and rites of reconciliation (the Eucharist, penance). Not all these sacraments had to be administered in church – extreme unction was

[1] Duffy, *Stripping of the Altars*, 137–8; Hutton, *Rise and Fall*, 5–68.
[2] Barclay, *Eclogues*, 34, 233; Vergil, 306–7.
[3] *Mary of Nemmegen*, 79.

usually given at the bedside of the dying person – but the Eucharist nearly always was. The Eucharist, otherwise called the mass,
is a ritualized supper at which the priest consecrates bread and
wine at an altar (representing both a table and a place of sacrifice). In orthodox teaching the bread and the wine are converted,
at the moment of consecration, into the body and blood of Jesus
Christ, sacrificed for the salvation of his followers. These elements – the consecrated bread (the host) and wine – were con-
sumed by those present in a context of formal prayer. People
varied considerably in the number of times they attended confes-
sion and received the Eucharist in the course of the year, but all
who were confirmed were expected to hear mass once a week and
to receive the host at least once a year.[4] Normal social obligations must have usually ensured so much, and for many people
attending mass was a daily event. The centrality of the mass in
everyday Christian experience in the late Middle Ages meant that
the broken body of Christ was an image that recurred in a wide
range of cultural contexts.[5]

Beside this set of integrative social practices, the teaching of the
church supplied a self-conscious set of behavioural norms that
were inculcated from childhood by parental and clerical instruction, by sermons and by the visual and dramatic arts. For ease
of learning, principles were structured into various sets – the ten
commandments, Jesus's summary of the law into the two main
principles of loving God and loving one's neighbour, the seven
works of mercy (feeding the hungry, giving drink to the thirsty,
clothing the naked, visiting prisoners, visiting the sick, harbouring strangers, burying the dead), the seven virtues (faith, hope,
charity, prudence, justice, fortitude, temperance) and, the seven
deadly sins (pride, envy, anger, lechery, avarice, gluttony, sloth).[6]

The church's teaching also supplied a structure of ideas to live
by, based on its formal creeds, or statements of belief, formalized into twelve articles of faith. Its insistence that truth is self-
consistent, and that (except by a miracle) it can only be learned
from an authoritative source, appealed to reason. Even an illiterate
Christian could, in time, understand the purpose of human life,
the experience of deprivation and pain, the foundations of ethical
obligation, the sense of the sacred, the efficacy of prayer, and the
symbolic meaning of a large part of cultural activity. Furthermore,

---

[4] Swanson, *Church and Society*, 276.
[5] S. Beckwith, *Christ's Body: Identity, Culture and Society in Late Medieval Writings*,
London 1993; Rubin, *Corpus Christi*, 302–6.
[6] E.g. *Catholic England*, 54.

the gospels, the epistles and medieval prophetic tradition all implied that as the body of Christ, in which salvation might be found, the church ought to be united. As an international body, the church was united under a single pope.[7] At the local level, this ideal of unity was annually proclaimed, and often ritualized in the form of processions, especially in the Corpus Christi celebrations that had become one of the high spots of the liturgical year.[8]

A large institution that teaches the road to beatitude is in a vulnerable position. To the extent that the church successfully taught the virtues by which the working of the Holy Spirit might be recognized, it laid itself open to increasing refinements of criticism. Different shortcomings were expressed in literary stereotypes – the priest's ignorance, the rector's avarice, the monk's gluttony, the friar's hypocrisy, and so on – which predictably demonstrated that the church was not a perfect embodiment of its own best principles. There were inevitably personal antagonisms between some priests and some parishioners over some issues, some of which resulted from legitimate grievances.[9] The idea that the church needed reform was universal, in varying degrees. Wolsey's legatine authority was extended several times between 1518 and 1524 expressly to allow him to undertake the necessary measures.[10] Many complaints were in fact taken seriously. A determined effort was made to raise the educational standards of the clergy to meet the rising demands being made on them, and laxity amongst monks and priests was often corrected. Comparatively little criticism, meanwhile, was directed at the established practices of the church. The evidence of wills suggests that aspects of religion that were to come under destructive criticism in coming generations – the veneration of saints, the saying of masses for the dead – were deeply rooted. The church was able to withstand innumerable criticisms of its performance in detail because of its strong hold over the basic loyalties of its members.

Church and Kingdom

Although the church was an international body, people in the late Middle Ages did not normally feel themselves to be torn between

---

[7] M. M. Harvey, 'Unity and Diversity: Perceptions of the Papacy in the Later Middle Ages', in R. N. Swanson (ed.), *Unity and Diversity in the Church*, Studies in Church History, xxii, Oxford 1996, 146.

[8] Rubin, *Corpus Christi*, 245–71.

[9] *Catholic England*, 262–7.

[10] Gwyn, *King's Cardinal*, 265n, 267, 278.

two allegiances. This was partly because of the endorsement of royal authority by the church. It was also a result of the way in which the potential for collision between church and state was institutionally contained. In the rhetoric directed against the church after 1529, much was said about the independent power of churchmen. Henry VIII himself said in 1532 that he had found the clergy to be 'but half his subjects, yea, and scarce our subjects'.[11] Simon Fish, the Lollard pamphleteer, whose *Supplication for the Beggers*, printed on the continent in 1528, had earned him Henry VIII's favour, asked what could be done about the overweening pride of the clergy. 'What remedy? Make laws against them? I am in doubt whether ye be able. Are they not stronger in your own parliament house than yourself?'[12] Fish greatly exaggerated the extent to which churchmen in fact challenged royal authority. This can be illustrated by examining appointments to ecclesiastical office, the extent of ecclesiastical jurisdiction and the principles of ecclesiastical taxation.

The nomination of bishops by the king had long been a routine matter. Though new episcopal appointments had to be made in the papal consistory court at Rome, the king was expected to made his wishes known. From 1492 the system by which he did so was well established. A leading cardinal at Rome, a member of the consistory, was appointed as 'cardinal protector of England', and rewarded for his services by being appointed to an English bishopric. To nominate a new bishop the king wrote to the pope and the cardinal protector. The latter defended the king's wishes in consistory, and the new bishop was duly 'provided' by the papacy. Eight letters by which Henry VIII nominated English bishops still survive in Rome from the period 1514–23, when Giulio de' Medici was cardinal protector of England. In the case of the bishopric of Hereford in 1516, for example, letters were sent to the pope and to Giulio de' Medici four days after the old bishop's death on 18 April. They nominated Charles Booth, who was a royal councillor. Within three months Giulio de' Medici had collected a small dossier of evidence to support Booth's candidacy, and he duly defended his case. Booth was formally provided to the bishopric of Hereford on 21 July.[13] In February 1517 the estates of the bishopric (the temporalities) were restored to him by the king, who had held them during the vacancy. Booth

[11] Scarisbrick, *Henry VIII*, 299.
[12] Fish, *Supplicacyon*, 8.
[13] Swanson, *Church and Society*, 13; W. E. Wilkie, *The Cardinal Protectors of England: Rome and the Tudors before the Reformation*, Cambridge 1974, 50, 151.

then did homage to the king and swore fealty, the normal feudal
ritual between a dependent and his lord, renouncing anything in
the papal documentation that might be prejudicial to the king's
rights.[14]

Not surprisingly, bishops were men with whom the king could
work. In this respect the episcopate became more secular under
Henry VII than before.[15] Some bishoprics were given as rewards
for ministerial service, as in the case of John Morton, who became
bishop of Ely (1479–86), and who was later made archbishop
of Canterbury (1486–1500) in return for outstanding services
to the cause of Henry Tudor between 1483 and 1485. Richard
Fox, a loyal servant of Henry VII from the beginning, became
successively bishop of Exeter (1487–92), Bath and Wells (1492–
4), Durham (1494–1501) and Winchester (1501–28).[16] Thomas
Wolsey was another conspicuous example of a ministerial bishop.
He was briefly bishop of Lincoln (1514) and then archbishop
of York (1514–30). While remaining archbishop of York he was
also successively appointed to Bath and Wells (1518–23), Durham (1523–9), and Winchester (1529–30).[17] Morton, Fox and
Wolsey were exceptionally important officers of state, and not all
bishops were so central in government affairs. But most of the men
appointed to the wealthier sees had assisted the government in some
capacity or other.[18] Some had helped as royal agents in Rome, like
John Clerk, bishop of Bath and Wells (1523–41). Others were
diplomats, like Nicholas West, bishop of Ely (1515–33), who
served the king in Scotland, France, Germany and Castile.[19]

To say that such men were but half the king's servants was an
odd way of looking at them. In effect, the crown used clerical
patronage as a way of paying its leading servants. Many bishops
were too busy in royal service to give much personal attention to
their dioceses, which had to be entrusted to deputies. William Smith,
bishop of Lincoln (1495–1514), complained to Sir Reginald Bray
about his long-enforced absence from his diocese as president of
the council of the Marches. In 1516 Richard Fox saw his resigna-
tion from office as keeper of the privy seal as an opportunity to

[14] C. Harper-Bill, *The Pre-Reformation Church in England, 1400–1530*, London 1989,
98–9.
[15] M. Condon, 'Ruling Elites in the Reign of Henry VII', in C. Ross (ed.), *Patronage,
Pedigree and Power in Late Medieval England*, Gloucester 1979, 110–12.
[16] E. B. Fryde, D. E. Greenway, S. Porter and I. Roy, *Handbook of British Chronology*,
3rd edn, London 1986, 229, 242, 247, 256, 277, 283.
[17] Gwyn, *King's Cardinal*, 4.
[18] Thomson, *Early Tudor Church*, 49.
[19] Fryde *et al.*, *Handbook*, 229, 245.

turn from worldly concerns to his spiritual duties.[20] These bishops evidently thought it appropriate to describe their absenteeism as a matter for conscientious regret, though one beyond their control. It is doubtful whether Wolsey ever felt this way, though shortly before his death he spoke in the same sense to Sir William Kingston, who had him under arrest: 'If I had served God as diligently as I have done the king, he would not have given me over in my grey hairs.'[21]

Even lower down the church, amongst the parochial and unbeneficed clergy, the notion that the church was some sort of fifth column cannot be taken seriously. The crown itself had considerable rights of ecclesiastical patronage, appointing clergy to churches permanently in the king's gift and to other benefices that the king temporarily controlled following the death or forfeiture of his tenants, or at times when bishoprics and abbeys were controlled by the crown pending the appointment of new bishops and abbots.[22] Many other appointments to benefices were made directly by lay patrons. Moreover, many unbeneficed clerics were little more than the personal servants of the laity, employed to officiate in their households or pray for the souls of their deceased relatives. The world of clerical appointments was one of heavy interaction between religious and secular interests.

In the course of the Reformation great play was made with the independence of ecclesiastical jurisdiction. Each bishop had a consistory court for his diocese, normally presided over by an official to whom he delegated his judicial responsibility. Below the consistory court there was a subordinate structure of archdeacons' courts. In the diocese of York, for example, there were five archdeacons – West Riding, East Riding, Richmond, Cleveland and Nottingham. There was no hard and fast division between the business of consistory and archdeaconry courts; it was often a matter of indifference where a case was heard, and there was some conflict of jurisdictions. Some of the business of the courts was 'office' business, initiated by their own agents following local investigations or on the strength of information received, but most of it was 'instance' business brought to the court by petitioners and plaintiffs.[23] The church courts administered not the common law of

---

[20] M. Bowker, *The Secular Clergy of the Diocese of Lincoln, 1495–1520*, Cambridge 1968, 4, 16–17; Gwyn, *King's Cardinal*, 17.
[21] Cavendish, 178–9.
[22] Swanson, *Church and Society*, 72–4.
[23] Swanson, *Church and Society*, 160–6; A. H. Thompson, *The English Clergy and their Organisation in the Later Middle Ages*, Oxford 1947, 51–61.

England but the canon law of the church, which was in force – with many local variations – throughout western Europe.

Nevertheless, in the course of past wrangles between church and state the domain of ecclesiastical law had been narrowly defined. The church retained jurisdiction in a miscellaneous array of cases that affected the laity – probate of wills, matrimonial causes, sexual misdemeanours, heresy and superstition, disputed revenues from spiritualities, and clerical offences. Church courts were meanwhile excluded from many branches of jurisdiction in which the interests of churchmen were intimately involved. They were not allowed to consider cases in which the title to property was in question. Bishoprics, abbeys, priories, friaries, colleges and hospitals all had their own estates, but litigation relating to their property rights, or involving the rights of their free tenants, was subject to English common law. So was any litigation relating to the presentation of priests to churches. Some priests were appointed by churchmen and some by laymen, but in no case of any dispute was this a matter for the ecclesiastical law. In practice, then, the king had jurisdiction over many church affairs.[24] Above the archbishops of Canterbury and York was the pope, and churchmen and laymen alike might appeal to Rome if big issues were at stake. However, any appeal abroad which impinged on the status of the common law, or infringed the royal prerogative, could be interrupted. This was the effect of the current legal interpretation of the statute of praemunire of 1393, which was held to outlaw any ecclesiastical encroachment upon the rights of the king or the common law. An infringer of the statutes might suffer permanent imprisonment and the loss of all movable goods.[25] This legislation made it possible for the English kings to keep the jurisdiction of the church courts narrowly confined.

Even Wolsey's powers as papal legate from 1518 were more a comment on the power of the crown than of the independence of the church. They were acquired with royal approval in the first place,[26] and on occasion the king made direct use of them. In 1528, for example, Henry proposed several appointments that Wolsey should make in accordance with his special authority.[27] Wolsey's reform policy, too, was sometimes geared to royal concerns. Amongst his most controversial acts was to impose a legatine

---

[24] The palatinate of Durham was no exception, since the same distinction between ecclesiastical law courts and common-law courts was maintained there as elsewhere.

[25] R. L. Storey, *Diocesan Administration in Fifteenth-Century England*, Borthwick Papers 16, 2nd edn, York 1972, 27, 30–2.

[26] Pollard, *Wolsey*, 165–72; Scarisbrick, *Henry VIII*, 69.

[27] *SP*, i, 311; cf. i, 287, 289, 318–19.

inspection upon the Franciscan Observants of Greenwich in 1525. The friary was a recent royal foundation, attached to Greenwich Palace – Henry VIII had himself been christened there in 1491– and in 1524–5 it was under suspicion of harbouring heretics under the king's very nose.[28] Wolsey's downfall in 1529 also illustrates well the dependent status of his power over the church, for after the king had taken away his secular office he proceeded to indict him in the court of king's bench under the statute of praemunire. This was a very deliberate demonstration of the power of the crown to regulate the independence of even the most mighty churchman in accordance with English law.[29]

Critics of the church frequently implied that its wealth was somehow at the service of the papacy. Peter's pence or Romescot, which went back before the Norman Conquest, was supposed to be an annual tribute to the papacy from all English householders, though its collection was haphazard, and probably only about £200 a year left the country. Another source of papal income was from fees for papal bulls and all sorts of papal dispensations. The most lucrative of these were service taxes, based on the annual value of bishoprics or abbacies, payable when the pope in consistory provided or translated an archbishop, bishop or abbot to office, or confirmed an episcopal or abbatial election; they averaged about £2212 a year between 1476 and 1500 and £1447 between 1501 and 1533.[30] Fees also had to be paid for all sorts of indulgences, some of which were sold in large numbers ostensibly for crusading purposes. In 1500 the pope granted what was known as a jubilee indulgence, which was believed to have 'great sums of money' out of the country, though no estimate of the actual amount can be made.[31] The outflow of money from the country had been a matter for public concern since the late fourteenth century, and parliaments had periodically adopted measures to prevent merchants from exporting coins from England. The export of money to Rome was resented, and Simon Fish was vehement on the subject.

Yet in this, as in other respects, the independence of the church

---

[28] Gwyn, *King's Cardinal*, 275–6; K. Brown, 'Wolsey and the Ecclesiastical Order: The Case of the Franciscan Observants', in Gunn and Lindley, *Cardinal Wolsey*, 219–38; S. Thurley, 'Greenwich Palace', in D. Starkey (ed.), *Henry VIII: A European Court in England*, London 1991, 23–4, 26.

[29] Gwyn, *King's Cardinal*, 593–4.

[30] W. E. Lunt, *Financial Relations of the Papacy with England, 1327–1534*, Cambridge, Mass. 1962, 16–18, 48, 169, 305, 717.

[31] Vergil, 118–21; Lunt, *Financial Relations*, 471. Indulgences were documents whereby, in exchange for a financial contribution to church funds, the pope formally remitted penalties that would otherwise have to be paid for sins committed.

had been effectively contained by the monarchy. English kings had long obstructed papal claims to tax the church directly, and had indeed developed regular procedure for taxing the clergy for their own ends. Between 1485 and 1534 the papacy could on average extract about £4816 a year from the English church. The king, meanwhile, extracted from it two and a half times as much – about £12,500 a year, of which about £9000 was from direct taxation.[32] The church had been integrated into the taxation system, even though taxes had to be approved by its own representative bodies, the convocations of Canterbury and York, rather than by parliament. Convocations operated in tandem with parliament, and were generally summoned at about the same time. When Henry VIII was planning war with France in 1512, for example, parliament voted three 'fifteenths and tenths'. In the same year, the convocation of Canterbury granted four tenths of clerical incomes and the convocation of York granted three tenths. In 1523, for Henry's second war with France, the two convocations granted about half a year's income of all benefices, the payment to be spread over five years.[33]

Churches

The late medieval church was a large and complex organization, whose most visible manifestation was the proliferation of church buildings across the land. In 1500 England and Wales had twenty-one cathedrals, about 8800 parish churches, about 265 houses of monks, 306 houses of regular canons, 183 houses of mendicant friars and 142 houses of nuns and canonesses.[34] There was also a thick scattering of private and non-parochial chapels associated with wealthy households, guilds, hospitals, colleges and out-of-the-way villages. These different churches may be divided for convenience into two principal divisions. The first, comprising parish churches and most chapels, was devoted to the use of laymenand was served by secular clergy (clergy who did not belong to a religious order). The second group, comprising monasteries, priories, nunneries and friaries, was used by religious communities of monks, regular canons, friars and nuns, and was served by

---

[32] Scarisbrick, 'Clerical Taxation', 45–50.

[33] F. C. Dietz, *English Public Finance, 1485–1641*, 2nd edn, 2 vols, Urbana 1964, i, 93–4; Gunn, *Early Tudor Government*, 142.

[34] D. Knowles and R. N. Hadcock, *Medieval Religious Houses: England and Wales*, 2nd edn, London 1971, 494; Swanson, *Church and Society*, 1, 4.

regular clergy (clergy belonging to a religious order). Cathedrals cannot be easily classified in these terms because bishops had responsibilities towards clergy of both kinds, and eight English cathedrals (Canterbury, Durham, Ely, Norwich, Rochester, Winchester, Worcester and Carlisle) had monastic communities attached to them.

The importance of churches as centres for the administration of the sacraments, especially of the mass, has already been touched on. A further distinctive feature of the late medieval church was the saying of masses for the souls of the dead. It was believed that after death most souls went not directly to Paradise but to the intermediate world of Purgatory where they were purified by means of appropriate penance, and this purification might be accelerated by the prayer and sacrifice of the living. Prayers for the dead were offered in every sort of church or chapel, and people could endow masses for their own souls or for those of family, friends and benefactors. This practice had considerable impact on the social characteristics of religion in the late Middle Ages. It provided for many more auxiliary priests than could otherwise have been funded, particularly in urban parishes. It increased the opportunities for hearing mass. It also placed the hiring and firing of priests into the hands of great variety of people.[35]

In the late Middle Ages laymen participated more actively in the life of their local churches than ever before. The authority of the church was compatible with some exercise of control by the laity both within parochial organization and outside it. Parish organization required lay parishioners acting as churchwardens to administer parish property and to maintain church buildings and furnishings; a number of surviving sets of churchwardens' accounts give rich information about this side of parish life.[36] Outside parish organization were many guilds and fraternities, whose membership and activities were controlled by laymen. They characteristically provided both for the saying of masses on behalf of deceased members and for other social activities of a convivial and practical nature. Some of these guilds assumed considerable political importance, like the wealthy guild of the Assumption of the Virgin Mary in Westminster, which by 1500 was acting as a 'surrogate town council'. Active concern with the church in the community easily spilled over into concern for

---

[35] *Catholic England*, 224–5; Duffy, *Stripping of the Altars*, 301, 368–76; Thomson, *Early Tudor Church*, 178–87.
[36] Duffy, *Stripping of the Altars*, 596–600.

charitable acts enjoined by the church's teaching, and there is now considerable evidence of the thought given by testators to the way in which their wealth might be put to worthwhile causes after their death. An interesting implication of these activities is that even the most conscientiously orthodox parishioners were becoming more independent of the beneficed clergy in some of the most meaningful aspects of their religion.[37]

The lives of monks, regular canons, friars and nuns differed according to the particular rules of the different religious orders. Though the liturgy of their communities was more elaborate and continuous than that of parish churches, the eucharist was just as central to their practices. The religious orders had long lost the enthusiastic patronage of the nobility that had once held them at centre-stage in the history of the church. The great days of monastic foundations, when kings and leading landowners were willing to give extensive estates to maintain monks, had been before the year 1200. Even the greatest magnates of the fifteenth century had not used their vast properties to create new monastic houses, but had preferred to endow chantries, which were cheaper. Meanwhile the families who had endowed monasteries in the distant past had died out, leaving the monks to pray in perpetuity for the souls of ancient benefactors. By the 1520s, none of the thirty monasteries in Norfolk founded by lay families was in the patronage of the family that had founded it. The idea that monks and nuns were particularly devout people was undermined by literature that stressed their privileges and their fallibility. Direct observation might lead to the same conclusion; the hundred or so servants employed in Westminster Abbey could hardly doubt that the monks did themselves proud. An active concern for religion in everyday life amongst both laity, secular clergy and the preaching orders had reduced the status of those whose rule was designed to cut them off from other Christians. Even the great monasteries attached to cathedrals – a distinctively English tradition – failed to project clear religious values that the outside world could admire.[38]

Yet opinions of monasticism in the late Middle Ages were no

---

[37] P. H. Cullum and P. J. P. Goldberg, 'Charitable Provision in Late Medieval York: "To the Praise of God and to the Use of the Poor"', *NH*, xxix (1993), 24–39; G. Rosser, *Medieval Westminster, 1200–1540*, Oxford 1989, 285–93; G. Rosser, 'Parochial Conformity and Voluntary Religion in Late-Medieval England', *TRHS*, 6th ser., i (1991), 173–89; Tanner, *Church*, 91–110.

[38] R. B. Dobson, 'English Monastic Cathedrals in the Fifteenth Century', *TRHS*, 6th ser., i (1991), 170; Harvey, *Living and Dying*, 153, 210–11; B. Thompson, 'Monasteries and their Patrons at Foundation and Dissolution', *TRHS*, 6th ser., iv (1994), 120–1.

more unanimous than those concerning any other aspect of the church. An analysis of 'the lay view' of monasticism on the eve of the Reformation has to take account of expressions of affection for individual houses from all ranks of society. Friaries were closer to the everyday life of the church than monasteries, but even the latter were often remembered in testamentary bequests. An analysis of over 3000 wills proved in the diocese of York between 1520 and 1535 shows that one-third included a bequest to a friary, and one-sixth to a monastic house. Some houses occur more frequently than others, but the wide range of beneficiaries does not suggest that corruption was thought to be common. Usually money was left for the singing of masses for the soul of the testator. This practice were not confined to the north. Thomas Paycocke of Coggeshall, an Essex clothier who died in 1518, was a brother of the Crutched Friars of Colchester, to whom he bequeathed £5 for their prayers. He left bequests to other local friaries in Colchester, Maldon, Chelmsford, Sudbury and Clare, but also to the abbot and convent of Coggeshall.[39]

At a time when the horizons for development amongst the regular clergy were constricted for want of patronage and funds, new opportunities for Christian involvement were opening up for wealthier and better-educated laymen. They became more inclined to meditate about their religion, even if their meditation was not rooted in Bible study; books of hours, an aid to private devotions of the laity, were becoming widespread, to the point that it paid Paris publishers to commission special editions for England. There were at least six editions of the Sarum hours published by Simon Vostre before 1512, and the market was still developing in the late 1520s, when François Regnault began to capture it.[40] One of the implications of growing lay participation in religious activity was the intrusion of differences of wealth, personality and belief into an area of local society where they had not been so prominent in earlier centuries. By the end of the fifteenth century the social status of laymen could be assessed by the guilds they attended, their contribution to parish organisation, their literacy, or their provision for intercessory masses.

[39] G. F. Beaumont, 'Paycocke's House, Coggeshall, with some Notes on the Families of Paycocke and Buxton', *Transactions of Essex Archaeological Society*, ix (1906), 322–4; C. Cross, 'Monasticism and Society in the Diocese of York, 1520–1540', *TRHS*, 5th ser., xxxviii (1988), 132–4; Tanner, *Church*, 119–25.

[40] Duffy, *Stripping of the Altars*, 227–9. 'Hours' in this context means prayers and devotions for specific times. For a manuscript example, see A. F. Sutton and L. Visser-Fuchs, *The Hours of Richard III*, Stroud 1990.

The Church and Education

Because the church embraced everyone, and its doctrine was necessary for salvation, formal instruction in its principles was carried deeper into society than any comparable instruction in law. The illiterate layman was not fed the same fare as the university theologian, but the church maintained a common ground of fundamental beliefs (especially those formalized in the creeds) and a common ground of ritual (especially that of the Eucharist) that anchored all orthodox Christians in the same faith. Though inevitably a large part of popular religion overlapped with magic, and was tolerated because it was difficult to disentangle from more orthodox forms of prayer and ritual, church courts actively suppressed practices that departed most flagrantly from Christian values – particularly those designed to harm neighbours. Four times a year parish priests were expected to expound in English to their parishioners the creed, the ten commandments, Christ's summary of the law, the seven works of mercy, the seven virtues, the seven deadly sins and the seven sacraments. This educational practice had been initiated in 1281 and was retained up to the Reformation.[41] Historians who have studied late medieval religion differ in their assessment of the effectiveness of this teaching in achieving homogeneity of belief. Some are impressed by the formal homogeneity of beliefs and practices throughout the church, and can show that the Christianity of the college chapel had innumerable similarities to that of the village church. Others are more interested in the wide variety of magical rituals and beliefs that were tolerated or encouraged by churchmen.[42]

Bishops were amongst the most active in the late medieval fashion for endowing grammar schools, and the church did nothing to hamper innumerable lay initiatives designed to make schooling more readily available. The fourteenth and fifteenth centuries witnessed the growth of lay education, both within households and in schools. The educational role of households deserves more emphasis than it has traditionally received; there was quite widespread literacy among townspeople, including women, and many children learned to read at home. The number of reading and singing schools, often taught by parish clergy, as well as endowed grammar schools, multiplied from the late fourteenth century to the point that by 1529 there were well-established schoolmasters

[41] *Catholic England*, 51–8.
[42] Duffy, *Stripping of the Altars*, 2–3, 53–4, 266–98; K. Thomas, *Religion and the Decline of Magic*, London 1971, 25–50.

even in small towns like Banbury, Ewelme and Chipping Norton, all in Oxfordshire. Much of what they taught was geared to training people to participate in the liturgy of the church.[43] Most beneficiaries put their learning to some practical use in trade, estate management or law. Others, however, went on to become priests. Probably 90 per cent of all priests had received no more formal education than what such schools could offer.[44] They nevertheless had to demonstrate an adequate level of competence to receive a benefice; when Lord Clifford presented a clerk to the church of Londesborough in 1520, the dean of York declined to admit him on the grounds that 'his cunning is marvellous slender. I have seen few priests so simple learned in my life.' Between 1500 and 1532, 42 per cent of the beneficed clergy in Norwich were university graduates.[45]

The university world of the late Middle Ages provided a general intellectual training that was a possible high-road to ecclesiastical promotion, even though it did not relate closely to the practical needs of clerical office and did not guarantee being given an ecclesiastical benefice. There were only two universities, Oxford and Cambridge, of which Oxford was the larger, and numbers were growing at both. In this period most students lived in halls or private lodgings rather than in colleges, which were a specialized institution for more advanced studies. Some halls were maintained by religious orders, so that their members could study at university without living outside their rule, and the number of monks attending university rose during the fifteenth century. Only a few of the newer colleges – New College and Magdalen College at Oxford and King's College, Cambridge – provided places for undergraduates. It is not known how many students attended the universities at any given moment, but the number was probably over 1000 at each. Study for a BA often started at the age of fourteen or fifteen, and students had often graduated by the time they were eighteen. Conscientious university teachers were expected to thrash idle students.[46]

---

[43] N. Orme, *Education and Society in Medieval and Renaissance England*, London and Ronceverte 1989, 57; Swanson, *Church and Society*, 304; Tanner, *Church*, 110–12.

[44] C. Haigh, *English Reformations: Religion, Politics and Society under the Tudors*, Oxford 1993, 42.

[45] *Clifford Letters*, no. 17, p. 84; Tanner, *Church*, 28–30.

[46] H. S. Bennett, *The Pastons and their England*, 2nd edn, Cambridge 1932, 103–5; Dobson, 'English Monastic Cathedrals', p. 168; T. A. R. Evans, 'The Number, Origins and Careers of Scholars', in Catto and Evans (eds), *History*, 485–92, 533–8; M. Keen, *English Society in the Later Middle Ages, 1348–1500*, Harmondsworth 1990, 245–6; Thompson, *Transformation*, 351–2.

The syllabus for a first degree at Oxford was spread over twelve terms (four years), and consisted largely of secular disciplines. These were defined as the seven liberal arts, divided between the *trivium* (grammar, rhetoric, logic) and the *quadrivium* (arithmetic, music, geometry and astronomy). The *trivium* was a basic course in academic writing, and the *quadrivium* grounded students in analysis of the numerical properties of things. The old system of teaching, based on lectures on prescribed Latin texts that a master or bachelor read out sentence by sentence with comments, was giving way to one more dependent on private study. Many of the authors read by students for the BA degree were non-Christian, even before the influence of the Italian renaissance on university studies, simply because teaching material from the Ancient World was still, in many subjects, the best available. For example, the study of grammar used parts of the voluminous *Institutiones Grammaticae* of the sixth-century Latin author Priscian, a work containing numerous illustrative examples from classical prose-writers (especially Cicero) and poets (especially Virgil and Horace). Rhetoric and logic were studied through Latin translations of various works of Aristotle (384–322 BC) as well as the *Topica* of the Latin author Boethius (*c.*AD 480–524) and extracts from major Latin poets. The *Arithmetica* and *Musica* of Boethius were read for the arithmetic and music courses. The course in geometry was rooted in the *Elements* of the ancient Greek mathematician Euclid (who worked around 300 BC), and the astronomy was based on the *Almagest* of the Greek geographer and astronomer Ptolemy (who worked around AD 127–48). A student who went on a further three terms to study for an MA concentrated on the philosophy of Aristotle. Though university students lived in an environment of theological competence, only a minority ever registered for degrees in theology or ecclesiastical law, and even students who were going to be priests usually left off university study without such specialization.[47] In other words, the universities, then as now, more often provided students with a high-quality general education than with vocational training.

Dissidents

Church and state between them had considerable apparatus for preventing the dissemination of ideas that challenged orthodox

---

[47] J. M. Fletcher, 'Developments in the Faculty of Arts, 1370–1520', and Evans, 'Number, Origins and Careers', in Catto and Evans (eds), *History*, 323–4, 494–5.

doctrine, and from time to time they used it. Anybody could depart from orthodox teaching in some particulars through ignorance or carelessness, but this was no problem for the authorities so long as such beliefs were not deliberately propagated, and so long as those making them came into line when required to do so. Culpable heresy implied wilful persistence in defiance of authority, and such resistance usually implied that more than merely private opinion was at stake. The tiny minority of the population that ventured into this perilous territory comprised men and women with an over-riding allegiance to a dissident group. Some were rebel clergy. It was to be several centuries before European states started to treat religious unorthodoxy as a matter of indifference; in the late Middle Ages, eradicating heresy was a joint concern of church and state. Richard III's administration required incoming sheriffs to swear 'to destroy and make to cease all manner heresies and errors commonly called Lollardries within your bailiwick from time to time to all your power'.[48]

Through most of the period 1471–1529, Lollardy was the only active heresy in England. It originated at Oxford University in the 1370s amongst the followers of John Wyclif, and departed from orthodoxy in its understanding of the sacraments of the church, as well as on other major issues.[49] From the Establishment's perspective, the Lollards' chief characteristic was hostility to the proliferation of sacred rites and to the hierarchy of persons which the orthodox recognized as necessary to God's scheme of salvation, but which Lollards saw as fictitious barriers between God and man. Lollards rejected the orthodox interpretation of the seven sacraments as channels of divine grace. They challenged the clerical control of biblical learning, and circulated English translations of the Bible in manuscript form. They objected to the priestly claim to have the power to absolve sin, still more to the remission of sin by means of indulgences. They opposed both the practice of praying to saints as intercessors between man and God, and, by association, the use of images in churches. They recommended the expropriation and redistribution of clerical wealth. They regarded the existence of monks and friars as a denial of Christian values, on the grounds that their ideals of holiness were founded on rules separating them from the common life of the church.[50] A man or woman accused of Lollardy might be expected to deviate from orthodoxy in one or more of these points.

---

[48] *Harley 433*, 176.
[49] For the sacraments, see above, pp. 148–9.
[50] Hudson, *Premature Reformation*, 289n, 349–51.

The Lollard movement was not centrally organized, and its members did not formally separate from the established church. To that extent it lacked two attributes of an archetypal sect. Even as a body of beliefs its coherence is doubtful, since Lollards had no mechanism for maintaining uniformity. Lollardy had other sectarian features to some degree – a distinct literature, a conviction of superior righteousness, the self-conscious affiliation of its adherents to the group, frequent contact between members, a network of communication between different cells, and a formidable willingness amongst some of those involved to sacrifice themselves for the cause. There were groups in some towns, and there were also rural networks – especially in northern Essex, in southern Kent round Tenterden, and in the mid-Thames valley and the Chilterns, between High Wycombe, Amersham, Uxbridge, Newbury and Burford. Nevertheless, the heresy had been successfully contained in the early fifteenth century; its adherents had been prevented from creating an organization to rival the church and from recruiting more than a tiny minority of the population. The threat of Lollardy to the Establishment was slight, to judge from the pacific stance of most Lollards and the absence of missionary intent. No new Lollard writings of any significance are known to date from the period after 1471, though the tract called *Wycklyffes Wycket* possibly dates from as late as the 1470s.[51] Though Lollards were increasingly prosecuted in the church courts from about 1485, the reasons for this are not well understood. Perhaps political stability under the Tudors created more opportunities for taking a hard line.[52] Or it may be that Lollards became more numerous, despite persecution, as standards of lay education rose.

In the 1520s Lutheranism emerged as a new threat to the Establishment, and rapidly became troublesome because of the number and resources of its friends abroad. Martin Luther, a monk of Wittenberg, attacked the practice of raising funds for the papacy by means of indulgences in 1517. By 1521, when he defied the Emperor Charles V at the Council of Worms, his ideas had become widely disseminated in Germany. Luther was excommunicated as a heretic by a papal bull of 15 June 1520, and the following year his ideas were condemned by the Emperor Charles V at Worms, first verbally on 19 April, then by edict on 26 May.[53] Meanwhile,

[51] A. G. Dickens, *Lollards and Protestants in the Diocese of York, 1509–1558*, London 1959, 8; Hudson, *Premature Reformation*, 18, 449–52, 456.

[52] C. Cross, *Church and People, 1450–1660*, Glasgow 1976, 15; 31; Hudson, *Premature Reformation*, 447.

[53] *Documents*, 85–9.

on 12 May 1521, an English public campaign against him was opened by Cardinal Wolsey with a burning of books in St Paul's churchyard in London. Between April and June that year the king, aided by a small team of theologians, wrote and published his *Assertio Septem Sacramentorum* ('Affirmation of the Seven Sacraments') against Luther's writings.[54] Despite such prompt measures of resistance, Lutheran books began to circulate in England, especially in London. In Cambridge a little group of sympathizers met in the White Horse Tavern, and in Oxford from 1526 Luther had a similar following amongst the bright young men appointed to Wolsey's own foundation of Cardinal's College. Luther's teaching was in some ways less radical than Lollardy, particularly in his theology of the Eucharist, but there were enough similarities for the ecclesiastical authorities to combat it as a reinforcement of the old heresy rather than something fundamentally new.[55] They avoided unnecessary martyrdoms, however, and successfully managed to persuade leading preachers to abjure their beliefs: Robert Barnes at another book-burning in February 1526, Thomas Bilney and Thomas Arthur in December 1527. Only five heretics of any kind were burned in Wolsey's time. The church's attempts at suppression were supported by the great weight of popular opinion throughout the kingdom, and by the educational establishment, including the university authorities.[56]

There was no immediate danger of revolution from below in 1529. The chief interest of Lollards and early Lutherans for historians is that their ideas, though outlawed and unpopular, illustrate much broader and partly-concealed tensions within the church. Amidst a great deal of official vagueness and diversity about what constituted superstition and magic, heretics were inclined to be aggressively on the sceptical side, though there were differences among them too.[57] The importance that they ascribed to the religious education of the laity is of particular interest. Perhaps the most puzzling aspect of ecclesiastical policy for a modern observer is the discouragement of bible-reading in the vernacular, at a time when more and more works were being translated into English and printed. The synod of Oxford, that banned the Lollard Bible in 1408, had seemed to allow for the possibility of some future authorized version of the Bible in English, but in fact no new translation was available until Tyndale's (illegal) New Testament

[54] Rex, 'English Campaign', 86–9.
[55] Hudson, *Premature Reformation*, 494–507.
[56] Brigden, *London*, 112, 158, 162; Rex, 'English Campaign', 89–95.
[57] Aston, *Lollards and Reformers*, 135–92; Hudson, *Premature Reformation*, 301–9.

came to England in 1526.[58] The fear of authorizing vernacular scripture, which was particularly acute in England, derived from the threat of heretical belief, and the invention of printing accentuated the dilemma of the authorities. Orthodox teaching depended upon a particular, historically developed interpretation of the scriptures, and it required more than the unaided intellect to read the Bible in the approved way.[59] This argument, however, could be read as a self-interested defence of the clergy as a status group privileged by education, and did not begin to meet the Lollard critique. Though in the end Lollardy won its argument about lay education, that victory was to pose intractable problems for the uniformity of religious belief that had hitherto been a Christian ideal.

---

[58] Cross, *Church and People*, 15; M. Deanesly, *The Lollard Bible*, Cambridge 1920, 319.
[59] Aston, *Lollards and Reformers*, 132; Deanesly, *Lollard Bible*, 293.

9

The Law

Those who ruled England in the king's name through the shires and boroughs of the land had a strong attachment to the institutions that gave them a title to their property and a public role in the affairs of the kingdom. If educational privilege and ordination justified the separate status of the clergy, it was surely legal title and legal responsibility that, in various ways, defined the special status of the gentry and nobility. The law figured prominently in their education. Together with Christian teaching it formed a sophisticated world of thought and practice common to men in public life, and it supplied much of the language in which the business of the realm was transacted. It would be difficult to exaggerate the influence of legal concepts upon the political thinking of the ruling elite during the late Middle Ages.[1] The law even buttressed national pride. Sir John Fortescue, whose ideas on monarchy have been cited in another context, argued that English institutions were unlike those of neighbouring countries and superior; the French were ground down with taxes, 'but, blessed be God, this land is ruled under a better law'. Fortescue believed English common law to be of very great antiquity – pre-Roman, in fact – and consequently superior to any other known legal system. 'So it would be wrong to deny, or even to doubt, that the customs of the English are not merely good but the best.' He was not alone in his profoundly traditionalist reading of history. If English law was set up by Brutus the Trojan, as Edward Hales supposed in a lecture delivered in the Inner Temple in 1512, then it was already old at the time of Julius Caesar's invasion.[2]

The most formal source of law was the procedure by which the king approved bills put to him in parliament to make them

---

[1] Ives, 'Common Lawyers', 189–91.
[2] Fortescue, *Governance*, 2; Fortescue, *De Laudibus*, 38–40; Baker, 'Introduction', 33.

statutes. Statutes sometimes originated with drafts prepared by the king's officers, but often they began as private petitions brought to parliament.[3] When the king approved new laws in these circumstances they were entered on the statute roll, and were subsequently cited by reference to the year in which they were authorized.[4] Only by this form of legislation could the king create new criminal offences that endangered the lives and liberties of his subjects. A less formal type of legislation, whose authority was not precisely defined at the time, was by royal proclamation, which was used sometimes to urge the enforcement of statutory regulation, and sometimes for general commands that could not await another meeting of parliament.[5]

To a considerable extent, however, English law was constituted not by statutes and ordinances but by the tradition of the common law, some of which was formalized in written treatises, but much of which was transmitted orally through a highly developed system of instruction. Lawyers spoke of the common maxims and general customs of the law, meaning the principles that were passed on through the teaching methods of the inns of court. To some extent this teaching involved dialogue with those past actions at law whose details were available. The most convenient collections of law reports were the annual collections known as year books, which had been compiled ever since Edward I's reign for teaching and study. Yet these represented only a small part of the business of the courts, they lacked the status of official legal records, and they did not constitute a fixed corpus of knowledge to which all lawyers had access. There is no evidence that Westminster Hall had a law library where they might be consulted. Moreover, even the original records of the courts did not systematically record the legal grounds for individual judicial decisions. There was no way of recovering most of what had happened in past decisions, 'for much water flows through the mill of which the miller knows nothing', as a lawyer wrote in 1463–4. As this implies, the concepts of case law and legal precedent were only weakly developed. Though year books were sometimes cited in court, judges were not bound by decisions of their predecessors if they wished to interpret the common maxims of law differently.[6]

Of course, law was not simply a way of thinking about rights

[3] G. R. Elton, 'State-Planning in Early Tudor England', *EconHR*, 2nd ser., xiii (1960–1), 434–6.

[4] Above, p. 130.

[5] Heinze, *Proclamations*, 30–7.

[6] Baker, 'Introduction', 159–63; Simpson, *Legal Theory*, 84.

and wrongs but also comprised a complex set of procedures. Knowing the details of how to see particular cases through the courts constituted a most important part of legal knowledge, especially among the lower branches of the profession, whose income derived from advising clients. But though the professionals commanded the higher mysteries of the law, a great deal of legal knowledge, as of Christian teaching, was widely shared. A larger proportion of the population was involved in lawsuits then than now, chiefly because litigation was relatively much cheaper. In addition, the jury system, one of the most striking features of the English common law, ensured that people in every town and village throughout the kingdom knew well some principles of substantive law and had regular experience of some of its routine procedures. Only a minority of common pleas, brought to court in private legal actions, were ever carried through to formal judgement, since most were settled by agreement out of court or by the default of one of the parties. However, in those cases that were carried through to the end jurors were required to judge the truth, and sometimes to assess damages. At all levels of procedure in criminal law, grand juries – usually of twelve men – were required on oath to bring charges against those suspected of indictable offences so that the accusations might be judicially investigated. Except at the very lowest level of policing in manor and borough courts, a different jury, the petty jury, was the required to assess the evidence in individual cases and to decide the truth of the matter. Criminal proceedings under common law were also open to the public.[7]

The considerable emphasis on formal correctness in legal procedure, together with its complexity, meant that the law often operated more as a game than as an arbiter of rights and wrongs. In one aspect it was a merely artificial construct, defining what litigants could do, rather than what they should do, and it provided ample scope for non-violent aggression by the strong or knowledgeable against the weak and ignorant. A lawsuit was 'a contest in which each party was ready to use whatever means lay at hand to outwit the other',[8] and knowledge of the law was often equivalent to knowledge of the rules of chess. There were people in all ranks of life who saw legal procedure as something to be exploited for personal gain in hammering others into

---

[7] J. Bellamy, *Crime and Public Order in the Later Middle Ages*, London and Toronto 1973, 121–5, 140–5; Gunn, *Early Tudor Government*, 95–9.
[8] Hastings, *Court of Common Pleas*, 211.

submission. The third duke of Buckingham, who initiated 128 lawsuits in the central royal courts of common pleas and king's bench, evidently used the law as a mode of outright aggression.[9] This merely tactical function of the law in interpersonal conflict is as much a part of the late medieval and early modern scene as its operation as the protector of rights. Amongst some of the most ruthless tacticians were Edward IV, Richard III, Henry VII and Henry VIII.

Law and Kingdom

It was evident to the most casual observer that respect for the law was closely allied to respect for the crown. Unlike modern governments, those of the Middle Ages did not seek to make their reputation by the volume or quality of their legislation since the perceived problem, as usually defined, was the implementation of existing laws rather than the creation of new ones. For this kings needed the cooperation of the nobility and gentry, especially those in office as sheriffs and justices of the peace. In principle such goodwill was not hard to secure, since the need for better law enforcement was one of the commonplaces of political discourse. When kings struck grand attitudes over law and order, their leading subjects were prepared to be impressed. The Crowland chronicler writes with approval of Edward IV's travelling about with his justices 'sparing no one, even of his own household, from being hanged if he were caught stealing or killing'. All kings of the period made comparable gestures as an accepted part of kingcraft. In preparing for Henry VII's first parliament in 1485 the king's justices met to discuss how to tackle problems relating to law and order, and agreed that they were powerless to enforce statutes relating to violent crime, excessive wages, vagrancy, and corruption in local courts without a general consensus to do so on the part of the lords and gentry of the realm. They decided to ask the lords and commons who attended parliament to swear to uphold all these laws, and that general oath-taking was a principal item of business on 19 November.[10]

The positive measures taken by successive kings to deal with lawlessness inevitably responded to contemporary analysis of what was wrong. As in our day, some observations concerned the prevention of crime and some the effectiveness with which it was punished.

---

[9] Harris, *Edward Stafford*, 96.
[10] *Crowland Continuations*, 136–7; EHD, *1485–1558*, 532–4.

The former of these concerns gave rise to an interesting body of legislation to be discussed in chapter 10. The latter – the enforcement of law – was generally held to be problematic because of the abuse of power by local magnates. This concern is readily intelligible, if only because any threat to the judicial integrity of the common-law courts undermined the security of freehold property and private contracts. A recurrent nightmare that governments sought to allay was that yeomen or gentlemen might lose their inheritances to more powerful opponents. The fear of local corruption prompted recurrent measures to contain the private deployment of armed force and to suppress practices by which powerful men were able to intimidate weaker rivals. Under Edward IV, in 1468, a parliamentary act had repeated earlier legislation against giving distinctive clothing, or clothing marked by a heraldic badge to servants other than menials, administrative officials and legal advisers, since the proliferation of such liveried retainers was one of the ways in which the powerful were tempted to make their presence felt. The act had also made it easier to bring charges before the king's courts and to secure a conviction.[11] This legislation was amongst the points that the nobility was sworn to observe in 1485, and in 1486 Henry established by a judicial ruling that all forms of retaining were covered by it except household service and legal counsel.[12] He drove hard against the illegal formation and deployment of aristocratic retinues, introducing new legislation in 1495 and 1504. He also set up a special conciliar tribunal to deal with accusations of illegal retaining, though the court had so little business that it is unclear how long it continued to function.[13]

The idea of placing potential troublemakers under bonds to keep the peace – so that they would have to pay money penalties if they defaulted – was commonly employed by fifteenth-century law courts. Henry, however, employed this same technique to create obligations directly to himself, and did it so systematically that this became a distinctive feature of his reign between 1502 and 1509. For this purpose he used a variety of formally drafted legal documents that committed defaulters to paying sums of money to the crown if they failed to behave themselves. Some bonds were intended to enforce the payment of debts, and so had direct financial implications for the crown; others were concerned only with keeping the peace, so that the prime purpose was defeated

---

[11] Bellamy, *Bastard Feudalism*, 82–5.
[12] Gunn, *Early Tudor Government*, 39–40.
[13] Bellamy, *Bastard Feudalism*, 127–30.

if the king had to collect a penny. Often bonds were the result of legal decisions, and so reinforced the link between royal authority and the efficacy of the courts. The multiplication of legal bonds symbolized in very tangible form the strengthening of the bonds of duty owed to the king by his subjects. Because of the unpopularity of his father's rule, Henry VIII backtracked on the extensive use of bonds and recognizances, but he did not abandon his father's insistence that noblemen should be respectful of the law and pay their debts to the crown, and in practice he was prepared to use their indebtedness as a means to enforce their subordination.[14]

The most sustained government posturing on law enforcement came from the king in council. Since the mid-fourteenth century the council had met in the star chamber, on the east side of Westminster Hall, which was so called because it was decorated with stars on the walls or the ceiling.[15] Conciliar jurisdiction in cases involving serious offences was long established, and in particular the council was responsible for investigating cases where there was *prima facie* evidence of miscarriages of justice in lower courts. Such activity was not extensive in Edward IV's reign, but he gave the court maximum authority by his frequent attendance.[16] One of Henry VII's earliest responses to the problem of livery, maintenance and embracery was a conservative measure in 1487 to set up a high-powered tribunal of ministers and justices to act on the evidence of written petitions to the chancellor.[17] This body did not attract a significant amount of business, and in reality there was little institutional change during his reign in the way the council operated. In Henry VII's reign the council was receiving on average about 13 petitions a year, of which no more than a tenth concerned genuine criminal offences.[18]

From the time of his appointment as chancellor in 1515, Wolsey enthusiastically used his place in the council to convey a government message about the effectiveness and fairness of its law enforcement. It is from this time that we can confidently speak of the court of star chamber as a normal part of the legal system rather than as an occasional device. On 2 May 1516 Wolsey made an important speech before the king in council about the

---

[14] Gunn, *Early Tudor Government*, 56–7; Harris, *Edward Stafford*, 164–5; T. B. Pugh, 'Henry VII and the English Nobility', in Bernard, *Tudor Nobility*, 66–72.
[15] Colvin, *History of the King's Works*, i, 545–6.
[16] Ross, *Edward IV*, 303.
[17] 3 Henry VII, c. 1: *SR*, ii, 509–10.
[18] Guy, *Cardinal's Court*, 15–17.

need to enforce the law impartially, and this was followed by an ostentatious drive against members of the king's own council for illegal retaining. Between 1516 and 1519 he used the star chamber to punish corruption in local government, making an example of some prominent local knights.[19] All this must have been with Henry's connivance. The earl of Northumberland was imprisoned in the Fleet prison. In August 1517, following an affray between Justice Piggott and the servants of Sir Andrew Windsor over a wardship, Wolsey wrote to the king of his hope 'to see them learn the new law of the star chamber which, God willing, they shall have indifferently ministered to them according to their deserts'.[20] In an agenda drawn up in 1519 of matters that the king had in mind to discuss personally with his council, the first item was the king's intention 'that an order shall be taken for the true, equal and indifferent administration of justice and his laws, and to exclude the abuses and corruption of the same'.[21] This deliberate, repeated emphasis on pulling down the law-breaking mighty from their seat is the kernel of truth in the accusation that Wolsey was against the nobility. The chief advantage of the court of star chamber to the government lay in its propaganda value for expounding and exemplifying principles of law and order, rather than in the amount of business it handled. Though it became necessary to organize the council's activity more formally, the number of cases it handled was still only about 120 a year.

Such political concern with law and order could potentially conflict with the traditions of the legal profession. This was chiefly apparent during Wolsey's chancellorship, at a time when he was making his reputation for administering effective justice a key feature of the royal concern for law and order. In the star chamber, according to Cavendish, 'he spared neither high nor low but judged every estate according to their merits and deserts'.[22] Lawyers became concerned during the 1520s that this policy was not the same thing as judging in accordance with the law. Wolsey had no legal training, and was inclined to be authoritarian in the interests of what he though to be equitable; 'like most laymen, he had supreme confidence in his own common sense'.[23] The number of cases he handled was only a small proportion of the total, but

---

[19] Guy, *Cardinal's Court*, 30–1; J. A. Guy, 'Wolsey and the Tudor Policy', in Gunn and Lindley, *Cardinal Wolsey*, 70–1.
[20] *LP*, ii (2), 1539.
[21] British Library, Cotton MSS, Titus B.i, fo. 191r.
[22] Cavendish, 24.
[23] Baker, 'Introduction', 77.

it looked as if the government was set to undermine professional learning. The danger was exaggerated, since Wolsey often worked in close consultation with the chief justices, and his style proved to be only a passing phase. After him – starting with Sir Thomas More in 1529 – English chancellors were common lawyers, with a more profound respect for legal precision. But as long as Wolsey was chancellor he was a worrying illustration of the way a politician's concern for law and order could part company with that of the legal profession.

Courts

The two principal royal courts all sat in Westminster Hall for a total of about 100 days in the year, though this was divided into four legal terms (Michaelmas, Hilary, Easter, Trinity).[24] These were the court of common pleas and the court of king's bench. The court of common pleas handled principally cases involving real estate, debt and detinue (that is, the withholding of goods or livestock rather than money), though it also handled quite a lot of private suits alleging breach of the peace, which in the later Middle Ages came under the general heading of actions of trespass. King's bench did not handle cases involving real estate; its basic responsibility was actions for 'trespass', and for lawsuits against prisoners of the crown. It was widening it range of competence, however, by allowing litigants to initiate lawsuits by bill of complaint rather than through the more rigid process of issuing a formal writ.[25] Such statistics as we have show that common pleas received 6200 separate actions in the Michaelmas term of 1482, and that king's bench received 1000 actions in the Michaelmas term of 1488.[26] Having declined under the Yorkists, activity in these courts partially recovered during Henry VII's reign to a peak in 1509–10, only to decline again sharply between then and 1529. This was chiefly because of short-term crises like epidemics that caused the courts to close, and had little to do with the development of the jurisdiction of chancery and the king's council, though some common lawyers were inclined to blame Wolsey for their loss of fees.[27] A less busy royal court, the court of the exchequer, met in the exchequer chamber in Westminster

[24] Baker, *Legal Profession*, 82.
[25] Baker, 'Introduction', 53–61.
[26] Guth, 'Enforcing Late Medieval Law', 86–7.
[27] Brooks, *Pettyfoggers and Vipers*, 80–3.

Palace, adjacent to the Great Hall. It dealt primarily with debts owed to the crown and with pleas against royal officials, including local receivers and collectors such as sheriffs. Some of its business also concerned offences against parliamentary statutes and royal proclamations, mostly to do with smuggling.[28]

The court of chancery, which also met in Westminster Hall, was unlike the common law courts so far discussed in that it was an equity court, which meant that the chancellor could use his personal authority to administer justice in a limited range of situations – including some relating to settlements of property – where there was no remedy in common law. As a court it had several advantages for litigants. Not only did the chancellor, whose court it was, have great personal authority as a senior minister of the crown, but the procedures by which defendants were summoned to appear were exceptionally prompt and effective. A litigant could initiate a plea by petition ('bill') rather than having to choose a particular form of action and follow the fixed process initiated by a standard writ. For these reasons, lawyers devised various loopholes by which their clients' cases were diverted from the common-law courts into chancery, with the result that the latter grew at the expense of the former. By using the pretext that the defendant was withholding vital legal documents, and so preventing a trial at common law – another area of equity jurisdiction – lawyers from the 1470s onwards were managing to bring to chancery a wider range of cases concerning title to land.[29] The number of petitions in chancery rose from 243 a year on average between 1470 and 1475 to 553 between 1475 and 1485, and then stayed at about that level till 1529.[30] The activities of chancery provoked some dissatisfaction amongst lawyers attached to the common law courts, and while Wolsey was chancellor (1515–29) his activities here, as in star chamber, bred the accusation that the common law was being undermined by arbitrary judgements. His high-handedness in chancery lacked the political justification it had in star chamber, but he was to some extent justified by rigidities in the common-law courts.[31]

Even at the centre in Westminster, the judicial system that attracted lawyers' veneration looks chaotic to a modern eye. It called for great faith to see an integrated system of thought or

[28] Guth, 'Enforcing Late Medieval Law', 84–5; Guth, 'Notes', 104, 111–12.
[29] A. Fox and J. A. Guy, *Reassessing the Henrician Age: Humanism, Politics and Reform, 1500–1550*, Oxford 1986, 187–9.
[30] Brooks, *Pettyfoggers*, p. 54.
[31] Baker, 'Introduction', 24–32, 77–82; Gunn, *Early Tudor Government*, 76–81.

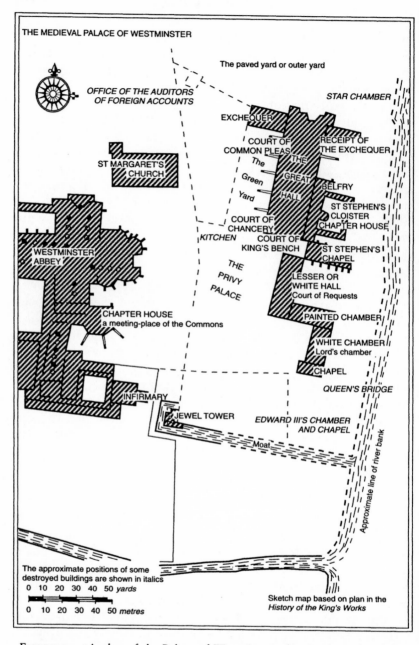

FIGURE 9.1 A plan of the Palace of Westminster, showing how the courts of common pleas, king's bench, the exchequer, chancery and (approximately) the star chamber were distributed in and around Westminster Hall. The plan also shows the Painted Chamber, where parliaments often opened, the White Chamber, where the lords subsequently sat, and the chapter house of Westminster Abbey, a meeting-place of the commons (*based on a plan in Colvin, History of the King's Works*)

practice. A broader look, taking into account all the local courts of medieval England, reveals a highly devolved structure. Counties were important units of delegated jurisdiction, and so were chartered boroughs. Manors had manorial courts, often with some responsibility for basic policing operations as well as for litigation between individuals. Urban guilds often had jurisdiction over their members for the enforcement of craft regulations. Some of the law enforced in these local courts was statute law, but this took on some exotic local colourings when it was differently interpreted in different courts, and there was an large mass of local custom and by-law relating to many aspects of social life. Boroughs and manors had their own legislative powers to the extent that they could formulate what was existing 'custom', or create new by-laws to meet new contingencies. Even the family may be regarded as a unit of law enforcement, since heads of households, usually men, were expected to be responsible for subordinate members.

Most of the responsibility for enforcing criminal law was in the hands of amateurs, while the professional lawyers made their piles from the fees they received for handling private litigation relating to lands, debts and trespasses. Local courts handled the great bulk of criminal jurisdiction as well as minor policing activity relating to unruly behaviour, vagrancy, pollution and trading offences. The king and parliament rarely set up any adequate machinery for the enforcement of new statutes or royal ordinances, and depended heavily on the goodwill of those who manned local courts.[32] Only the most serious crimes, which were beyond the competence of lesser courts, received the attention of the king's justices; they were reserved for the assizes in each county twice a year. Criminal cases might also be dealt with in the court of king's bench at Westminster either in the first instance or on appeal or by adjournment from lower courts, but in practice very few criminal proceedings were initiated there. The attorney-general rarely initiated criminal prosecutions before the council by virtue of his office.[33] The principal burden of maintaining order and enforcing the criminal law was borne locally by justices of the peace, by virtue of their statutory duties relating to criminal and economic offences. The justices, commissioned county by county, were obliged to hold quarter sessions at least four times a year, 'that is to say, at the feast of the Annunciation of Our

[32] Guth, 'Enforcing Late Medieval Law', 95–6.
[33] Guy, Cardinal's Court, 18.

Lady, Saint Margaret, Saint Michael and Saint Nicholas, and more session if need be, after their discretion'.[34] None of this apparatus was new; the duties of the justices of the peace were increasing between 1471 and 1529, but the institutions through which they worked had been in place since the fourteenth century.

The handling of private litigation was also a matter that affected the king's reputation and authority, since if litigants lost faith in the even-handedness of the courts, or their willingness to act, there was a danger of their taking the law into their own hands. Private lawsuits were the main business of all the central courts at Westminster. Like criminal jurisdiction, however, private litigation in late medieval England was conducted in a wide range of courts, whose diversity gave litigants a choice of strategies, and did not preclude the same grievance being pursued in several places simultaneously.[35] Local courts could be both cheaper and quicker than the king's courts, provided that the defendant could be compelled to put in an appearance. The usual technique for this was distraint – that is, seizure of possessions of the accused by the officers of the court. Urban courts attracted a lot of commercial business, especially concerning small and local debts. The Colchester borough courts, for example, received an average of 255 pleas of debt each year between Michaelmas 1476 and Michaelmas 1482, and of these 72 per cent were for sums below £2.[36] The object of taking opponents to court was in most cases to put pressure on them to come to terms. The king's courts gave judgement in only about a tenth of the pleas brought before them, and in all the other cases either the dispute was settled privately or the plaintiff withdrew from the prosecution. The procedures whereby disputes were resolved were sometimes quite formal. There was a long tradition of arbitration in medieval England, and especially in complex financial disputes this was likely to lead to the most satisfactory solutions. The fact that so many disputes were settled out of court does not mean that legal knowledge were not involved in resolving them, since professional lawyers were often employed in such business. Giving relevant advice, and acting as arbitrators, was one of the ways in which lawyers earned their keep, and the long vacations between legal terms gave them ample time to take on such business.[37]

---

[34] *Boke of Justices of Peas*, fo. Aiii.
[35] Guth, 'Enforcing Late Medieval Law', 82.
[36] R. H. Britnell, *Growth and Decline in Colchester, 1300–1525*, Cambridge 1986, 207–8.
[37] Ives, *Common Lawyers of Pre-Reformation England*, 126–30.

Law and Education

The heart of the world of law was very easily defined in the period 1471–1529, as it had been for some time before. It stretched from the grounds of the Middle Temple and Inner Temple on the north bank of the Thames as far as the grounds of Gray's Inn. Within this small area were not only the four inns of court (Middle Temple, Inner Temple, Lincoln's Inn and Gray's Inn) but also a further ten inns of chancery. The fourteen inns had chambers for about 1200 residents, of whom about 400 were active in the courts. Justices and serjeants-at-law, the cream of the profession, were not allowed to live in the inns. They could either belong to one of two serjeants' inns, in Chancery Lane and Fleet Street, or they could acquire their own property.[38]

The largest group of residents in the inns of court and chancery were in various stages of pupillage, since they strongly rivalled the universities as centres of higher education for those who could afford it. It was usual to start learning law at one of the inns of chancery about the age of seventeen or eighteen and then transfer to the inns of court later. On average entrants to the inns of court were about twenty or twenty-one. Perhaps as many as 6000 men were admitted to the inns between 1471 and 1529, the majority of them only for a general education with a legal bias.[39] Having learned enough, or decided that the law was not for them, most returned to their homes in the provinces with mixed memories of life in London and an enhanced understanding of their place in the social order. Large numbers of English gentlemen had spent time in London in this manner, picking up the terminology, jokes and prejudices of the legal profession, and learning what to do – or, perhaps more significantly, what not to do – in the performance of their duties. Probably fewer than a third of all entrants became lawyers in any professional sense, and many of those who did had no formally recognized qualifications. A modicum of legal knowledge might make a man employable as an estate officer, auditor or accountant.

Long before the invention of printing, there was a strong manuscript tradition of instruction in the law through legal treatises written by highly professional lawyers. A beginner in law needed to know something about substantive law and something about procedure. The most useful area of the former, especially for the

[38] Baker, *Legal Profession*, 79, 93–5.
[39] The estimate is recalculated from Baker, *Legal Profession*, 95.

child of a propertied family, was land law. So a student might start with the *Old Tenures*, a late fourteenth-century work for law students, first printed by Richard Pynson, London's principal law printer, about 1494. It started at the top of the social scale, with tenure by knight service, and then worked down to villeinage and precarious tenures.[40] The student might then proceed to the lengthier *New Tenures*, a work written around 1465–75 by Sir Thomas Littleton for the private instruction of his son, first published and printed in partnership by John Lettou and William de Machlinia in about 1482. This book dealt with a single branch of the law systematically, and explained it according to principles of substantive law, and as such it has been acclaimed as embodying a fundamentally new approach to the teaching of law.[41]

Procedural law was an arcane discipline that required extensive study of the writ system that had developed since the reign of Henry II. Different writs issued by chancery implied different procedures through the courts and different possible outcomes at the end of the trial. The basic book here was another late fourteenth-century work, *The Old Natura Brevium*; it too was first printed by Pynson about 1494. Forty years later, in 1534, William Rastell recommended the *Old Tenures*, the *New Tenures* and the *Old Natura Brevium* as constituting together an ABC of law.[42] They made a good educational foundation for a future landed gentleman, especially if combined with a manual on the statutory duties of a justice of the peace.

A more advanced legal education required further attention to the way in which cases were handled through the courts, and meant learning how to proceed if a plea was contested. English common law provided for an adversarial battle of wits between the attorneys of the contestants, and the heights of expertise in the legal profession involved learning the rules of this particular game by attending practical exercises, known as moots, in the inns of court.[43] Though the tradition was heavily dependent on oral transmission, lawyers showed considerable interest in the more accessible written evidence available to them from the past,

---

[40] *Old Tenure*, vii–viii, xv.
[41] A. W. B. Simpson (ed.), *Biographical Dictionary of the Common Law*, London 1984, 316; Simpson, *Legal Theory*, 274–6.
[42] Simpson, *Legal Theory*, 83.
[43] Baker, 'Introduction', 142–3; A. Harding, *The Law Courts of Medieval England*, London 1973, 115; S. E. Thorne and J. H. Baker (eds), *Readings and Moots in the Inns of Court in the Fifteenth Century, ii: Moots and Readers' Cases*, Selden Society cv, London 1990, xlv–liv.

particularly in the year books, many of which were available in manuscript. They could use such evidence in the daily course of legal debate, as well as to augment their pleading in court with appeals to older wisdom.

When Lettou and Machlinia started to print year books in about 1481–2, they chose books from the mid-1450s for the purpose. Between about 1490 and his death in 1530 Pynson produced over ninety volumes of them.[44] The value of having reports on past cases to hand is further illustrated by Anthony Fitzherbert's *Abridgement*, published in 1514–16, which contained notes on 13,845 cases going back through the year books and beyond, as far as *Bracton's Notebook* from the reign of Henry III. It was a vastly more ambitious compilation than anything earlier, and has been described as 'the earliest serious effort to systematize the entire corpus of law', though it includes no cases later than 1501.[45] It would be wrong to argue from the somewhat antiquarian nature of much law publishing that lawyers and their students had no interest in recent decisions, since manuscript year books continued to be made and circulated, and lawyers were encouraged, probably from their apprenticeship days, to compile their own collections of reports.[46] The reason why the printers concentrated on older year books seems to have been simply that the reports they contained were less easily obtainable than more recent ones and so could be expected to sell better. Some seemingly antiquarian law publishing was nevertheless the result of pure laziness. In 1506 or thereabouts Pynson printed a little manual for justices of the peace listing their statutory duties, setting out the forms of writs they were most likely to meet, and adding a sample collection of criminal proceedings. To judge from its contents, the text must have been about fifty years old.[47]

Collections of judicial precedents were particularly likely to appeal to those intending to make law a career. Many high-flyers in the legal profession, as in the church, came from relatively obscure families, or from disadvantaged positions within more eminent families. To reach the top, however, required both a high order of natural ability and considerable devotion to study.

[44] Abbott, *Law Reporting*, 13–16; Baker, 'Introduction', 161–3; F. L. Boersma, *An Introduction to Fitzherbert's Abridgement*, Abingdon 1981, 27; Simpson, *Legal Theory*, 79–80.
[45] Abbott, *Law Reporting*, 13; Boersma, *Introduction*, 15, 31–5; T. G. Watkins, in Simpson (ed.), *Biographical Dictionary*, 180.
[46] Baker, 'Introduction', 169, 178.
[47] *Boke of Justices of Peas*, iii–vi.

Anthony Fitzherbert was born to a family of Derbyshire gentry about 1470, but being a younger child was left propertyless when his father died in 1484. From 1490, or earlier, his mother supported him through the early years of a legal education at Gray's Inn. He was presumably 'called to the bar' about 1496-8. This expression referred to a particular structural arrangement in the hall of an inn of court that was needed when moots were held as exercises in pleading; a barrister was someone who could be trusted to argue cases 'at the bar'. By 1471 this had become recognized as a mark of status within the inns, comparable to graduation in the universities. It was an acknowledgement of proficiency that led to private employments in which proven legal competence was a desideratum. After about ten years, the normal gap, Fitzherbert was 'called to the bench'. The bench was another physical object, presumably at the end of the hall, on which senior members of an inn were seated when moots were held. A bencher was expected to deliver some formal lectures on the statutes of the realm. Fitzherbert was now technically equipped to act as advocate in the courts of the exchequer, king's bench and chancery when an opportunity should arise. At this point, in 1509, amongst his other commitments he was appointed recorder of Coventry, which meant that, in return for a retaining fee, he gave his professional opinion on difficult cases that cropped up in the borough court, and on other legal business affecting the borough, perhaps occasionally attending the Coventry court in person. A man might wait a long time as a bencher; the next promotion was to the post of sergeant-at-law, but the number of sergeants was usually fewer than ten, and promotions to fill the ranks of the deceased and the promoted were infrequent. Fitzherbert was fortunate in that he had to wait only until 1510, at which point he joined the elevated brotherhood at the head of the legal profession, wearing a distinctive habit and linen coif, and with the right to act as advocate in the court of common pleas. He was also now eligible to be promoted as a judge, but had a long wait for his turn to come. He was nevertheless fully employed; in 1512 he resigned as recorder of Coventry because 'he had so great business by reason that he was serjeant of the law'. In 1514-16 he published his *Abridgement*, so establishing himself as the greatest legal scholar of his day, and in 1516 he was made king's serjeant, which meant that in exchange for another small salary he was retained by the king. He was knighted probably by February 1522, and in the Easter term of 1522 he was made a judge in the court of common pleas. Such were the delays and tribulations involved in getting to the top, even for the most able.[48]

Many men became professional lawyers without reaching anywhere near these heights. There were numerous clerical posts for men with legal education – well over 100 in the royal courts at Westminster. The largest single group of lawyers was that of professional attorneys, who gave legal advice to clients and represented them in the courts at each stage of litigation. Often they had strong links with particular towns or regions of the country, and represented litigants with whom they had such local links. Attorneys working in the main courts had to be examined by judges, sworn in and formally registered. In 1480 there were perhaps about 290 attorneys operating in the courts of common pleas, king's bench and the exchequer, though many of these were also officers of the courts. Below the attorneys in status were solicitors and accountants, who had no recognized status in the courts, but who were able to attract some business in advising clients or drafting legal documents. Many of them belonged to the inns of court. One of their most important responsibilities was to advise their clients about the most appropriate form of action at law for each particular case. These various activities in the lower branch of the legal profession had analogies in local courts throughout the kingdom, especially in the towns.[49]

The Triumph of Law and Order?

Inculcating respect for law and order was high on the government's declared agenda throughout the period 1471–1529, and historians have used the quality of law enforcement as one of their principal indicators of the quality of successive regimes. They have generally been sceptical about the claims of kings and their ministers to be restoring law and order. Probably it was harder for a nobleman or gentleman to get away with murder under Henry VIII than under Henry VI, since the government was primed to make exemplary cases of prominent delinquents. Whether that means that the country was more law-abiding in 1529 than in 1471 is a different question, and probably not one for which any definite answer should be expected.

It is legitimate to express a moderately optimistic view of the

[48] *Coventry LB*, 635; Boersma, *Introduction*, 2–6; Thorne and Baker, *Readings and Moots*, liv–lvii.
[49] Baker, *Legal Profession*, 84–93; Brooks, *Pettyfoggers*, 19, 160.

rule of law in political affairs. By the later fifteenth century the principle of government in accordance with law had been established in England for over two centuries. *Magna Carta*, with its principle that no free man should be imprisoned, deprived of property, outlawed, exiled or destroyed without the judgement of his peers, had a great traditional hold on political values. Yet the ease with which the legal rights of the king's opponents had come to be openly disregarded during the third quarter of the fifteenth century is striking. This no doubt is attributable to dynastic conflict and recurrent civil war. Between 1450 and 1485, and chiefly as a legacy of the armed conflicts of 1450–61, the rights of the king's subjects to trial by their peers were severely compromised in political cases. The difference between dying in battle and being killed following defeat in battle, or following subsequent capture, was ignored. After the battle of Tewkesbury in 1471, for example, Lancastrian fugitives were slaughtered in Tewkesbury Abbey and in the parish church at Didbrook, about ten miles away.[50] Henry VI was murdered in cold blood. Thomas Fauconberg was beheaded secretly and without trial in the same year. None of those in the way of Richard, duke of York, was tried by his peers in 1483, and Edward V and his brother just disappeared from view. It was no accident that Richard III's memory suffered sorely at the hands of two of the most conscientious early Tudor chancellors, Morton and More. When Tudor historians described the horrors of the mid-fifteenth century, the breakdown of political legality was prominent in the images they selected.

One of the greatest and most important contrasts between the Tudors and their predecessors was their respect for legal form, even though this was quite compatible with using legal procedure for political ends and, if necessary, inventing both charges and evidence. In this respect Richard III's defeat in 1485 was a turning-point. Between 1485 and 1529 no opponents of the crown were put to death except in battle or after some legal process, whether by trial or attainder. The law of treason was particularly useful for solving particular political problems, as in 1495 when Sir William Stanley was executed, in 1499, when Perkin Warbeck and the earl of Warwick were executed, and again in 1521, when Henry VIII dealt with the duke of Buckingham. Men wept at the duke's fate, but he was technically guilty, so the judges said, and law must have its course.[51] Thomas More, who himself had

---

[50] Hammond, *Battles*, 97–9.
[51] Hall, 624.

described the lawless machinations of Richard III, was to be the victim of quite a different pattern of political ruthlessness in 1535. Legal establishments that cooperate to do a government's dirty work are unattractive things – less attractive to some people than impulsive violence – and the proceedings of Tudor state trials will raise the hackles of a modern reader more often than not. Nevertheless, the preference of the Tudors for working within the law was far more characteristic of medieval tradition than the cavalier principles of the Yorkists, and by all accounts their subjects seem to have valued the change.

In other respects it is unclear whether all the official bluster on law and order by successive kings brought much positive gain. It had some effect in reducing outrageous contempt of court, such as that characteristic of the worst days of Henry VI; such scandals had always been exceptional, but their suppression was at least a cosmetic gain. Wolsey's pontificating in council, even if it gave rise to professional misgivings, was probably effective in reducing the risk that disputes over property would lead to 'land wars' out of court, and it is possible that his activities did something to raise the professional integrity of the judges themselves.[52] If so, one achievement of government policy was to ensure that a larger proportion of disputes between individuals were handled either by arbitration or through the courts, rather than by private feuding. Maybe it was whistling in the dark, but Wolsey repeatedly asserted that something had been achieved. In August 1517 he told the king that 'Your laws be in every place indifferently ministered without leaning of any manner', and in February 1518 he reported that 'the kingdom was never in greater harmony'. Later, in July 1527, he reported to the king that Kent 'was not more quiet this twenty year than it is now'. In the interim, of course, he had had an uprising on his hands in 1525.[53]

Meanwhile, large areas of law enforcement were little affected either by the activities of central government or by any developments in the practices of the courts. The capture and conviction of common criminals remained a haphazard and unconvincing business, to the extent that in parts of the country the operations of the courts had nothing to do with the level of crime. In the Welsh marcher lordships it was common for lords to impose general fines on their tenants rather than hold the courts that might judge malefactors. As the tenants of Hay complained in

[52] Baker, 'Introduction', 80; Bellamy, *Bastard Feudalism*, 131–4.
[53] *SP*, i, 196; Pollard, *Wolsey*, 73.

1518, this practice of 'redeeming the sessions' was one that punished the law-abiding rather than the criminals, since 'such persons as do not offend, but be of good rule, bear more charge to the redeeming of the said sessions than the offenders do'.[54] On the northern borders the courts were quite unable to contain the organized crime of the men of Tynedale and Redesdale, who raided southwards with impunity; there were said to be up to 100 thieves from the borders in Hexham every market day in 1515, 1516 and 1522.[55] Over the whole kingdom, any reduction in criminal activity was probably confined to the more readily identifiable political and social elite rather than to groups lower down the social scale. That means that any success the Yorkist and early Tudor kings achieved in enhancing respect for the law should be counted as political success in controlling the loyalties of the propertied classes rather than as a more fundamental advance towards a law-abiding society.

[54] *Marcher Lordships*, 43.
[55] R. Robson, *The Rise and Fall of the English Highland Clans: Tudor Responses to a Medieval Problem*, Edinburgh 1989, 78–9.

Part IV

Economy

The Secular Social Order

Discussing past societies is partly a matter of discovering ways in which people at the time thought about their world, partly a matter of describing that world in terms of modern concepts, and both tasks are equally important for a rounded understanding. This chapter concerns chiefly concepts that were held in the late Middle Ages, ideals of social rank, family, community and commonwealth, so it portrays this world in a somewhat static and idealized way, but such an approach is nevertheless essential if we are to understand the values by which people lived. The following two chapters, and particularly the last, look at society in ways that are foreign to later medieval thought, but which are necessary for relating that world to ours.

There were two necessary requirements for being a duke, earl, viscount, marquess or baron, these being the five ranks of nobility at the time (in descending order). The first was an income sufficient to maintain an appropriate life-style, and that meant that most noblemen received at least £400 a year apiece, while the wealthiest earls and dukes had up to £3000.[1] The second requirement was recognition of one's noble title by the king. Older peerages were acknowledged in this period by a personal summons to parliament to sit in the upper house. If the king wished to create a new peer he issued letters patent to declare the new promotion.[2] There was usually a ceremony at court, after which the new peer would be summoned to parliament. If a noble family maintained its estates and avoided political disasters, titles passed by heredity from father to son. But if a family's income fell too low, royal recognition was withdrawn and the peerage lapsed. This happened,

---

[1] Cornwall, *Wealth and Society*, 143–4.
[2] J. R. Lander, *Conflict and Stability in Fifteenth-Century England*, 3rd edn, London 1977, 169.

for example, to the earldom of Kent on the death of Earl Richard in 1524; he had wasted his inheritance as a result (it was said) of excessive gambling, and there was not enough substance or reputation left to justify ennobling his heir.[3] If a peer miscalculated sufficiently seriously to be condemned as a traitor, this again led to the lapse of his title unless the condemnation was later reversed.

Below the nobility were the gentry, a category invented by later writers to embrace three social ranks that were distinguished in the late Middle Ages – knights, esquires and gentlemen. There were probably only about 6500 men who thought of themselves as belonging to any of these three categories around 1500, and with their immediate families they constituted less than 2 per cent of the total population of the kingdom.[4] Some urban gentlemen earned their status in borough administration and law, and remained firmly wedded to the life of the towns. Some professional lawyers and minor administrators were also categorized as gentlemen by the late fifteenth century. But for the most part the different grades of gentry, like the nobility, had homes in the country, lived from landed revenues and had some degree of lordship over men, even if only a single small manor, or no manor at all.[5]

A few families in these three categories accumulated wealth to rival that of the less affluent nobility, especially amongst those who acquired fortunes in the service of the king.[6] Sir William Compton, groom of the stool in the king's privy chamber, had an income of £1655 in 1524. However, few had incomes of over £300 a year in the 1520s, and many would-be gentlemen had to manage with £20 or less.[7] The minimum annual income needed to qualify for appointment as a justice of the peace was £20,[8] but there were some families on the lower margin of gentility who received less. In 1474 Edward IV wrote to Coventry requiring that all gentlemen and other inhabitants of the city with an annual income of £10 or more should turn out to meet him when he came to the town.[9] To be considered a gentleman, a man had

[3] G. W. Bernard, 'The Fortunes of the Greys, Earls of Kent, in the Early Sixteenth Century', *HJ*, xxv (1982), 684–5; T. B. Pugh, 'Henry VII and the English Nobility', in Bernard, *Tudor Nobility*, 74.
[4] Cornwall, *Wealth and Society*, 147; Lander, *Limitations*, 24.
[5] Carpenter, *Locality and Polity*, 89–90; Horrox, 'Urban Gentry', 22–44.
[6] G. W. Bernard, 'The Rise of Sir William Compton, Early Tudor Courtier', *EHR*, xcvi (1981), 754–77; M. Condon, 'From Caitiff and Villain to Pater Patriae: Reynold Bray and the Profits of Office', in M. A. Hicks (ed.), *Profit, Piety and the Professions in Later Medieval England*, Gloucester 1990, 137–68.
[7] Cornwall, *Wealth and Society*, 144.
[8] S. M. Wright, *The Derbyshire Gentry in the Fifteenth Century*, Chesterfield 1983, 2.
[9] *Coventry LB*, 413.

Table 10.1   Leaders of provincial society and their incomes, 1524

Rank	Number	Normal range of incomes (£)	Lowest income recorded (£)	Highest income recorded (£)
Peer	60	400–1400	40	2920
Knight	500	120–200	20	1655
Esquire	800	50–80	5	618
Gentleman	5000	10–20	2	160

Sources: J. C. K. Cornwall, Wealth and Society in Early Sixteenth-Century England, London 1988, 144–7; J. R. Lander, Conflict and Stability in Fifteenth-Century England, 3rd edn, London 1977, 168n

to support his family without the need for demeaning manual work, so that the appropriate education for his children was in social arts and book-learning rather than in the acquisition of productive skills. Table 10.1 shows the normal range of incomes for peers, knights, esquires and gentlemen in 1524, but also illustrates how widely spread incomes in fact were amongst the exceptionally fortunate or unfortunate members of each category.

Knights usually received an income appreciably more than the £40 a year supposed to be the minimum income needed to support the title. In law, any freeholder earning £40 a year was required to be knighted and to be available for the king's service in this capacity, but in practice it had long been recognized that more like three times this sum was needed.[10] The status of a knight, like that of a noble, had to be accredited by the king or his representative in a ceremonial dubbing. The rank of esquire was not ceremonially bestowed, but it was not one that could be easily assumed. Some men descended from noblemen or knights used 'esquire' as a courtesy title, some used it as a prescriptive title, following the example of their forebears, and others became entitled to use it as prominent officers of the crown.[11] Unlike knights and esquires, gentlemen did not owe their status to any particular form of recognition, and families could emerge into their ranks by buying land and simply describing themselves as of gentle status. Families wanting more official recognition of their gentility

[10] E. Acheson, A Gentry Community: Leicestershire in the Fifteenth Century, c.1422– c.1485, Cambridge 1992, 39; Cornwall, Wealth and Society, 9; Wright, Derbyshire Gentry, 3.
[11] Carpenter, Locality and Polity, 89.

obtained it by applying to the king's heralds for armorial bearings granted under the heralds' letters patent, for which they had to pay the fees demanded.[12]

Nobility and gentry between them constituted the ruling echelons of provincial society, so it is not surprising that their status was acknowledged by means of a variety of publicly recognizable indicators. There were recognized ways to address such men in conversation – 'my lord' or 'sir' for the nobility, 'sir' for the gentry. Noblemen, knights, esquires and many gentlemen had armorial bearings and lesser emblems that could be displayed on their buildings and furnishings. Styles of housing were regular indicators of rank, particularly in the countryside. Usually there could be no mistaking the difference in size and grandeur between the residence of a nobleman and that of an ordinary knight. Though castles were associated with the nobility, and manor houses more with the gentry, the contrast between the two architectural forms was breaking down in detail. Some manor houses had castle-like features, as at Edmund Bedingfield's manor of Oxburgh Hall (Norfolk), which was fortified under a royal licence of 1482. Meanwhile, aristocratic castles were no longer being built primarily for defensive purposes; the architect of Thornbury Castle (Gloucestershire), which was being built for the duke of Buckingham at the time of his execution in 1521, hesitated whether to call it a castle or a manor.[13] Most of the residences of these families were inherited from the past, and since this was not one of the great ages of reconstruction, surviving examples of contemporary taste are not numerous. Something remains of Lord Hastings's castle-building at Ashby de la Zouch and Kirby Muxloe (both Leicestershire) and of the duke of Buckingham's similarly aborted work at Thornbury, however, and amongst manor houses of the period may be mentioned Ashbury Manor (Berkshire) of about 1488 and Compton Wynyates (Warwickshire), built for Sir William Compton about 1515–20.

The environment of a distinguished home could also present telling signs of the status and wealth of its owner. Around the residences of both nobility and gentry, the construction of parks had acquired such value as a status symbol that this had become a chief reason for enclosing land. Wivenhoe Park, where Essex

---

[12] Carpenter, *Locality and Polity*, 90; D. A. L. Morgan, 'The Individual Style of the English Gentleman', in M. Jones (ed.), *Gentry and Lesser Nobility in Later Medieval Europe*, Gloucester 1986, 17–18.

[13] Thompson, *Decline of the Castle*, 60.

University now stands, was so created by the earl of Oxford between 1502 and 1509.[14] The local influence of distinguished families was likely to be evident in their parish churches, which they often developed as mausoleums. It was not uncommon for families who paid for the rebuilding or modernization of churches to have them ornamented with family emblems. At Thornbury (Gloucestershire) can be seen the knot of the Staffords, and at Lavenham (Suffolk) the star of the de Veres. The homogeneity of the symbolic forms by which authority was represented across the social divides between crown, nobility and gentry is striking, and parallels the same concerns with inherited title and worth that were held to justify both royal and seigniorial authority in the first place. The intelligentsia played with the contrast between inherited gentility and moral gentility – as, most notably, in Henry Medwall's play of *Fulgens and Lucrece*, written for Cardinal Morton's household in the 1490s[15] – but in political reality the second counted for nothing without the first.

The 98 per cent or so of the population below the level of the ruling elite was subdivided into yet more social ranks. In the countryside, though peasants shared some class interests in confrontation with their landlords, they were deeply divided by wealth and status. The wealthier ones, those most heavily engaged in commercial agriculture, were often referred to as yeomen. This group overlapped with the lower ranks of the gentry, into which they sometimes aspired to rise, and the contiguity between the two groups is suggested in the oldest surviving ballad of Robin Hood, printed probably in the years 1510–15:

Lythe [= attend] and listen, gentlemen
That be of freebore blood;
I shall tell you of a good yeoman,
His name was Robin Hood.

The economic bounds of the yeomanry are difficult to define at either the top or bottom end, but its members were mostly farmers earning between £2 and £10 a year, after the payment of rents and wages to any employees they might hire.[16] Below the yeomen

[14] R. H. Britnell, *Growth and Decline in Colchester, 1300–1525*, Cambridge 1986, 253.

[15] Medwall, 3, 31–89.

[16] R. B. Dobson and J. Taylor, *Rymes of Robin Hood: An Introduction to the English Outlaw*, Gloucester 1989, 71, 79; J. C. Holt, *Robin Hood*, London 1982, 119.

were peasants with smaller holdings, sometimes classified as husbands or husbandmen. In the *Gest of Robin Hood* already mentioned, Robin instructs his followers to respect such men: 'But
look ye do no husband harm / That tilleth with his plough.'[17] The
word 'husband' here is closer to its older meaning of 'master of
a household' than to its modern reference to any married man,
and refers to the ability of the husbandman to support himself
and his family from his own land. As the words of the ballad
suggest, the life of the husbandman was necessarily one of agricultural work on his land the year round. At a still lower level
of income and status were cottagers and labourers who characteristically depended for their living upon wage-earning. In the
towns, the population below the ranks of the merchant class
might be similarly divided between tradesmen and artisans, who
were characteristically self-employed, and labourers, who depended
upon wages.[18]

Differences of rank below the ranks of nobility and gentry were
similarly reflected in the quality of homes. Amongst the wealthier
peasantry and urban artisans there were comfortable and well-
constructed houses that allowed a generous amount of space for
each occupant. Many of these survive, sometimes in good number
as at Lavenham (Suffolk). They usually used a wooden framework constructed on stone foundations, with panels of wattle
and daub between the timbers. Though thatch was common, many
of the more substantial houses were tiled, even in rural areas. In
East Anglia and south-eastern England two-storeyed houses were
numerous. Even the smallest artisan's house was likely to contain
a workshop, a living-room and a bedchamber. The cottages of
the poor, meanwhile, usually had only a single room for the whole
family.[19]

Distinctions of wealth within village and urban populations
were accompanied by distinctions of legal status. The nobility
and gentry were freeborn by definition, and a common assumption to that effect was made of the yeomanry, who were regarded
as the backbone of English archery. Lower down the ranks of
countrymen the position was more confused. Heavy labour services, once a defining characteristic of serfdom, had almost disappeared, so that most rents were paid in money or in grain. Many
families had escaped from personal serfdom during the course of

[17] Dobson and Taylor, *Rymes of Robin Hood*, 80.
[18] Dyer, *Standards of Living*, 15, 20.
[19] Dyer, *Standards of Living*, 162, 167–8; Phythian-Adams, *Desolation*, 81.

the fifteenth century either by negotiation with their manorial lords or, more commonly, by moving away from the village of their birth and starting a new life elsewhere.[20] In a much diminished form, however, servile status still survived, and it entitled landlords to impose financial obligations and other duties on certain countrymen who were accounted their villeins. Moreover, even without the complication of serfdom, English village society was structured according to hierarchical distinctions that determined many aspects of daily life and activity – the sources of a family's wealth, hours of leisure, quality of diet, and forms of action with other villagers.[21] In the towns, too, a distinction was strongly maintained between freemen (or burgesses) who had the right to trade as they wished freely, without paying tolls, and those who were not free and were not allowed to trade. The difference corresponded quite closely to that between the artisans and labourers, the former being tradesmen or craftsmen and the latter their dependants, and is one that will have to be re-examined in the course of discussing the borough community.

Families

Any discussion of concepts of social order must include some account of the family, the context in which most education relating to ethical and political issues was conducted. In the play known as *Calisto and Melebea*, which was printed about 1525, householders in the audience are warned by Danio, the father of the well-brought-up heroine, to teach their children 'some art, craft or learning':

The bringers-up of youth in this region
Have done great harm because of their negligence,
Not putting them to learning nor occupations:
So, when they have no craft nor science,
And come to man's state, ye see th'experience,
That many of them compelled be
To beg or steal by very necessity.[22]

The arts and crafts of which Danio speaks would be appropriate for families below the ranks of the gentry, and learning would be

---

[20] M. Bailey, 'Rural Society', in Horrox, *Fifteenth-Century Attitudes*, 158–9.
[21] Blanchard, 'Social Structure', 318–30.
[22] *Calisto and Melebea*, ll. 1065–71.

more appropriate for the ranks above, though there were some opportunities, as we have seen, for bright boys from the ranks of the wealthier peasantry or townspeople to embark on a legal or clerical career.

There were many other respects, of course, in which families differed according to their social status and economic circumstances, and not all household units corresponded to a standard married couple with their children. On the one hand, families of the merchants and the better-off artisans and yeomen farmers, like those of the nobility and gentry, were extended by the addition of domestic servants. Urban craftsmen often had at least one apprentice resident in their homes. A cottage was unlikely to house more than a single nuclear family, without servants. Meanwhile, in the lower ranks of society there were some very small households, headed by widowers or widowers. Unmarried women sometimes lived alone or with other spinsters, but this arrangement, rational though it might seem, was inhibited in towns by the suspicion that it implied a brothel. In 1492 the Coventry authorities required healthy 'singlewomen' under the age of fifty to take service in another household until they should marry.[23] Differences in household size were closely paralleled by the size of houses, except that overcrowding was more marked lower down the social scale.

Parental authority was formally recognized by modes of demeanour and address. These are best recorded, in literature and surviving correspondence, for the upper ranks of society. About 1474, when in his mid-twenties, William Stonor opened a letter to his father with the words 'My right reverent and worshipful father, I recommend me unto your good fatherhood in the most humble wise that I can or may, meekly beseeching your fatherhood of your daily blessing'; this was standard filial style in addressing either parent. In conversation, polite children addressed their father as 'sir'. Husbands and wives in polite society showed each other a similar formal respect in public contexts, women addressing their husbands as 'sir' or 'husband', and men addressing their wives as 'dame' or 'wife'.[24]

Childhood dependence was shorter than it is now. Even in the highest ranks of society, the period of formal education was rarely prolonged beyond the late teens, and men might be exposed to

---

[23] *Coventry LB*, 545.
[24] *Stonor Letters*, 228; H. S. Bennett, *The Pastons and their England*, 2nd edn, Cambridge 1932, 72–3; Phythian-Adams, *Desolation*, 89.

the full rigours of military campaigning and battle by that time. Edward, prince of Wales, heir to the Lancastrian dynasty, fell in battle at Tewkesbury at the age of seventeen. Lower down the social scale economic exigencies often required that children should become productive members of the household at a tender age. It was common for both boys and girls to leave the parental home in their teens to work elsewhere either as apprentices or as servants. This meant that artisan and peasant households often contained only the younger children of the householder, together perhaps with servants, while the older sons and daughters worked elsewhere away from their parents as 'young men' and 'maids'. Men and women alike achieved their own homes only at marriage, which was usually in their early or mid-twenties; first marriages were usually between partners of about the same age.[25]

The level of economic dependence upon a male householder varied considerably between families. Women often made a very considerable contribution to the income of their households, either through cooperating with their husbands on the farm or in the workshop, or by pursuing some commercial activity of their own. Many, for example, were active brewers and sellers of ale, either retailing it from their own homes or selling it to the keepers of inns and alehouses. Women might engage on their own account in other service trades like nursing, laundering and dealing in second-hand clothes, or in manufacturing industries like spinning, candle-making and hand-milling. However, women's work was less valued, and more poorly paid, than men's work. There was a strong prejudice in favour of protecting male employment at the expense of women when times were hard, and opportunities for women deteriorated in towns like York that had fallen on hard times. Women were also very poorly represented in the various civic ceremonies by which borough communities defined their composition and common interest.[26]

The paternal role in the household was dominant, and backed up by custom and by the law, which gave each man the right to manage his wife's property and also made him responsible for her debts. In practice, where a household had both a husband and wife in residence, they generally shared authority over subordinates,

[25] Goldberg, *Women*, 225–32; Phythian-Adams, *Desolation*, 84–5.

[26] J. M. Bennett, '*Ale, Beer and Brewsters in England: Women's Work in a Changing World, 1300–1600* (New York and Oxford, 1996); Goldberg, *Women*, 132–5, 155, 278–9; C. Phythian-Adams, 'Ceremony and the Citizen: The Communal Year at Coventry, 1450–1550', in Holt and Rosser, *Medieval Town*, 58–9.

and the wife was usually in command when her the husband was away from home. The authority of householders to discipline and punish extended not only to children of the family but also to resident apprentices and servants, who had exchanged the authority of their own parents for that of a master and mistress. Because marriage was such an important determinant of a family's status, connections and wealth, parents, particularly fathers, were expected to have a say in the matrimonial choices of their children, and especially among the propertied classes this could amount to considerable pressure to accept a particular partner. There were nevertheless external restraints on male authority in common law and ecclesiastical law, and though these did not always prove very effective in reality, they could be enforced if family members were sufficiently determined. A man was not entitled to sell any property his wife might hold by gift or inheritance, unless he had her formal consent to do so. Nor was he entitled to compel his children to marry without their consent, and compulsion of this sort provided grounds for later divorce.[27]

Communities

The idea of community is an awkward one in the ordinary course of comment on medieval society. Since most settlements were very small by today's standards it would be apposite to describe them as face-to-face communities, in which most families not only knew each other but knew quite a lot about each other. However, in modern English the word community sometimes has egalitarian or romantically conservative connotations which are inappropriate to the Middle Ages because they cut across the way that people then thought of their world.

There was a definite sense of public good in medieval communities, which was often invoked in exhorting people to virtue. 'Every man after his power and degree should principally put him in devoir and labour for the advancement of the common profit of a region, country, city, town or household.'[28] Yet the common good in question, at least in the minds of the writers of the texts we have, always required the preservation of clearly defined social

[27] Goldberg, *Women*, 275.
[28] *Boke of Noblesse*, 57.

rank; each member of a community, of whatever social rank, should know his or her place. The symbolism in terms of which communities were understood was that of the body whose members function in different ways and with differing degrees of honour. In the community of the borough, as of the realm, there was a head and there were feet, and their status and associated rights were not the same. The description of the society by means of corporeal imagery, in order to represent the maintenance of existing distinctions of rank and traditions of authority as natural and just, was central to all models of society, and it received expression in the language of social degree, in the details of constitutional forms, and in the style of public ritual.[29]

Both village and town communities had a definite part to play in local government and society. Surviving records from the medieval countryside are mostly from landed estates, since parish records from this period are quite rare, and though they illustrate well the nature of lordship they do not do justice to the role of the village community in rural organization. Open-field systems predominated in a broad swathe of country stretching from Durham in the north, southward through Yorkshire and the Midlands to Dorset and Hampshire in the south, and here villages were agrarian units that required some common management. In some cases the regulation of open fields was the responsibility of manorial courts, but there were many villages whose territory was divided between several manors and where there was no single manor court that all villagers attended. In such cases people must have organized their fields through some alternative means; at Harlestone (Northamptonshire) in 1505 they had a standing committee of nine good men, presumably appointed at some village meeting. Even outside open-field country, common pastures and woods were often carefully regulated. Throughout the countryside, villages were responsible for assessing and collecting taxes imposed by parliament. Sometimes the lord of a manor was heavily involved in this proceeding, but some villages held general meetings, or entrusted the task to responsible assessors. In addition, in so far as they constituted a parish, villagers had a church building and its activities to maintain, and this involved both raising money and organizing events. Some parishes had systems of poor relief, as at Nayland (Suffolk), whose churchwardens were bequeathed a tenement as a perpetual almshouse in 1495. It was a common

---

[29] Chrimes, *English Constitutional Ideas*, 312–13.

practice for villagers to organize help-ales, bride-ales and church-
ales, at which ale was sold with a view to donating the proceeds
to some charitable cause. Many villages had parish guilds that
combined religious devotion with conviviality.[30]

The extent of local government was necessarily wider in urban
communities, and many towns had a formal measure of self-
government granted them by charter. This went along with a
distinctive legalistic concept of community, meaning a body of
townsmen with shared privileges and shared obligations defined
by a borough charter. Not all urban residents of a borough were
members of the urban community in this special sense. Men were
able to become free burgesses, and so share in borough privileges,
only by inheritance from their fathers, by completing an apprenticeship within the borough, or by finding sponsors and buying
themselves in. To become a freeman of Hull, for example, cost
£2 up to 1498 and £1 thereafter, but the latter sum, lowered in
response to hard times, still represented about two months' wages
for a skilled worker. Freemen shared the liberty of choosing their
own senior officials from the wealthier amongst them, and of participating in various economic freedoms. They had a strong incentive to maintain the legal distinction between themselves and the
unfree because it protected them from some forms of commercial
competition and made it easier to control their employees. At the
same time, they were obliged, as freemen, to assume responsibility to the king for the proper running of the town and the collection of royal dues. The administrative and political operations
of a chartered borough were more extensive than those of a village
community, often extending to responsibility for walls and bridges,
the enforcement of law and order, and the holding of courts of
law, presided over by the town bailiffs or mayor. All the main
boroughs were expected to return members of parliament. Borough
communities frequently owned and managed property and other
sources of regular income with which to meet their obligations to
the crown. The borough of Grimsby in 1492 had a regular income
of over £27, mostly from the rent of property, though £2 came
from tolls on trade.[31]

Towns had existed before there were town charters, however,
and it would be a mistake to place so much stress upon the legal

---

[30] W. O. Ault, *Open-Field Farming in Medieval England*, London 1972, 75; J. M.
Bennett, 'Conviviality and Charity in Medieval and Early Modern England', *P&P*, cxxxiv
(1992), 19–41; Dyer, 'English Medieval Village Community', 407–18.
[31] S. H. Rigby, *Medieval Grimsby, Growth and Decline*, Hull 1993, 120; Rigby, *English
Society*, 160–5.

aspects of urban communities that other essential facets of town life are overlooked. Many of the most striking features of late medieval urban culture had little to do with borough status; they are to be found in Westminster, whose inhabitants had never sought self-governing independence. One aspect of this culture was the formation of a large number of internal communities of various sorts, especially craft guilds and religious fraternities. Another was in the pride that townsmen placed in their streets and buildings, especially their parish churches. In urban society, as in the countryside, the ritual year was an important focus of communal activity that did not depend upon any particular form of urban administration, even if public ceremonies were used to display the authority of borough officials where they existed.[32]

Urban ritual was often developed to display the hierarchical character of urban communities, especially in the festivities organized by many towns for the feast of Corpus Christi (meaning 'the body of Christ'). On these occasions the politically recognized members of the urban community of the borough were symbolically identified with Christ's body, and different urban groups, mostly organized according to the urban crafts, assumed obligations to contribute to a grand procession or put on plays within a centrally planned structure. Where there were town councils, they regulated participation in such festivals by formal ordinances, and individuals and groups could be fined for failing to do what was expected of them. The different status accorded to different groups was publicly paraded, and sometimes gave rise to rivalry. The form of these celebrations implied that the different rights and duties of various groups of townsmen, the inequalities of status that distinguished them, and the antagonisms that divided them, should all be interpreted in the context of a natural and sacralized order.[33]

The Commonwealth and Social Legislation

Having warned householders in his audience of their duty to educate children in their charge, Danio, in *Calisto and Melebea*, proceeds to widen the responsibility for education:

[32] D. Palliser, 'Urban Society', in Horrox, *Fifteenth-Century Attitudes*, 142–3; G. Rosser, 'The Essence of Medieval Urban Communities: The Vill of Westminster, 1200–1540', in Holt and Rosser, *Medieval Town*, 216–37.

[33] James, 'Ritual', 16–47; Phythian-Adams, 'Ceremony', 238–64; M. Rubin, *Corpus Christi: The Eucharist in Late Medieval Culture*, Cambridge 1991, 266–7.

The heads and rulers must first be diligent
To make good laws, and execute them straitly (= strictly)
Upon such masters that be negligent . . .
If the cause of the mischiefs were seen before
Which by conjecture to fall [= occur] be most likely,
And good laws and ordinances made therefore
To put away the cause, that were best remedy.[34]

This idea that the unemployment leads to crime, and that its causes should be tackled by legislation, was a commonplace of the age, building upon earlier traditions of medieval thought, but carrying them further in some directions.

One of the most useful rhetorical expressions in the repertoire of political propagandists for the crown, petitioners, and other special pleaders from the mid-fifteenth century onwards was 'commonwealth', or 'commonweal' (usually two separate words), for which there is no exact equivalent in current English. Much the same meaning was conveyed by 'public weal' or 'politic weal', which was used as an idealized expression for the state, with resonances that linked it to ideals of justice, truth and social harmony.[35] 'The common wealth of this realm, or of the subjects or inhabitants thereof', wrote Edmund Dudley in 1509, 'may be resembled to a fair and mighty tree growing in a fair field or pasture, under the covert or shade whereof all beasts, both fat and lean, are protected and comforted from heat and cold as the time requireth.' On the surface this was a pacific ideal. On the other hand, since internal unity would make England more defensible against external enemies and enable the king to pursue his just causes abroad, commonwealth was also a concept with military relevance, if required. The author of *The Book of Noblesse* developed a number of representative commonwealth themes while exhorting Edward IV to recover his rights in France.[36]

The particular issues that people thought legitimate to put before the king as problems affecting the commonwealth depended upon their particular packages of interests and perceptions, so that the legislative activity of the period illustrates numerous points of tension and conflict between social groups. Sometimes the government can be shown to have an agenda of its own, to increase its

---

[34] *Calisto and Melebea*, ll. 1073–5, 1079–82.
[35] A. Fox and J. A. Guy, *Reassessing the Henrician Age: Humanism, Politics and Reform, 1500–1550*, Oxford 1986, 124–5. 'Commonwealth' translates the Latin *respublica* from which the English 'republic' derives.
[36] Dudley, 31; *Boke of Noblesse*, 57, 65–70.

capacity to raise taxes and armies, but large amounts of legislation were more the response to representations from particular
non-government interests. Some proposals might be classified
as issues of class conflict, such as the government's concern to
strengthen the ability of employers to discipline their employees.
Others had more to do with preserving differences in the formal
ordering of social rank by styles of dress, and so on, and these
may be classified as areas of status conflict. Other measures are
difficult to explain by reference to interests of any kind, and can
be interpreted only in terms of a deep-seated fear of moral disorder born of individualism. John Russell, bishop of Lincoln, in
preparing a sermon for Richard III's parliament of 1484, put the
last point of view very clearly: 'Would God that our people of
England, where every man now severally studieth to his own
singular avail and to the accomplishing of his own singular affection, would think upon his own body, the common and public
body of the realm, where, of right, a great person is oft times but
a small member.' These different concerns may illustrated by the
response of various administrations to one of the concerns that
Russell picked out for special mention – the decay of the commonwealth 'by closures and emparking, by driving away of tenants and letting down of tenantries'.[37]

Because kings and their ministers believed that the conversion
of arable land to pasture and parkland, and the enclosure that
accompanied it, caused landlessness and depopulation, they attempted to halt and reverse it.[38] A military aspect of this concern
was apparent in Henry VII's early statutory measure to prevent
the growth of farms and to protect arable husbandry on the Isle
of Wight in 1490, on the grounds that the security of the realm
required the island to be 'well inhabited with English people'. In
the same year the king renewed the chartered privileges of New-
port (Isle of Wight) and granted the burgesses additional sources
of income.[39] A more general enactment to protect arable farming,
approved in the same parliamentary session as that for the Isle of
Wight, again urged the defence of the realm as a principal consideration, but argued further that in the country as a whole the
conversion of arable to pasture created unemployment and the
destruction of churches.[40] The question then lay dormant for

[37] Chrimes, *English Constitutional Ideas*, 180–1.
[38] Thirsk, 'Enclosing and Engrossing', 213–18.
[39] 4 Henry VII, c. 16: *SR*, ii, 540; *VCH, Hants.*, v, p. 257.
[40] 4 Henry VII, c. 19: *SR*, ii, p. 542. For the date of these measures, see *SR*, ii, 524n
and *Rot. Parl.*, vi, 437.

several decades, but the military concern with conserving manpower did not go away, and helps to explain why the belligerent Henry VIII became antagonistic to enclosures between his wars. Enclosure surfaced as an issue in 1514, following the French campaign of 1513 and the exceptionally high grain prices of the years 1512 and 1513. A royal ordinance of 1514 or 1515 mentions scarcity of food, unemployment and crime as the results of pasture farming and the engrossment of farms. A statute of 1515, for 'avoiding pulling down of towns', elaborated yet further the arguments against pasture farming, and ordered that no land was to be enclosed and turned to pasture if this caused the decay of even a single dwelling.[41] Cardinal Wolsey followed up this statute with commissions of enquiry in 1517 and 1518 to receive information over most of the kingdom about illegal enclosures created since 1488.[42]

All categories of landlord engaged in the enclosure of land for pasture, and there are examples of conflict between landlords and tenants as a result, such as those between the third duke of Buckingham and his tenants at Thornbury (Gloucestershire). Though such conflicts perhaps brought the enclosure to the attention of the government as a continuing phenomenon, they were much less frequent than they became after 1530, and were not numerous enough to explain why the government should choose to antagonize landlords.[43] Nor was enclosure anything new. A change in land use towards pasture had been a marked feature of agrarian development since the mid-fourteenth century, and many of the examples of decay that met the traveller's eye in the 1520s were the result of change over a period of nearly 200 years. John Rous, who wrote a lengthy denunciation of depopulating landlords into his *History of the Kings of England*, which he dedicated to Henry VII in the years 1489–91, says there that he had presented a bill on the subject in the Coventry parliament of 1459 and in several subsequent parliaments, but that on each occasion his labour had been wasted.[44] The new public concern over enclosure under the Tudors corresponded to a range of other government concerns about manpower, food supplies, employment and social order.

---

[41] *Tudor Royal Proclamations*, 122–3; 6 Henry VIII, c. 5; 7 Henry VIII, c. 1: *SR*, iii, 127, 176–7. The statute was at first authorized to be enforced only until Christmas 1515, but was made permanent later that year. For the format of references to statutes, see above, p. 130.

[42] *Domesday of Enclosures*, i, 9–11.

[43] Harris, *Edward Stafford*, 83–5, 276; R. B. Manning, *Village Revolts: Social Protest and Popular Disturbances in England, 1509–1640*, Oxford 1988, 27, 38.

[44] Rous, 120–1.

Legislation to help employers to control their employees was another issue of government concern directly related to a recurrent area of class tension, and one where the government backed traditional authority. Regulation of wages by parliamentary statute, originally introduced as a response to the Black Death, remained a fixed principle of legislation. A revised act of 1495 was repealed in 1497 because it threatened penalties against masters as well as servants, so that the former did not want to enforce it, but it was re-enacted in 1512 without the offending clause. This measure fixed maximum wages and regulated the length of the working day, including the length of breaks.[45] Other new laws extended the suppression of games-playing by servants outside the Christmas season. In addition to handball, football, quoits, dice and skittles, which were prohibited under older legislation, after 1478 servants were banned from playing closh, half-bowl, hand in and hand out and 'quekeboard'.[46] This legislation was motivated partly by the idea that servants who played these games impoverished themselves and resorted to crime to recoup their losses. The government contributed its own agenda to this legislation by adding that it was also intended to encourage young men to practice martial arts with the longbow. The suppression of unlawful games was considered to be a vital part of maintaining the peace.[47]

Unrest about the supposed erosion of status distinctions is well demonstrated by legislation relating to consumption. It was widely believed that extravagant dress was a source of impoverishment and social friction.[48] In 1483 Edward IV approved a statute to regulate the dress of men of all social degrees, from his own family down to servants and labourers. Previous legislation was not being observed, and, so it was said, the resulting extravagance meant that the realm had fallen into great misery and poverty, and was likely to deteriorate further. Labourers, for example, were not to wear cloth costing more than 2s a yard. The statute aimed to make men content with their status. It had the secondary object of restricting imports, since no one below the rank of

---

[45] 11 Henry VII, c. 22; 12 Henry VII, c. 3; 6 Henry VIII, c. 1: SR, ii, 585–7, 637; iii, 124–6.

[46] 12 Richard II, c. 6; 11 Henry IV, c. 4; 17 Edward IV, c. 3; 11 Henry VII, c. 2; 19 Henry VII, c. 12: SR, ii, 57, 163, 463, 569, 656–7. Closh was a game like croquet and quekeboard was a form of chequers. Half-bowl was 'a game played with a hemisphere of wood and fifteen pins of a conical form': O.E.D., under 'Half-bowl'.

[47] 17 Edward IV, c. 3; 11 Henry VII, c. 2; 19 Henry VII, c. 12: SR, ii, 463, 569, 656–7; Henry VIII repeated instructions for their enforcement in 1511, 1526, 1527 and 1528: Tudor Royal Proclamations, i, 88–9, 152–3, 174, 180.

[48] Boke of Noblesse, 80; Fitzherbert 1523, fo. 52v.

lord was entitled to wear foreign cloth.[49] Henry VIII's ostentatious displays of wealth were notorious, and contrasted strikingly
with the low-key court ceremonial of his father's last years.[50] Yet
the first parliament of his reign overhauled the law relating to
apparel, and this legislation was again renewed at length in 1515
and 1517. The most ambitious measure of this kind was a proclamation of 1517 to restrict the number of courses men in different ranks of society might have at a single meal. Cardinals did
rather well.[51]

Unemployment was feared as another feature, or cause, of disorder in the commonwealth. Some of the measures taken were oppressive measures to suppress beggars and vagrants. Orders were
repeatedly given by royal proclamation to enforce older rules for
dealing with vagrancy by setting suspect idlers in the stocks, and
sending the disabled back to the place of their birth or the place
where they last lived for as much as three years, and two new
statutes dealing with the problem were made under Henry VII.[52]
Some legislation, however, was designed to protect or create
employment. In 1519 one of the items that Henry VIII intended
to discuss with his council was 'how the commodities of this his
realm may be employed to the most profit and wealth of his own
subjects, and how the idle people of his said realm may be put
in occupation'.[53] The government's protectionist measures were
usually in response to petitions from private interests, but whatever the pressure group behind them a number of scattered measures taken for the common weal of the realm have a consistently
aggressive, bullionist, protectionist stance that they share with
the fourteenth and earlier fifteenth centuries.[54] Richard III's legislation of 1483 to regulate the quality of English cloth and to
ban fifty-seven varieties of imported manufactures is the outstanding mercantilist package of the period, and owes something
to his need for friends.[55]

[49] 17 Edward IV, c. 3: SR, ii, 463.

[50] S. Anglo, 'The Court Festivals of Henry VII: A Study Based upon the Account Books
of John Heron, Treasurer of the Chamber', Bulletin of the John Rylands Library, xliii
(1960), 20, 26.

[51] 1 Henry VIII, c. 1; 6 Henry VIII, c. 1; 7 Henry VIII, c. 6: SR, iii, 8–9, 121–3, 179–
82; Tudor Royal Proclamations, i, 128–9.

[52] Tudor Royal Proclamations, i, 17, 33–4, 89–90, 127, 174; 11 Henry VII, c. 2; 19
Henry VII, c. 12: SR, ii, pp. 569, 656.

[53] British Library, Cotton MSS, Titus B.i, fo. 191r.

[54] E.g. 3 Henry VII, c. 11; 4 Henry VII, c. 11: SR, ii, 520, 535–6; 6 Henry VIII, c. 12:
SR, iii, 132.

[55] 1 Richard III, cc. 8, 12: SR, ii, 484–9, 495–6.

One of the features of all this social and economic legislation was the difficulty of enforcing it in any systematic way. The only thing to do, in some cases, was to encourage informers to spy on their neighbours and report the fact to the authorities, sometimes in exchange for a statutory reward. Henry VII's statute against unlawful retainers in 1504 encouraged informers to lay information before either the king and his council attendant, or the chancellor in star chamber, or the court of king's bench.[56] In 1528, people were urged to send the cardinal information in confidence about anyone they knew who had infringed the statutes against enclosure. In December 1528, when grain prices were high, the king's subjects were instructed to inform their local JP's of any known case of high prices, and in particular of anyone who deliberately engineered high prices by cornering supplies.[57] Most of this commonwealth legislation had little effect as an instrument of social change, but it gives a valuable insight into the political discourse of the period concerning matters we should now think of as social policy.

[56] 19 Henry VII, c. 14: SR, ii, 659.
[57] Tudor Royal Proclamations, i, 174–5, 180–1.

11

Market Economy

In Thomas More's land of Utopia, people scorned gold and silver, and the goods that farmers and artisans produced were distributed according to need.[1] In England, by contrast, love of gold and silver characterized kings and their servants, and the livelihood of all their subjects depended in some degree upon the circulation of coin. A large part of the gold and silver of the realm was in the form of plate, works of art and sacred vessels. But the quantity and qualities of coin produced by the king's moneyers, most of it at the Tower of London, were a matter of public concern because of its use both in internal trade and in trade with foreign merchants.

The most flexible system for citing sums of money was in units of pounds sterling, shillings and pence, the pound being equivalent to 20s and the shilling to 12d. A common alternative, especially for large contracts, was to state sums of money in terms of marks, the mark being equivalent to two-thirds of a pound (13s 4d). This second system was much less flexible than the first because few sums could be expressed conveniently as multiples or fractions of a mark. Of these accounting units – pounds, marks, shillings, pence – only the penny corresponded to a coin in normal use. The gold coin in most frequent use throughout the period was the golden angel, worth half a mark (6s 8d). The principal smaller coins in use, all made of silver, were the groat (4d), the half-groat (2d) and the penny, and these were the ones used for household purchases of food or fuel. A groat corresponded to a day's wage for an agricultural labourer across much of southern England throughout the years from 1471 to 1529.[2]

The value of money in circulation was about £1,400,000 in

[1] More, *Utopia*, 61–3.
[2] P. Bowden, 'Statistical Appendix', in Thirsk, *Agrarian History*, 864.

1526, but much of this was in coin appropriate for only a restricted range of business, since only about a quarter of the total value was minted in silver, the remainder being in the larger gold issues.[3] These figures should induce some caution about the extent to which late medieval society resembled our own. A money stock of some 12s a head of the population – and only 3s of silver a head – was not impressive by modern standards, even with the price level as it was in 1526. This was partly because average standards of living were much lower, and partly because much of what people required for everyday life was obtained without money. Skelton produced some characteristically outrageous mockery of barter amongst the poor in his poem 'The Tunning of Eleanor Rumming', written about the early 1520s, concerning a female brewer in Leatherhead, whose exclusively female clientele is able to get as drunk as it likes by exchanging clothes, footwear, mercery, utensils, foodstuffs, livestock and poultry for ale.[4] Nevertheless, key aspects of both class relationships and the relationship between the king and his subjects were monetized. Cash was used for paying wages, rents and taxes.

Towns, Industry and Trade

Dependence upon money and exchange was at its most apparent in towns, since the proportion of the population which could produce its own food was here smaller. Specialization in a single occupation was the exception rather than the rule, particularly in smaller towns like Ramsey (Huntingdonshire).[5] Many townsmen continued to have a stake in agriculture. For example, when the city council at York agreed to a request by Richard III that a piece of land should be permanently enclosed by the Hospital of St Nicholas, this led in 1484 to a 'riotous assembly or insurrection' and the embarrassed council had to backtrack, with the king's consent.[6] But self-sufficiency was not possible for most townspeople, many of whom had to purchase at least some of the means of everyday life.

[3] N. Mayhew, 'Population, Money Supply and the Velocity of Circulation in England, 1300–1700', EconHR, xlviii (1995), 243–5.
[4] Skelton, 214–30.
[5] A. R. DeWindt, 'The Town of Ramsey: The Question of Economic Development, 1290–1523', in E. B. DeWindt (ed.), The Salt of Common Life: Individuality and Choice in the Medieval Town, Countryside and Church, Kalamazoo 1995, 78–82.
[6] York House Books, i, 303–4; ii, 440–1; A. S. Green, Town Life in the Fifteenth Century, 2 vols, London 1894, i, 137n.

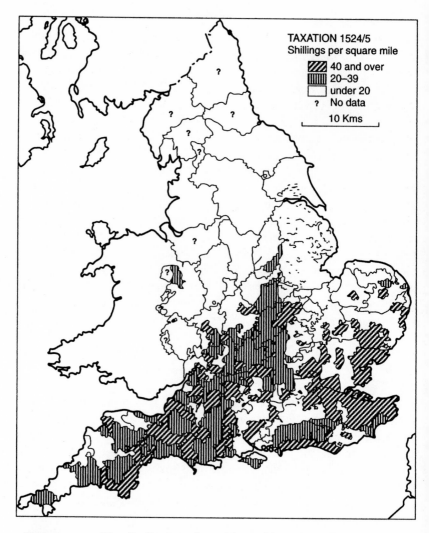

FIGURE 11.1   The distribution of taxable wealth in England, 1523–1524.
This shows clearly the greater concentration of taxable wealth in England
towards the south and west (*after J. Sheail, 'The distribution of taxable
population and wealth during the early sixteenth century*', Transactions and
Papers, The Institute of British Geographers, *LV (1972), 120, and on
additional information provided by Dr Sheail from PRO Exchequer Lay
Subsidies E. 179*)

To judge from the records of the subsidy of 1524–5, the wealth
of England was concentrated south and east of a line drawn from
the Severn to the Humber estuaries (see figure 11.1). England at
that time had only about ten towns with more than 6000 inhabitants. London, which was both England's major port and

close to the centre of government in Westminster, was by far the largest, with perhaps somewhere between 50,000 and 70,000. Norwich, with about 10,000, came second, and Bristol, Exeter, Salisbury, York, Canterbury, Newcastle upon Tyne, Coventry and Colchester were the other eight. Most of these larger towns showed signs of recent contraction, since the later fifteenth and earlier sixteenth centuries were not a good period for the economies of older boroughs. Most of them nevertheless retained extensive links in at least some aspect of their trade. London, Bristol, Exeter and Newcastle were major English ports; Norwich, York, Salisbury, Colchester and Coventry were all major cloth towns, even if reduced from their former pre-eminence by competition from elsewhere. The majority of the inhabitants in all these larger towns would have been dependent on earning money in some way in order to buy food, and perhaps about a third of their populations engaged at least part of the time in supplying food and drink to the rest in the form of bread, ale, fish and meat. London drew its supplies from an exceptionally wide area. When the king wanted to encourage the flow of grain to the city in 1522 he sent instructions accordingly to the sheriffs of eighteen counties – including Lincolnshire, Nottinghamshire and Derbyshire – though it may be that some recipients were at a loss to know what was expected of them.[7]

Urban characteristics were also marked in many places with fewer than 5000 people. There were about thirty-three more towns with between 2000 and 5000 people, and these included a number of port towns (Hull, Boston, King's Lynn, Great Yarmouth, Ipswich, Southampton, Plymouth, Chester) and some important centres of specialized manufacture (Crediton, Tiverton, Newbury, Hadleigh), as well as a number of cathedral cities and county towns.[8] Yet about 800 other places in England and Wales were marketing centres, both because they had resident populations needing to buy agricultural produce and because they had markets and fairs to serve them, and these places are conveniently classified as small towns, even though they had populations of a size today associated with village life. They characteristically engaged in supplying manufactures and services to villagers within a radius of ten miles or so, buying in exchange the produce of the

---

[7] *Tudor Royal Proclamations*, i, 134–5; R. B. Dobson, 'Urban Decline in Late Medieval England', *TRHS*, 5th ser. (1977), 1–22; A. Dyer, *Decline and Growth in English Towns, 1400–1640*, London 1991, 25–36, 66; Phythian-Adams, *Desolation*, 12; S. Rappaport, *Worlds within Worlds: Structures of Life in Sixteenth-Century London*, Cambridge 1989, 50n.
[8] Phythian-Adams, *Desolation*, 12.

countryside they required for food and raw materials. Many of them were described as boroughs by contemporaries, because some at least of their inhabitants occupied distinctive freehold burgage smallholdings beside or near the central market-place.[9]

Such was the little market town and borough of Northallerton, in the North Riding of Yorkshire, which had about 500 inhabitants in the late fifteenth century. In its high street, where a weekly market was held, there was a tollbooth, a market cross and stocks, for the punishment of minor crime, together with some permanent butchers' stalls. The town also had an inn, called the Swan. Amongst the residents were butchers, bakers and brewers to satisfy the predictable requirements of residents and visitors for food and drink; such processors of food were the largest buyers of incoming grain and livestock. But other occupations amongst the townsfolk – those of smith, plumber, wheelwright, slater, mason, plasterer, tanner, shoemaker, glover, weaver, shearman, dyer and tailor – demonstrate how even such a small place could be supplying manufactures to local consumers.[10]

It was impossible to tell, merely from the size of a late medieval town, how its trade split between local and long-distance transactions. Northallerton had no industrial importance outside its immediate surroundings, but some towns not much larger depended on mercantile connections over long distances, particularly for the sale of woollen cloth. Characteristically, the smaller towns that manufactured cloth of merchantable quality concentrated on producing some distinctive local type. The most expensive English cloths were whole broadcloths, whose dimensions were regulated by law to measure twenty-four yards by two yards. Half-cloths were simply half the length of whole cloths. Yet there was no single type or standard of English cloth. In the cloth towns of Suffolk and Devon the industry depended considerably upon straights, which were narrow cloths, regulated in 1483 to measure twelve yards by one. Kerseys were the same width as straights but half as long again. Parliamentary statutes also recognized numerous cheaper cloths that were exempted from statutory regulation – bastards, celestrines, cogware, florences, frizeware, kendals, packing whites, plunkets, rays, sailingware, says, stamens, vesses and worsteds. Some of these were highly localized, like vesses, which were made

[9] A. Everitt, 'The Marketing of Agricultural Produce', in Thirsk, *Agrarian History*, 468–75.

[10] C. M. Newman, 'Order and Community in the North: The Liberty of Allertonshire in the Later Fifteenth Century', in A. J. Pollard (ed.), *The North of England in the Age of Richard III*, Stroud 1996, 51–5.

in Suffolk. Between 1471 and 1529 the cloth industry was widely scattered, and in years of expansion many small towns and villages prospered at the expense of older-established manufacturing centres. Colchester, Coventry, Norwich and York, which had benefited from the expansion of the woollen industry in the later fourteenth and early fifteenth centuries, now lost ground to smaller towns.[11]

In eastern England the chief centres of cloth-making, outside Norwich and Colchester, were in southern Suffolk, notably at Lavenham, Long Melford and Hadleigh. There were pockets of less spectacular activity in Essex, as in Coggeshall.[12] In the south, in addition to Salisbury, there was a major concentration of manufacture, especially noted for white woollen broadcloths, around Trowbridge and Bradford-upon-Avon in western Wiltshire. Many of these cloths were exported to be dyed and finished abroad.[13] In Devon there were points of impressive development at Tiverton, Cullompton and, farther to the south, at Totnes. Tiverton specialized in coloured kerseys, Collompton in half-cloths (called 'dozens' because they were twelve yards long) and Totnes in straights, though all three centres produced some kerseys. Other commercially significant textiles from Devon were barnstaples (between 1470 and 1483) and tavistocks (between 1480 and 1483).[14] The Frome Valley in Gloucestershire was becoming known in this period for woollen cloths whose manufacture concentrated around Stroud in the parishes of Bisley, Minchinhampton and Nailsworth. The Stroud region was specially known for Bristol red.[15] Newbury (Berkshire) in the early sixteenth century became a centre of a region of kersey manufacture that stretched westwards into the Kennet Valley as far as Marlborough (Wiltshire).[16] In the north

[11] 14, 15 Henry VIII, c. 11: SR, iii, 217; J. N. Bartlett, 'The Expansion and Decline of York in the Later Middle Ages', EconHR, 2nd ser., xii (1959–60), 27–33; R. H. Britnell, Growth and Decline in Colchester, 1300–1525, Cambridge 1986, 192; Palliser, Tudor York, 162–3, 208–11; Phythian-Adams, Desolation, 49.
[12] E. Power, 'Thomas Paycocke of Coggeshall: An Essex Clothier in the Days of Henry VII', in E. Power, Medieval People, 11th edn, London 1986, 152–73; G. Unwin, Studies in Economic History, London 1927, 264, 266.
[13] E. M. Carus-Wilson, 'Woollen Industry', 133, 138–40.
[14] E. M. Carus-Wilson, The Expansion of Exeter at the Close of the Middle Ages, Exeter 1963, 17–19; E. M. Carus-Wilson, 'The Significance of the Secular Sculptures in the Lane Chapel, Cullompton', Medieval Archaeology, i (1957), 114; W. R. Childs, 'Devon's Overseas Trade in the Late Middle Ages', in M. Duffy, S. Fisher, B. Greenhill, D. J. Starkey and J. Youings (eds), The New Maritime History of Devon, 2 vols, Exeter 1992–, i, 79; P. Russell, The Good Town of Totnes, Exeter c.1964, 34, 45, 47.
[15] E. M. Carus-Wilson, 'Evidences of Industrial Growth on some Fifteenth-Century Manors', EconHR, 2nd ser., xii (1959–60), 190–7.
[16] Carus-Wilson, 'Woollen Industry', 140; Cornwall, Wealth and Society, 64.

PLATE 11.1   Paycocke's House, Great Coggeshall, Essex. Thomas Paycocke
the clothier inherited this house from his father in 1505, when it was newly
built. The house must have been intended for Thomas and his first wife,
since their initials (T. P. and A. P.) recur in the oak rafters of the hall; it
was perhaps built for them when they married. The elaborate wood carving
that decorates the house includes, as a repeated motif, the family's merchant
mark, an ermine tail. Pevsner describes it as 'one of the most attractive
half-timbered houses of England' (*The Conway Library, the Courtauld
Institute of Art*)

the manufactures of York were under threat from new developments around Halifax, Leeds, Wakefield and Bradford.[17] In north-
western England an increase in textile manufacture in south-east
Lancashire is on record from the 1490s, and there was also a
commercially vigorous textile industry in the southern Lake District centred on Kendal, Langdale and Grasmere.[18]

As these comments imply, the woollen industry spilled over
into places that lacked any central marketing function and cannot be considered urban. It is found on the manors of Worcester
Cathedral in the west midlands, and on those of Basingwerk and

---

[17] Palliser, *Tudor York*, 208–9.
[18] J. Kermode, 'The Trade of Late Medieval Chester, 1500–1550', in R. H. Britnell and
J. Hatcher (eds), *Progress and Problems in Medieval England*, Cambridge 1996, 289; A.
Winchester, *Landscape and Society in Medieval Cumbria*, Edinburgh 1987, 118.

Margam abbeys.[19] The weavers and spinners in such places produced goods for sale to merchants elsewhere, or on commission from them. Both this, and the small size of the smallest towns, illustrates well the absence of a hard and fast division in this respect between town and country. Many village populations contained smiths, carters, thatchers and carpenters supplying local needs, but more commercially structured industries, like woollen textiles, were also developing outside the towns either because their raw materials were produced in the countryside, as in the case of all the extractive industries, or for the sake of cheap part-time labour, or because their technology required water power that was not otherwise available. The application of water power to industry, usually to power a trip hammer, had affected the location of both textiles and metalworking. On the king's manor of Leeds (which was leased for ten years from 1483 by Richard III's secretary, John Kendall), the rent of the fulling mill doubled between 1462 and 1536.[20]

In some regions rural employment outside agriculture was available in mining industries, whose location was largely determined by the current state of geological and technological knowledge. A wide variety of products, whose profitability depended heavily on the level of overseas demand, was scattered from Cornwall to Northumberland. The most concentrated of the major mining industries, and the easiest to discuss, was tin, which was mined mostly in Cornwall, but with some working in Devon. The crown levied a tax on tin production, called coinage, whose centres of collection were Lostwithiel, Truro and (from 1492) Helston in Cornwall, and Ashburton, Chagford, Plympton and Tavistock in Devon; these roughly delimit the area of production. A good deal of what was produced was exported to markets in France, Spain, the Mediterranean and the Middle East, passing through Plymouth, Exeter, Southampton and London. Very little tin was available in Europe elsewhere in this period, and it was a necessary material for the manufacture of pewter and bronze.[21] Lead-mining and smelting was more scattered. The principal centre of the industry was between Wirksworth and Hathersage in northern Derbyshire, but there were lesser centres of mining and smelting in the upper reaches of Weardale, Teesdale, Arkengarthdale, Wensleydale,

[19] Dyer, *Lords and Peasants*, 345–6; D. H. Owen, 'Farming Practices and Techniques: Wales and the Marches', in Miller, *Agrarian History*, 245.
[20] *Leeds Documents*, 3–37; Carus-Wilson, 'Evidences', 192–7; Carus-Wilson, 'Woollen Industry', 143; Palliser, *Tudor York*, 208.
[21] Hatcher, *English Tin Trade*, 77–9, 120–2, 130–4.

Wharfedale and Nidderdale (Durham, West Riding of Yorkshire), in Flintshire and Cardiganshire in Wales, and in the Mendip Hills.[22]

A great deal of industrial activity was conducted by self-employed artisans in town and countryside, depending upon such marketing facilities as their local environment offered them. In towns manufactured goods were often sold from shops, which were more like workshops than modern retail outlets in so far as artisans made goods and sold them from the same premises. Shops were often attached to a producer's own home, though some were separate commercial constructions leased by landlords to artisans.[23] Heavy goods – metalware, bricks and tiles – were not suitable for sale from shops, and often required the purchaser to acquire them from the forge or kiln. The lessee of the bishop of Winchester's manor of Crawley in 1503–4 bought 6000 tiles, fifty hip tiles, twelve crests and thirty-six gutter hips from Richard Colswayne, and paid to have them carted from Richard's home back to Crawley.[24] If marketing activities needed to be more active, manufactures could sell their wares at annual fairs, which were numerous all across the country. The bigger ones drew custom over many miles throughout the period. Thetford Priory in Norfolk bought large numbers of nails, other ironware and basketry at Ely fair every year between 1499 and 1516 and took them back by boat.[25] Much of this trade involved little intermediary handling between craftsman and buyer.

However, the period 1470–1529 saw the expansion of a distinctive group of entrepreneurs in the textile industry who coordinated the various stages of production, and to that extent reducing the autonomy of the workmen they employed. Most cloth-making regions yield examples of such clothiers whose enterprise absorbed a significant proportion of local trade. At Lavenham Thomas Spring, who died in 1523 leaving a fortune of £3200, was famous for his importance as an employer in the textile industry, and the withdrawal of his capital from the industry after his death may have been more significant than high taxation in causing local unemployment and disaffection in 1525. There were many big names in the Wiltshire industry. James Terumber of Trowbridge (died 1488), who became legendary for his wealth, was remembered by the anti-

[22] Blanchard, 'Industrial Employment', 230, 238; Pollard, *North-Eastern England*, 38, 74–5; Williams, *Recovery*, 75.

[23] Palliser, *Tudor York*, 25, 33–4.

[24] N. S. B. Gras, *The Economic and Social History of an English Village*, Cambridge, Mass. 1930, 495.

[25] *Register of Thetford Priory*, i, 93–4, 117, 131, 149, 164, 178, 191, 205, 219–20, 233, 247, 260, 272, 284, 297, 309, 320, 331.

quary John Leland over half a century later. A later entrepreneur
in the region was Thomas Horton (died 1530), whose attractive
manor house still stands at Westwood. At Tiverton the principal
operator of the early sixteenth century was John Greenway (died
1529), whose ornate chantry chapel, decorated with scenes from
the life of Christ and a frieze of merchant ships, is to be seen in
the south aisle of the parish church. Collompton's leading cloth
merchant was John Lane (died 1529), whose chantry chapel has
angels clutching teasel-frames and cloth-shears. In Newbury,
John Winchcombe (died 1519) was long remembered as an innov-
ator who had put his workers together in a single workshop,
and he has accordingly been celebrated as a pioneer of factory
production.[26]

This entrepreneurial innovation was a direct response to a tight-
ening of the structure of English overseas trade, in which cloth had
a preponderant share. A growing concentration of exports along
the route from London to Antwerp enhanced the importance of
mercantile networks of trade and credit that connected the provinces with London, and benefited those entrepreneurs able to take
advantage of them. Earlier in the fifteenth century the English exporters had plied a number of trade routes, and sold cloth in a
corresponding variety of ports of call. After 1450, however, trade
with both the Baltic and with Gascony had dwindled away as a
result of war, economic contraction on the continent and political
weakness at home. Though cloth merchants still called themselves merchant adventurers, they operated on an unadventurous
set of routes. In the later fifteenth century, by far the most promising area for development was Brabant.

There were groups of merchant venturers in several provincial towns – notably York, Newcastle upon Tyne and Norwich –
though they were always most numerous in London. From 1462
they had appointed their own governor in the Low Countries.
The benefits of cooperation increased with the growth of trade in
the 1470s, and by the 1480s they constituted an effective pressure
group, centred on the London Mercers' Company. In 1486 the various groups set up a more formal organization using the mercers' resources for the purpose. They began to make their own ordinances
and to hold their own courts, whose records survive amongst
those of the Mercers' Company. At the same time, London interests

[26] Carus-Wilson, *Expansion*, 18; Carus-Wilson, 'Significance', 104–13; Carus-Wilson,
'Woollen Industry', 134–6, 141–2; Cornwall, *Wealth and Society*, 52, 63–4, 72–3; A. E.
Welsford, *John Greenway, 1460–1529, Merchant of Tiverton and London: A Devon
Worthy*, Tiverton 1984, 10.

began to dominate the trade as a whole. By 1500 about three-fifths of all overseas trade in the hands of English denizens was controlled by the merchant adventurers there. That explains why the Tiverton clothier John Greenway, who joined the London Drapers' Company in 1497, at some point joined the London Merchant Venturers' Company as well.[27] The strength of the Merchant Venturers was to some extent the direct result of favour showed by the government. York merchants tried to redress the balance in 1477 by petitioning Edward IV to give more representation to northern interests, but the king fobbed them off, and nothing changed.[28] Londoners benefited from their superior credit network; provincial merchants found it harder to raise commercial credit than Londoners did, particularly in the north. These developments built institutional rigidities into the conduct of overseas trade and had the effect of deterring new enterprise in the provinces.[29] The period 1471–1529 illustrates well the monopolizing spirit and love of exclusive privilege which, according to the eighteenth-century economist Adam Smith, comes naturally to merchants and manufacturers.

While the merchants of the east-coast ports remained committed to the North Sea trading area for their profits, those of Bristol had more connections with southern Europe. They also temporarily showed an awareness of new opportunities across the Atlantic. Between 1480 and 1505 deliberate attempts were made to explore westwards, at first in search of a legendary 'isle of Brazile'. In 1497, John Cabot, a Venetian explorer who had made Bristol his base, with more ambitious ideas of finding a sea route to Cathay, met with some nebulous success in exploring the coast somewhere in the stretch between Cape Breton and Cape Bauld, but he died in a second expedition the following year. Henry VII showed a tentative interest in these early voyages, and in 1502 granted a charter to a group of Bristol men who subsequently called themselves the Company Adventurers into the New Found Islands. Between 1503 and 1505 the king was receiving souvenirs of the north American coast, brought back from their voyages, and in these years England was still in the vanguard of exploration in the north Atlantic. Yet any commitments to long-term

[27] Carus-Wilson, *Medieval Merchant Venturers*, 143–82; H. van der Wee, *The Growth of the Antwerp Market and the European Economy (Fourteenth-Sixteenth Centuries)*, 3 vols, The Hague 1963, ii, 123; Welsford, *John Greenway*, 4–5.

[28] Pollard, *North-Eastern England*, 72.

[29] J. Kermode, 'Money and Credit in the Fifteenth Century: Some Lessons from Yorkshire', *Business History Review*, lxv (1991), 475–501.

exploration quickly evaporated. Explorers found nothing to raise their hopes for new trading opportunities, and only the fishermen who resorted to the Newfoundland fishing grounds benefited from new economic opportunities. The possibility of finding a route through to Asia was explored by Sebastian Cabot (John's son) in about 1508–9, and again by John Rut in 1527, but from 1505 onwards English interest in America was more in evidence amongst intellectuals than amongst merchants. Sir Thomas More's brother-in-law, John Rastell, attempted to lead a voyage of exploration to north America in 1517, but the ship carrying him abandoned him at Waterford in Ireland and went off to trade in France. The lead in exploring the New World was lost for several generations after England's early start.[30]

Agriculture and Trade

The idea of family self-sufficiency had long been a mirage even in the countryside, though a higher proportion of families approximated to it around 1500 than in modern industrial societies. Fitzherbert advised young farmers to save money in setting themselves up by learning how to make their own equipment, when this could be made of wood.[31] However, even the most substantial farmer had to sell produce to pay his rent and to buy products such as clothing, fish, tar, nails, locks and hinges, metal tools, plough irons, horse-harness and horse-shoeing – all this before there was any talk of luxuries.

Estimates of the proportion of grain that was sold are impossible from this period for want of appropriate farming records. Around 1300, when such records were kept, it has been estimated that 20–30 per cent of all grain produced was sold in England as a whole, and even more in the London region. Grain production had decreased considerably since then, following a decline in the number of people to be fed, but the proportion sold may have been at least as high, if not higher. Whereas in 1300 many households were heavily constrained to avoid selling grain by the number of dependants among their families and neighbours, these constraints were much looser in 1500. Although the number of townspeople and rural artisans had declined since 1300, there is no reason to suppose it had declined more than the population as a

[30] K. R. Andrews, *Trade, Plunder and Settlement: Maritime Enterprise and the Genesis of the British Empire, 1489–1630*, Cambridge 1984, 41–57; D. B. Quinn, *England and the Discovery of America, 1481–1620*, London 1974, 5–191.
[31] *Fitzherbert*, 15.

whole; the proportion of food buyers to food growers may even have increased. Much of the trade in agricultural produce was in the hands of peasant farmers, selling grain grown on their family lands or on plots of land leased from larger estates. Most of the grain trade was over distances up to ten miles, since it was expensive to transport bulky goods overland and most producers were within easy reach of some market town where there would be some regular demand for purchased foodstuffs. Only in rich agricultural areas near the coast, or near major rivers like the Severn, the Thames and the Trent, was grain carried in bulk over much longer distances. Though grain was more likely than industrial products to be retailed in an urban market, there were many informal modes of trading, especially by the big dealers. Private marketing was far from being a development of the early modern period.[32]

An important part of many farmers' incomes was earned from the sale of pastoral produce. Estimates for 1495 of the cash income of Roger Heritage, a wealthy yeoman farmer from Burton Dasset (Warwickshire), suggest that all his cash income was from his pastures, 40 per cent coming from selling the wool of 860 sheep, 20 per cent from sales of sheep and beef cattle, and the rest from dairying, the sale of surplus calves and the sale of rabbits. A comparable concern with pastoral farming as a source of cash is evident from the investments of Thomas Kebell, serjeant-at-law, who at the time of his death in 1500 had on ten properties in Leicestershire over 3500 sheep, kept for their wool, and 158 cattle in addition to the oxen needed for ploughing his lands.[33] Many areas of the country had converted resources to the production of meat, and in particular beef, much of which was sold to urban markets over long distances. In the Forest of Arden between 1490 and 1509 there was more land under pasture than under the plough, and cattle-ownership was widespread among peasant farmers.[34] There was a regular trade in cattle from Wales and the Midlands,[35] and from the north. In the early 1480s

[32] R. H. Britnell, *The Commercialisation of English Society, 1000–1500*, Cambridge 1993, 98–100, 123, 161; D. L. Farmer, 'Marketing the Produce of the Countryside, 1200–1500', in Miller, *Agrarian History*, 358–77.

[33] C. Dyer, 'Were There Any Capitalists in Fifteenth-Century England?', in J. Kermode (ed.), *Enterprise and Individuals in Fifteenth-Century England*, Stroud 1991, 12; E. W. Ives, *The Common Lawyers of Pre-Reformation England*, Cambridge 1983, 249–52, 440–2.

[34] Watkins, 'Cattle-Grazing', 19–21.

[35] Dyer, *Lords and Peasants*, 369; T. H. Lloyd, *The Movement of Wool Prices in Medieval England*, EconHR Supplement 6, Cambridge 1973, 27.

John Capell, who farmed at Porter's Hall in Stebbing (Essex),
was buying 'northern steers' at the fairs of Woolpit and Ely. In
Romford (Essex), where pasture farming was expanding from the
late fifteenth century, the reputation of the market as a source of
dairy produce and livestock for London buyers became so great
that it was able to attracted cattle-dealers from as far away as
Leicestershire.[36]

Wool was a highly commercialized commodity under the Yorkists and early Tudors, since almost all that was produced was
sold. Large quantities were marketed by some estate owners, like
the Townshend family in Norfolk, who at Michaelmas 1516 had
18,000 sheep divided between twenty-six flocks.[37] In some areas
the sheep-farms of large landowners were crowding out peasant
activity, as in Lakenheath (Suffolk),[38] but in the country as a whole
there were large numbers of sheep in the hands of minor landowners, like Roger Heritage, and of peasant farmers, who in some
regions constituted the main source of wool.[39] Village by-laws often
restricted the number of sheep that individual residents could put
on the commons, but some large peasant flocks are nevertheless
on record. On manors of the bishop of Worcester they sometimes
rose to 360 or more.[40] The wool trade was predominantly internal to the kingdom, since the main part of what was produced
went to supply the various cloth industries that have already been
discussed. The wool grown on the Townshend estates was sold
both to middlemen and direct to clothiers, and some buyers came
from a distance. In 1495, for example, Eleanor Townshend sold
120 stone to a woman from Hadleigh, a small Suffolk cloth town,
and another 360 stone was sent to a Lavenham cloth-maker working under contract to Richard Peper of Norwich.[41]

What was left of the wool export trade – by now only a small
part of the total – was also dependent upon wholesale dealers.
Most of it was in the hands of a privileged organization known
as the merchants of the Staple, who shipped wool to Calais, England's last remaining foothold of territory across the Channel,
though their monopoly was impaired by consignments of wool

---

[36] British Library, Add. Roll 66051 (I owe this reference to Professor L. R. Poos);
M. K. McIntosh, *Autonomy and Community: The Royal Manor of Havering, 1200–1500*,
Cambridge 1986, 226–7, 230.
[37] Moreton, *Townshends*, 166.
[38] M. Bailey, *A Marginal Economy? East Anglian Breckland in the Later Middle Ages*,
Cambridge 1989, 294–5.
[39] Lloyd, *Movement of Wool Prices*, 28.
[40] Dyer, *Lords and Peasants*, 325, 328.
[41] Moreton, *Townshends*, 173, 245.

shipped direct to Italy through the Straits of Gibraltar under licence from the crown. By the end of the period the Staple Company was in a sad plight. Its merchants were obliged, under an agreement with the king, to maintain the Calais garrison and to recoup the costs from the customs duty on wool exports, but their income did not cover their obligations. By 1527 they were 'piteously complaining' of their waning prosperity.[42]

There were still very many small farmers who only sold grain to pay their rents because they produced too little to think in terms of commercial profit. Yet even in East Anglia, where such smallholders were most numerous, a large number of peasants produced for the market. In the west midlands a contrast has been observed between the more open countryside of south Warwickshire, where holdings of thirty acres or more were in the majority, and the wooded country round Coventry where smallholders predominated. In many parts of the country the peasantry constituted the chief source of marketed produce. Some were able to transform the status of their families by acquiring for their children an education that launched them on a professional career. Such was Geoffrey Audley of Earls Colne, who was accumulating tenements there in Henry VII's reign, and whose lawyer son, Thomas Audley, eventually became chancellor of England.[43] The sources of commercial enterprise in this society cut across the categories of social status discussed in chapter 10, and penetrated well inside village communities.

Employment

Wage labour accounted for a smaller proportion of work in the late Middle Ages than in the modern world. Much of the labour of the countryside was by peasant farmers on their own lands, and in the towns the characteristic form of industrial organization was the self-employed artisan, often assisted by family members. Nevertheless larger farming units depended upon wage labour for many separate tasks. At the harvest of 1482 John Capell employed twenty-eight men and fifteen women, who were paid between them for a total of 241 days' work, and at other times of the year he paid workers for sowing, threshing, muck-

[42] *Tudor Economic Documents*, iii, 24–8.

[43] Britnell, *Growth and Decline*, 259; R. H. Britnell, 'Tenant Farming and Tenant Farmers: Eastern England', and C. Dyer, 'Tenant Farming and Tenant Farmers: The West Midlands', in Miller, *Agrarian History*, 614–18, 636–7.

spreading, harrowing, fetching and carrying, and maintaining farm equipment.[44] Building work was mostly performed by wage labour both in town and country. Many urban artisans, too, employed extra hands either as young apprentices or as journeymen, and the regulation of such employees was one of the recurring concerns of urban government.[45] Wage labour, then, was a regular feature of the late medieval economy, both in town and countryside. Families without enough land or trading capital were necessarily obliged to look for employment, and these probably accounted for the largest share of the workforce. However, even tenants with land were often under-employed on their own holdings, and would be consequently available for casual work if the terms were right.

Wages in the period 1471–1529 were high by the standards of most periods before the nineteenth century, and people who were fully employed could earn a comfortable livelihood. 'Fully employed' in this context is not a concept that is easy to interpret in the institutional context of the late Middle Ages, since very few wage-earners were specialized in one employment or employed on long contracts. Some agricultural workers on larger estates were employed by the year. John Capell paid 13s 8d in cash to John Royston 'for his year wages' in 1483, though most of what he received was probably in the form of food.[46] Apprentices were employed under contract for even longer periods, normally in exchange for board and lodgings, with very little cash. But wage labour was often very casual, and accounts often record only very short periods of work at daily rates of pay. This was not to the disadvantage of many wage-earners, who showed a high preference for leisure and a great reluctance to commit themselves to fixed hours of employment. Even discounting obvious prejudices in comments from the employing classes about the laziness of the workforce, there is reason to suppose that workers did not have to be 'fully employed' to earn a standard of living that suited them.[47]

In the newer centres of clothworking, manufacture was more dependent upon wage labour than it was in the older cloth towns. A number of the latter were still throughout the period able to stave off the dominance of capitalist entrepreneurship through the strength of their guild systems. Indeed, a number of towns

---

[44] British Library, Add. Roll 66051.
[45] Swanson, *Medieval Artisans*, 113–16.
[46] British Library, Add. Roll 66051.
[47] M. Bailey, 'Rural Society', in R. Horrox (ed.), *Fifteenth-Century Attitudes: Perceptions of Society in Late Medieval England*, Cambridge 1994, 163–8.

updated their guild regulations in the course of the period in order to protect the independence of cloth workers, as at Bury St Edmunds and Gloucester. Such older forms of industrial organization did not necessarily do badly. Given the right marketing opportunities, guildsmen long retained both their independence and their incomes, as apparently in the textile industries of Gloucester and Salisbury.[48] Yet independent artisans were less characteristic of the more rapidly growing industrial regions, where there was more variety of industrial organization. John Winchcombe's experiment with factory organization at Newbury is semi-legendary, and was certainly exceptional, but it was not uncommon for clothiers in small towns to have numerous dependent employees. Thomas Spring II of Lavenham, by his will made in 1486, left 100 marks (£66 13s 4d) to his spinners, fullers and weavers, to be distributed at the discretion of his executors.[49] Clothiers giving out wool to be broken, combed, carded or spun, yarn to be woven, or cloth to be fulled, were required by statute in 1512 to pay wages in ready cash and not in goods.[50] One advantage of smaller towns and villagers for such employers was that wages were lower; so, at least, it was believed in York, where damaging competition from clothiers in the West Riding was attributed to this cause.[51]

In towns with a strong reputation for some particular manufacture, industrial workers were more likely to be specialized in some particular occupation. One strand of evidence for this is the enforcement of apprenticeship regulations and craft-guild ordinances in the towns. These two institutions were closely linked, and many of their features, such as the demarcation of distinctions between crafts, regulation of hours of work, limitation of the number of servants each master might employ, and the binding of servants for fixed periods, imply that masters and servants alike spent their time in a single industry, at least for extended periods. In 1496 the ordinances of the Coventry cappers restricted the number of apprentices to two at a time for each master and imposed a minimum of seven years for the period of apprenticeship. Each newly-employed wage-earner in the industry had to be approved by the masters of the craft, to work for a weekly wage of 12d from six in the morning to six at night each day, and to

---

[48] Carus-Wilson, 'Woollen Industry', 140; Unwin, *Studies*, 265–6; *VCH, Gloucs.*, iv, 52, 59.
[49] D. Dymond and A. Betterton, *Lavenham: 700 Years of Textile Making*, Woodbridge 1982, 13, 68.
[50] 3 Henry VIII, c. 6: *SR*, iii, 28–9;
[51] Palliser, *Tudor York*, 208.

give (or receive) a week's notice before departing.[52] This implies that working at one occupation at a time was an expected norm.

Occupational specialization was least apparent in rural areas, where many farmers and their families, and not by any means only the least substantial, supplemented their incomes by working in mining or rural industry in periods of the year when farmwork was slack. Derbyshire lead-working, for example, depended heavily on the local peasant population turning out between the end of spring-ploughing and lambing (in April) and harvesting (in July and August).[53] In 1524, as we know from the Stannary records, 1169 tin-miners in Devon and Cornwall presented less than a thousandweight of tin during the course of the year, and it seems impossible that all these men were wholly dependent upon the mines. Many of them spent much of their time in other paid occupations in farm-labouring, fishing, building and other manual work.[54] In textile manufacturing, too, there were many who combined industrial work with peasant farming. Industrial work, and wage-earning, were not therefore solely for the landless, and did not imply a high degree of occupational specialization.[55]

Markets and Instability

The idea of a social order governed by market forces, in which individuals negotiate their own position in accordance with their capabilities and their interests, was not one in which early sixteenth-century statesmen placed any confidence. Yet patently there were features fundamental to this society's normal working that depended upon individual decision-taking and negotiation rather than either tradition or government direction. This had many politically unmanageable implications for the social order. If normal patterns of trade were interrupted, thousands of families might lose their livelihood. The furthest writers went in the direction of economic analysis was to recognize the necessity of money, markets and other trading institutions and the need for the king and other lords to safeguard them. Yet the livelihood

[52] *Coventry LB*, 572–4; Swanson, *Medieval Artisans*, 112–14.
[53] Blanchard, 'Miner', 93–100.
[54] G. R. Lewis, *The Stannaries: A Study of the English Tin Miner*, Cambridge, Mass. 1924, 187; J. Hatcher, 'Myths, Miners and Agricultural Communities', *AHR*, xxii (1974), 59.
[55] Blanchard, 'Miner', 104; I. S. W. Blanchard, 'Rejoinder: Stannator Fabulosus', *AHR*, xxii (1974), 68.

of artisans could not be guaranteed by government fiat, since it depended chiefly on how much was spent and what people chose to buy. The destruction of markets observed by John Rous in the west midlands resulted, he said, from a decrease in the number of people who bought goods from craftsmen and in turn sold them foodstuffs.[56] Even in these circumstances, however, the experience of vulnerability bred frequent complaint that markets were failing to meet the need of the commonwealth, and that the king and his councillors should do something about it.

Within the domestic economy, the farmers' dependence on the weather meant that supplies of food and raw materials were not the same from year to year. When supplies were poor, there were crises in London, and many of the poor went hungry almost everywhere. The most serious period of dearth followed the harvest of 1527, which was ruined by heavy rain through the previous winter, spring and early summer. Commissioners were appointed in each county to search out hoards of grain in barns and stacks and to compel farmers to market their surpluses at a reasonable price. Evidence from a block of ten parishes in rural Essex shows that even in rural areas supplies were seriously deficient in the winter of 1527–8. The king's commissioners estimated that their inhabitants had less than a quarter of the breadcorn they would need before the next harvest, and so would have to make bread with peas, beans or oats. Even so, they would not be able to supply all their needs. At the same time, relief supplies from the Baltic were impeded by the turn of English foreign relations towards France and against Charles V. The duke of Norfolk was afraid of serious disorder amongst the poorer inhabitants of East Anglian towns. This episode did Wolsey's reputation no good, since his alliance with Francis I of France was already unpopular for other reasons.[57]

The uncertainties and risks implied by dependence on trade were particularly acute amongst the minority of the population whose livelihood depended upon their ability to sell manufactures abroad. Overseas markets never had the chance to grow uninterruptedly for long. England's own continental wars, in 1475, 1489–92, 1512–14, 1522–5 and 1527 were not the only destabilizing events, since trade was often deterred by conflict in which England was not directly involved. In the summer of 1477, for

[56] Rous, 121–2.
[57] Hall, 736, 744–6; LP, iv (2), 1781–2; D. Dymond, 'The Famine of 1527 in Essex', Local Population Studies, xxvi (1981), 29–34; S. J. Gunn, 'Wolsey's Foreign Policy and the Domestic Crisis of 1527', in Gunn and Lindley, Cardinal Wolsey, 174–5.

example, buyers of English wool stayed away from Calais because of French military activity on the nearby borders of Burgundy, and in 1482 conflict between France and Burgundy deterred merchants both from Calais and from Antwerp. Stoppages of trade were sometimes ordered deliberately to put diplomatic pressure against Burgundian authorities, as in the general restraint of trade with Burgundy in 1483–4, or Richard III's prohibition of trade with Bergen-op-Zoom in April 1484. Henry VII more than once put a ban on trade with Burgundy because of the support given to his enemies by Margaret of York. If shipping were protected by carrying additional manpower, or by having the king's ships to protect them, freight charges inevitably rose steeply.[58] Some branches of the English economy between 1471 and 1529 were sufficiently vulnerable to fluctuations in overseas demand for this to be the chief feature of their history. The coal, lead and iron industries of Durham, for example, were all governed by opportunities of trade through Newcastle upon Tyne in the early sixteenth century, and this made them vulnerable to a wide variety of economic and political disturbances.[59] The political implications of industrial instability are evident from the fact that in hard times manufacturers framed petitions to parliament about the decay of the commonwealth – especially if they were well organized like the Norwich worsted makers, who were the subject of a series of statutory protective measures to prevent the supposed decay of the industry between 1495 and 1515.[60] Even though the economy around 1500 was so much less dependent upon commercial exchange than that 500 years later, many groups of people experienced the conflicts of interest and unpredictable changes of fortune that are so common today.

---

[58] Carus-Wilson, *Medieval Merchant Venturers*, 165, 166–7, 171; Hanham, *Celys*, 36–8, 284–6, 293, 295.

[59] I. S. W. Blanchard, 'Commercial Crises and Change: Trade and the Industrial Economy of the North-East, 1509–1532', *NH*, viii (1973), 77–8.

[60] 11 Henry VII, c. 11; 12 Henry VII, c. 1; 5 Henry VIII, c. 4; 6 Henry VIII, c. 12; 14, 15 Henry VIII, c. 3: *SR*, ii, 577–8, 636; iii, 94, 132, 209–12.

12

Economic Development

E conomic development between 1470 and 1529 has long been
seen as a problem area. The period falls between the great
slump of the mid-fifteenth century and the inflation of the sixteenth century, but has failed to earn itself any distinctive label.
Its economic history has variously been seen as one of stagnation
or recovery, partly because different strands of evidence relating to
it are not easily reconciled. The question whether an economy, and
the number of people it sustained, was growing, standing still or
declining can usually be answered very directly for modern economies because of the large amount of relevant evidence collected
by governments, but such questions impose a strain on the evidence to be found from the Middle Ages. This chapter rounds off
the analysis of the years 1471–1529 by examining what may be
said about this interesting but less tangible aspect of the period.

Export Trade

The aspect of aggregate economic performance which can be
addressed with greatest confidence is that of exports, for which
there survives the statistical evidence of the customs accounts.
These show that after a lengthy period of trade depression, the
volume of cloth exports grew at an average rate of 1.65 per cent
a year between the later 1460s and the later 1520s, so that by the
latter period the annual volume of exports was approaching three
times what it had been during the former. This increase was
achieved principally in two sharp bursts, one in the ten years
before Henry Tudor captured the throne in 1485, the other in the
ten years before Henry VIII succeeded him in 1509. Export growth
slowed down appreciably in the second and third decades of the
sixteenth century (table 12.1).

Table 12.1 Annual English exports of wool and cloth, 1465–1529 (five-year averages)

Years	Woolsacks	Cloths
1465–9	7944	35,446
1470–4	7673	?
1475–9	7970	?
1480–4	7309	55,108
1485–9	8081	(47,929)
1490–4	6002	56,802
1495–9	9587	(59,660)
1500–4	7171	78,790
1505–9	7165	83,203
1510–4	7418	83,415
1515–9	7609	88,881
1520–4	6356	82,677
1525–9	4628	94,656

Where figures are missing from particular ports in particular years, estimates have been made averaging the nearest six available years, balanced three on each side of the gap. No figure is raised by more than 4.5 per cent as a result of this operation. The bracketed figures for cloth exports are averages of fewer than five years because of defective data for 1484–5 and 1494–6. Sources: E. M. Carus-Wilson and O. Coleman, England's Export Trade, 1275–1547, Oxford 1963, 62–74; A. R. Bridbury, Medieval English Clothmaking: An Economic Survey, London 1982, 120–2

Edward IV's devaluation of the coinage in 1464 and 1465 gave a boost to sales of cloth to the continent, at the expense of cloths from Brabantine textile industries. Some of these cloths went south to Portugal, Spain and Gascony, or south-west into northern France.[1] The chief buyers, however, were a group of firms from southern Germany who, having evolved a new technology, the *Saigerprozess*, for extracting silver from polymetallic cores that included argentiferous copper, were able to trade each of these precious and non-precious metals through a Europe-wide distribution network, whose primary foci were the major fairs of Brabant, at Antwerp and Malines and Bergen-op-Zoom. From there southern Germans carried cloth to be sold through the Rhineland, southern Germany, and farther east in Poland, Hungary and Austria. Antwerp became the chief meeting-point for English cloth

[1] Childs, 'Devon's Overseas Trade', 88; G. V. Scammell, 'English Merchant Shipping at the End of the Middle Ages: Some East Coast Evidence', *EconHR*, 2nd ser., xiii (1960–1), 328.

exporters and German buyers – indeed, the link contributed power-
fully to the city's development as the commercial capital of north-
western Europe.[2] Throughout the period 1471–1529 England's
export trade was heavily dependent upon this particular route.

The importance of the trade to the Brabanters enabled English
negotiators to extract favourable terms from the rulers of the
Low Countries. On 24 November 1467 England agreed a thirty-
year commercial treaty with the Burgundian Netherlands, and
this was confirmed by a more committed freeing of trade between
the two countries in 1478. The treaty triggered a boom in cloth
exports through to the early 1480s. The renewed surge of exports
from the end of the fifteenth century can be attributed to further
successful negotiations between England and Burgundy in February 1496. The so-called *Intercursus Magnus*, or Great Treaty, gave
English merchants freedom to trade throughout the dominions of
the duke of Burgundy, except in Flanders. The duties to be paid
by English merchants were negotiated, and many trading procedures were regulated to reduce the occasion for disputes. English merchants were also promised rapid justice in the Archduke's courts.[3]
The agreement had teething troubles, and impediments to its working had to be smoothed away in 1497 and 1499,[4] but from the
beginning of the new century exports again expanded rapidly.
The early sixteenth century has been described as 'one of the great
free trade periods of modern English history'.[5] The treaty was
renewed in 1502, and a treaty even more favourable to English
merchants was negotiated in April 1506 in exchange for England's
recognition of the Archduke Philip as king of Castile. However,
Philip died before this was ratified, and a treaty that was finally
agreed in 1507 simply restated the *Intercursus Magnus*.[6]

[2] I. Blanchard, 'International Capital Markets and their Users', in I. Blanchard, A.
Goodman and J. Newman (eds), *Industry and Finance in Early Modern History*, Stuttgart
1992, 13–25; I. Blanchard, 'Credit and Commerce from the Mediterranean to the Atlantic
in the Sixteenth Century', in H. A. Diederiks and D. Reeder (eds), *Cities of Finance*,
Amsterdam 1996, 21–34; Fisher, 'Commercial Trends', 97; J. H. Munro, 'Monetary
Contraction and Industrial Change in the Late Medieval Low Countries, 1335–1500', in
N. J. Mayhew (ed.), *Coinage in the Low Countries (880–1500)*, British Archaeological
Reports, International Series, 54, Oxford 1979, 118; H. van der Wee, *The Growth of the
Antwerp Market and the European Economy (Fourteenth-Sixteenth Centuries)*, 3 vols,
The Hague 1963, ii, 83.
[3] R. B. Wernham, *Before the Armada: the Growth of English Foreign Policy, 1485–
1588*, London 1966, 68.
[4] *Foedera*, v, 82–7, 113–14, 136–9; J. H. Munro, *Wool, Cloth and Gold: The Struggle
for Bullion in Anglo-Burgundian Trade, 1340–1478*, Toronto 1972, 171–8; van der Wee,
Growth, ii, 123.
[5] Fisher, 'Commercial Trends', 101.
[6] Chrimes, *Henry VII*, 234.

Table 12.2   Indices of English grain and wool and general prices, 1465–1529 (1450–99 = 100)

	Grain	Wool	Composite index
1465–9	99	108	105
1470–4	95	104	98
1475–9	91	94	87
1480–4	123	115	128
1485–9	104	110	99
1490–4	99	94	105
1495–9	96	97	94
1500–4	125	93	107
1505–9	99	93	98
1510–4	107	109	106
1515–9	122	129	112
1520–4	144	106	144
1525–9	164	116	146

Sources: P. Bowden, 'Statistical Appendix', in J. Thirsk (ed.), *The Agrarian History of England and Wales, IV: 1500–1640*, Cambridge 1967, 839–42, 846–8; H. P. Brown and S. V. Hopkins, *A Perspective of Wages and Prices*, London 1981, 29

Though cloth exports were the biggest success story, the customs accounts also record an increase in mineral exports. Lead was especially notable in the port of Hull, whose share of the trade increased from about a half at the beginning of the period to perhaps two-thirds or more by the end. Both in Derbyshire and Weardale the output of lead-miners grew, between the 1460s and the 1530s, despite falling lead prices. The available estimates suggest an annual national output of 311 tons in 1473 (itself the result of rapid recent growth) and of 715 tons by 1531 (see table 12.3).[7] Tin was exported through London and through the southern and south-western ports, Southampton, Poole, Exeter, Plymouth and Fowey. In the export of lead and tin, as in that of cloth, there was a falling-off in performance after about the beginning of Henry VIII's reign. As table 12.3 shows, lead exports grew significantly more rapidly between 1471 and c.1510 than between c.1510 and 1529. Tin and pewter exports were similarly at their highest in 1507–8 and subsequently declined (see table 12.4). Coal exports through Newcastle probably increased

[7] See also I. Blanchard, 'Labour Productivity and Work Psychology in the English Mining Industry, 1400–1600', *EconHR*, 2nd ser., xxxi (1978), 24.

Table 12.3   Estimated English production and export of lead, 1464–1531 (tons)

Date	Production	Export
1464	80	80
1473	311	311
1490	350	450
1508	625	600
1513	500	575
1518	750	800
1523	350	350
1527	800	800
1531	715	715

Source: I. Blanchard, *International Lead Production and Trade in the 'Age of the Saigerprozess', 1460–1560*, Stuttgart 1994, 310 (figure A3–7) with additional information from Professor Blanchard.

gradually from the 1490s, despite a series of trade crises, but again growth was not sustained throughout the period. The 1520s were a period of lower exports before a resumption of growth after 1530.[8]

Developments in overseas trade created increasing prosperity not only for manufacturing and mining centres but also for some port towns, though the number of beneficiaries was more restricted than it had been in an earlier phase of export growth in the later fourteenth century. London was the chief of them. A rising proportion of English cloth exports was shipped from the Thames – 53 per cent of it in the five years 1465–9 and 79 per cent in 1524–8. The Merchant Adventurers traded as individuals, but the company chartered ships, organized their loading and negotiated details of sailing from the port of London and the freight rates to be charged.[9] The city's population had begun to recover by the end of this period, though the precise chronology is disputed. Westminster evidence suggests that recovery began there about 1470, and the same seems to be true of some of London's suburbs, though rents in Cheapside showed no tendency to increase until the middle of the sixteenth century. One estimate suggests that

[8] Blanchard, 'Commercial Crisis', 71–85; J. Hatcher, *The History of the British Coal Industry, 1: Before 1700*, Oxford 1993, 77, 487; J. F. Wade, 'The Overseas Trade of Newcastle upon Tyne in the Late Middle Ages', *Northern History*, xxx (1994), 33, 39–40.
[9] E. M. Carus-Wilson and O. Coleman, *England's Export Trade, 1275–1547*, Oxford 1963, 102–3, 115–16; E. M. Carus-Wilson, *Medieval Merchant Venturers*, 2nd edn, London 1967, 164.

Table 12.4 Average annual coinage of tin and exports of tin and pewter from England, 1465–1529 (mwt)

Years	Mwt presented for coinage	Mwt exported	% exported
1465–9	848	n.a.	n.a.
1470–4	915	n.a.	n.a.
1475–9	874	n.a.	n.a.
1480–4	n.a.	454	n.a.
1485–9	(919)	(465)	51
1490–4	(1133)	484	43
1495–9	(1066)	602	56
1500–4	1100	1051	96
1505–9	n.a.	1153	n.a.
1510–4	n.a.	888	n.a.
1515–9	1478	946	64
1520–4	1506	742	49
1525–9	1585	947	60

Calculations based on one year's figures are in brackets. A thousandweight (mwt) is 1200 lb.
Source: J. Hatcher, *English Tin Production and Trade before 1550*, Oxford 1973, 158–9, 168, 176–93

London's population grew from 50,000 in 1500 to over 63,000 in 1535, implying a growth-rate significantly higher than that of the kingdom as a whole.[10] Not all London's expansion was the result of growing exports, however, since much of it is attributable to the growth of inland trade and of government employment.

London's growth was not representative of the whole kingdom. Southampton's cloth exports increased from 1490 to 1523, but then suffered severe contraction, chiefly because of the withdrawal of the Londoners from trading there.[11] The Devon ports, especially Exeter, benefited from the recovery of trade to Spain, Gascony and northern France, from their proximity to a dynamic new textile industry in their hinterland, and from a strong fishing industry. Exports of cloth from Exeter increased between 1475 and 1502, particularly in the boom years 1497–1502, when the

[10] D. Keene, *Cheapside before the Great Fire*, London 1985, 20; G. Rosser, *Medieval Westminster, 1200–1540*, Oxford 1989, 174, 177; S. Rappaport, *Worlds within Worlds: Structures of Life in Sixteenth-Century London*, Cambridge 1989, 50.
[11] Carus-Wilson and Coleman, *England's Export Trade*, 148–9; C. Platt, *Medieval Southampton: The Port and Trading Community, A.D. 1000–1600*, London and Boston 1973, 219.

city's leading merchants traded through London, though from then on they declined.[12] Chester's trade expanded in all directions from the 1490s, and its merchants temporarily increased their share of the wine trade.[13] These were the relatively lucky towns. Other ports enjoyed no recovery phase to compare with that of Southampton and Exeter. Ports on the east coast trading with the Baltic continued to lose trade in competition with Hanseatic and German as well as London merchants. Probably no English port altogether escaped the impact of London's increasingly effective competition.[14]

Though the growth of overseas trade between 1471 and 1529 stimulated economic growth locally, and its regional effects on the structure of employment can often be observed, the more difficult task is to assess how significant it was to the economy as a whole. Many producers of export goods were unspecialized workers who made up their incomes from numerous sources. Thousands of lead-workers, for example, worked only sporadically at a low level of productivity.[15] It would be misleading, as an indicator of the impact of the growth of manufacturing and mining, to assess merely the number of people who might occasionally be employed. In order to have some meaningful standard for measurement it is better to think of employment in terms of the man-year equivalents needed to produce the goods in question, since this is the figure relevant to assessing their contribution to the economy as a whole – that is, it will suggest what proportion of the kingdom's labour force can be thought of as sustained by such activity. For this purpose the working year has here been defined as one of 270 days'.[16]

Flemish evidence shows a weaver might make ten broadcloths a year, which implies that the increase in cloth exports between the late 1460s and the late 1520s created about 6000 man-years of employment in weaving.[17] Perhaps another 6000 man-years

[12] E. M. Carus-Wilson, *The Expansion of Exeter at the Close of the Middle Ages*, Exeter 1963, 10–16, 28–9; Childs, 'Devon's Overseas Trade', 88; M. Kowaleski, *Local Markets and Regional Trade in Medieval Exeter*, Cambridge 1995, 92–5, 326.

[13] J. Kermode, 'The Trade of Late Medieval Chester, 1500–1550', in R. H. Britnell and J. Hatcher (eds), *Progress and Problems in Medieval England*, Cambridge 1996, 295–7.

[14] C. Phythian-Adams, 'Urban Decay in Late Medieval England', in P. Abrams and E. A. Wrigley (eds), *Towns in Societies*, Cambridge 1978, 167–8; S. H. Rigby, *Medieval Grimsby, Growth and Decline*, Hull 1993, 113–46.

[15] Blanchard, 'Labour Productivity', 12–13.

[16] D. Woodward, *Men at Work: Labourers and Building Craftsmen in the Towns of Northern England, 1450–1750*, Cambridge 1995, 131–2.

[17] J. H. Munro, 'Textile Technology in the Middle Ages', in J. H. Munro, *Textiles, Towns and Trade: Essays in the Economic History of Late Medieval England and the*

should be added to account for the preparatory crafts and another 3000 for the finishing crafts, making some 15,000 man-years in all. (The man-years in this context are not gender-specific, since a good deal of work in textiles was by women.) Over the same period the increase of nearly 900,000 lb of tin presented for coinage each year in Devon and Cornwall represented the output of fewer than 3000 full-time tinworkers.[18] Increases in the annual export of the lead industry between 1471 and 1529, according to the available estimates, did not exceed 700 tons, which represents fewer than 250 man-years.[19] On this calculation the increased exports of cloth, tin and lead between the late 1460s and the late 1520s could have been achieved by the creation of about 18,250 man-years of employment in these industries. This was no more than 1.7 per cent of the adult population aged sixteen and over in 1527.[20] The assumption in this calculation that all adults were fully employed is, of course, unrealistic; allowance must be made for a great deal of voluntary and involuntary unemployment. Even so, a net increase in employment of even four or five times the order the calculations suggest could have given only a very mild stimulus to aggregate growth over the period as a whole.

The export figures suggest that England's total manufacture of cloth started to revive during the 1470s, and if we follow through the implications of this we may reason that over the long term it favoured the expansion of wool growing. The increase in cloth exports between 1465–9 and 1525–9 would have required the equivalent of about 13,674 sacks of wool. Allowing for the concurrent decline in exportsof raw wool, this implies a net increase in the export of over 2 million fleeces.[21] Assuming constant English domestic consumption, the number of sheep maintained on English pastures would have increased by over 2 million. Some increase in sheep-farming can be demonstrated from independent documentary evidence. The sheep flocks of the Townshend family,

---

Low Countries, Aldershot 1994, item I, 17. The calculation in the text assumes that an English broadcloth needed the same amount of work as a Flemish one, on the grounds that the weight of wool was the same.

[18] Hatcher, *English Tin Production*, 85, 158–9.

[19] This is calculated on the evidence of productivity levels on Mendip: Blanchard, 'Labour Productivity', 24.

[20] Assuming an English population of 1.8 million, of which 60 per cent was adult: Campbell, 'Population', 145–54; Cornwall, *Wealth and Society*, 190, 213.

[21] This calculation assumes that a sack of wool made 4.33 cloths, that a sack weighed 364 lb avdp and that each fleece weighed 1.75 lb: Carus-Wilson, *Medieval Merchant Venturers*, xxiv; A. Hanham, *The Celys and their World: An English Merchant Family of the Fifteenth Century*, Cambridge 1985, 112, 115.

for example, increased from about 7000 sheep in twelve flocks at Michaelmas 1475 to 18,000 in twenty-six flocks at Michaelmas 1516.[22] Local evidence from the Breckland implies a recovery of sheep-farming in this same period.[23] The idea that sheep were eating up men became something of a government obsession under Wolsey.

It is tempting to deduce from these links that cloth exports brought prosperity for sheep-farmers. On the other hand, as suggested in chapter 10, the government's preoccupation with declining arable has caused the profitability of sheep-farming to be exaggerated. It is true that wool prices rose during the first three decades of the sixteenth century, but they did not diverge from the movement of grain prices before 1520, and thereafter the latter rose faster (table 12.2). There is little evidence of the conversion of arable to pasture except in circumstances where it was unwanted for tillage. Nor is it clear that the expansion of sheep flocks was as great as the export evidence alone might suggest. English domestic consumption contributed to the expansion of flocks in the period 1470–1500, and may have declined after about 1510, so that no clear conclusions about the magnitude or chronology of sheep-farming can safely be deduced from the export evidence alone.[24]

Internal Trade

Fluctuations in the economy as a whole were not determined by the export sector but in the much larger sector that satisfied domestic consumption. Substantial evidence from Derbyshire suggests a long-term cycle in the late medieval economy, its upswing lasting from the 1460s to the 1490s and its downswing from the 1490s to the 1520s, though the amplitude of the cycle was very restrained.[25] In the period of upswing, which was largely governed by the home market, demand for pastoral and arable products increased. Similar fluctuations, though not with identical phasing, are found in other parts of the country. On the estates of the

[22] C. E. Moreton, *The Townshends and their World: Gentry, Law and Land in Norfolk, c.1450–1551*, Oxford 1992, 164–6.

[23] M. Bailey, *A Marginal Economy? East Anglian Breckland in the Later Middle Ages*, Cambridge 1989, 293.

[24] *Duchy of Lancaster*, 16; Blanchard, 'Population Change', 436–9.

[25] *Duchy of Lancaster*, 11–13; Blanchard, 'Population Change', 434.

bishopric of Worcester there was some recovery of land values from the 1470s to the early sixteenth century, and then a recession in the 1510s and 1520s.[26] The income from fees and seals arising from litigation in the courts of king's bench and common pleas, which is probably an indicator of economic prosperity among property owners, shows no clear trend before 1487, growth up to about 1510, and then two decades of recession.[27] The upswing of the 1470s and 1480s was perhaps associated with the beginnings of demographic recovery, though gains made then were checked by epidemics in 1478–80 and 1490–1, and perhaps not sustained.[28] The problems of the period after 1510 were partly the result of bad harvests, but the chief obstacle to development in those decades was Henry VIII's belligerence, since rising tax levels were directly damaging to such economic prospects as those years had to offer. Skelton in 1522 expressed the view that high taxes led to falling investment, reduced employment, and impoverished townsmen. He made particular reference to one of the wealthiest clothiers of the day, Thomas Spring III of Lavenham:

Now nothing but 'Pay! pay!'
With, 'laugh and lay down,
Borough, city and town'.
Good Spring of La'nham
Must count [= reckon] what became
Of his clothmaking.[29]

Only a small part of the agrarian and industrial evidence at present lends itself to close analysis in terms of economic fluctuations. What there is suggest, even if only circumstantially, that over the whole period any impetus to long-term growth in the home market was not sustained, and that its long-term impact was slight. The development of the coal industry at inland sites such as Leicestershire suggests that there were some opportunities for expansion. Bailiffs' accounts from the lordship of Wollaton (Leicestershire) show output increasing from about 5000 tons a year around 1500 to 9000 tons in 1526.[30] There are also examples of growth in urban industries that can be attributed to domestic demand. One

[26] Dyer, *Lords and Peasants*, 288–90.
[27] C. W. Brooks, *Pettyfoggers and Vipers of the Commonwealth: The 'Lower Branch' of the Legal Profession in Early Modern England*, Cambridge 1986, 80–1.
[28] J. Hatcher, *Plague, Population and the English Economy, 1348–1530*, London 1977, 63–4.
[29] Skelton, 302; Hoyle, 'War and Public Finance', 75–99.
[30] Hatcher, *History of the British Coal Industry*, 166.

example, which probably attests the growth of the knitting industry, was the making of caps, as at Gloucester, Coventry and York.[31]
However, though the evidence of tin output and exports in table
12.4 is not wholly clear-cut, it suggest that the home market may
have lagged behind the overseas market between 1485 and 1529,
despite occasionally severe recessions in overseas markets. Studies
of towns other than those engaged in export industries characteristically demonstrate little impetus to growth, and current histori-
ography is more concerned with the hypothesis of urban crisis
and decline in this period than with claims to general urban
growth. Any development of the coal trade in Newcastle upon
Tyne was inadequate to prevent rents from falling in the later
fifteenth century.[32] Many smaller towns exhibit economic contraction or stagnation; the evidence from Northallerton shows no
signs of growth between 1471 and 1529.[33]

Especially in parts of the country where extensive pasture farming could be practised, rents often rose during the course of the
period all over the kingdom, reversing the downward trend of the
mid-fifteenth century. In the south recovery of rents in pastoral
areas began early in the period and then faltered after the first
decade of the sixteenth century. Some manors in the Breckland,
notably Brandon (Suffolk), recorded rising levels of rent from the
1470s, though such recovery was both slow, discontinuous and
patchy.[34] In the west midlands, which had a considerable commitment to cattle and sheep-farming, the evidence of the bishopric
of Worcester estates shows rising entry fines from the 1470s to
about 1510, as we have seen. A muted increase in pasture rents is
recorded in Sussex from the mid-1490s. Other evidence for pressure on resources in pastoral areas is supplied by the imposition
of rules to control the number of animals that villagers were allowed to graze on common pastures. On the bishop of Worcester's estates these became more numerous from 1479.[35] In the

[31] N. M. Herbert, *Medieval Gloucester*, Gloucester 1993, 52–3; C. Phythian-Adams,
Desolation of a City: Coventry and the Urban Crisis of the Late Middle Ages, Cambridge
1979, 44; H. Swanson, *Medieval Artisans: An Urban Class in Late Medieval England*,
Oxford 1989, 50–1.

[32] A. F. Butcher, 'Rent, Population and Economic Change in Late Medieval Newcastle',
NH, xiv (1978), 67–77; Pollard, *North-Eastern England*, 74.

[33] C. M. Newman, 'Order and Community in the North: the Liberty of Allertonshire
in the Later Fifteenth Century', in A. J. Pollard (ed.), *The North of England in the Age
of Richard III*, Stroud 1996, 50–1.

[34] Bailey, *Marginal Economy?*, 279–80.

[35] Dyer, *Lords and Peasants*, 331; M. Mate, 'Occupation of the Land: Kent and Sussex', in E. Miller (ed.), *The Agrarian History of England and Wales, iii: 1348–1599*,
Cambridge 1991, 129–30.

north, similarly, the income of the Percies from herbage the forest of Westward in Cumberland increased by 76 per cent between 1479 and 1524, and at Topcliffe in Yorkshire the revenue from leases of pasturage in their parks increased by 56 per cent over the same period.[36] Rents on Fountains Abbey pastures were increasing between the 1450s and the 1490s. Rent increases were general, both for arable and pasture, on Duchy of Lancaster manors in the High Peak and Middle Peak regions of Derbyshire. In contrast with the south, in northern England recovery of pasture rents was more striking between 1500 and 1550 than in the previous half century. This was associated with a more active market in land; the number of transfers of land in the West Riding recorded in the feet of fines at the Public Record Office increased over fourfold between 1510–14 and 1525–9.[37]

In many parts of England, however, and especially in the predominantly arable areas, there is little evidence for much of a recovery phase in the 1470s and 1480s, or of any long-term improvement for landlords before the 1520s.[38] In the north of England the records of the Percy estates in Northumberland, Cumberland and Yorkshire show that for the most part rents did not change, and this was not the result of administrative inertia. Similar stability is in evidence in Durham, and North Yorkshire around Northallerton.[39] At Billingham on the River Tees (Durham), this evidence of northeastern rents is supplemented by a series of tithe-corn receipts, which show that the level of crop production was unchanging from the 1460s to the 1510s (see table 12.5). Activity on the demesne lands of Elvethall Manor on the edge of the city of Durham increased in the 1460s, but Durham Priory then showed no propensity to expand crop or livestock output there between 1471 and 1514.[40] Rents were static in many parts of the south. Such evidence as survives for the Colchester region shows no hint of an upward movement of rents, at least up to 1514. The accounts recording the income from the estates of Rochester Bridge in Kent show that the rent levels of the years 1522–4 were no higher than those of the depressed years of the 1460s and 1470s. The leasehold rents on the estates of Merton College, Oxford, were static

---

[36] J. M. W. Bean, *The Estates of the Percy Family, 1416–1537*, Oxford 1958, 44.

[37] *Duchy of Lancaster*, 6–10; R. B. Smith, *Land and Politics in the England of Henry VIII: The West Riding of Yorkshire, 1530–46*, Oxford 1970, 218; Pollard, *North-Eastern England*, 59.

[38] Blanchard, 'Population Change', 435, 439, 442.

[39] Bean, *Estates*, 44–8; Newman, 'Order and Community', 50.

[40] R. A. Lomas, 'A Northern Farm at the End of the Middle Ages: Elvethall Manor, Durham, 1443/4–1513/14', *NH*, xviii (1982), 30, 40–1, 43.

Table 12.5   Tithe corn receipts at Billingham, 1460–1519
(annual averages)

Years (no. of years averaged in brackets)	Wheat and rye (bushels)	Barley (bushels)	Oats and peas (bushels)
1460–9 (3)	283	496	455
1470–9 (9)	297	497	518
1480–9 (7)	245	303	338
1490–9 (7)	262	396	406
1500–9 (9)	231	371	353
1510–9 (7)	322	435	409

Source: R. A. Lomas, *North-East England in the Middle Ages*, Edinburgh
1992, 111–12

between 1486 and 1521, and only two lessees in this period are
recorded to have paid entry fines.[41] An investigation of the evidence from the whole of Wiltshire concludes that the depression
of the mid-fifteenth century was arrested during the 1460s, and
that there followed a period of generally stable rents that lasted
to the end of the century even in parts of the county that were
benefiting from the growth of the cloth industry. Where there is
evidence up to the 1520s, as at Durrington and Wroughton, it suggests no significant recovery in this period.[42] At Kibworth Harcourt
(Leicestershire) the period 1450–1520 was one of stable rents, and
entry fines were rarely collected throughout the period. Entry fines
showed no general increase at Leighton Buzzard (Bedfordshire) between the later 1460s and the beginning of the sixteenth century.
At Whitchurch (Shropshire) levels of copyhold rent recovered by
1468 from an early fifteenth-century collapse, but there was no
such recovery in the rent from demesne land till 1525, and it was
only then, under the stimulus of inflation, that the earl of Shrewsbury began to increase his income from copyholders by raising

[41] R. H. Britnell, *Growth and Decline in Colchester, 1300–1525*, Cambridge 1986,
256–8; R. H. Britnell, 'Rochester Bridge, 1381–1530', in N. Yates and J. M. Gibson (eds),
*Traffic and Politics: The Construction and Management of Rochester Bridge, AD 43–
1993*, Woodbridge 1994, 81–4; T. A. R. Evans and R. Faith, 'College Estates and University Finances, 1350–1500', in J. I. Catto and R. Evans (eds), *The History of the
University of Oxford, ii: Late Medieval Oxford*, Oxford 1992, 681.
[42] J. N. Hare, 'Lords and Tenants in Wiltshire, c.1380–c.1520, with Special Reference
to Regional and Seigneurial Variations', unpublished Ph.D. thesis, London 1975, 161,
166, 174, 194; Hare, 'Durrington', 142.

entry fines.[43] Landlords who tried to raise levels of rent, like the third duke of Buckingham, were likely to meet stiff and effective resistance.[44] Evidence of rent increases becomes more common in the 1520s, when prices were rising, than in any earlier decades, but it is surprising how many estates showed little response to rising prices even in the 1520s.[45] In so far as rents are evidence for changes in the demand for land, then, new developments were far from being a general feature of the period.

Overall Economic Performance

On this evidence, the history of overseas trade and that of internal economy imply only patchy and localized development between 1471 and 1529, so that a high rate of economic growth is not to be expected. Even the meagre assessment of growth prospects to be derived from the evidence of England's export trade may be over-optimistic, since it cannot be assumed that all increased exporting contributed a net addition to national income. The fact that the new burst of cloth exports after 1496 was achieved without rising wool prices (table 12.2) strongly suggests that there was considerable slack in home demand at the time. In Derbyshire the timing of pastoral booms was governed by the home market, and not the overseas market; exports were more likely when wool prices in England were low.[46]

The rate of growth in this period cannot be reliably calculated, but it is unlikely to have been significantly large. The value of money in circulation is estimated to have amounted to about £900,000 in 1470, rising to £1,400,000 in 1526, implying an average rate of growth of 0.8 per cent a year between these dates, but since this increase was inflationary towards the end of the period the rate of growth of gross domestic product – one of the standard measures of economic growth – was lower.[47] Probably

[43] C. Howell, *Land, Family and Inheritance in Transition: Kibworth Harcourt, 1280–1700*, Cambridge 1983, 52, 62; A. Jones, 'Bedfordshire: Fifteenth Century', in P. D. A. Harvey (ed.), *The Peasant Land Market in Medieval England*, Oxford 1984', 244–5; A. J. Pollard, 'Estate Management in the Later Middle Ages: the Talbots and Whitchurch, 1383–1525', *EconHR*, 2nd ser., xxv (1972), 556–8.

[44] B. J. Harris, 'Landlords and Tenants in England in the Later Middle Ages: The Buckingham Estates', in R. H. Hilton (ed.), *Peasants, Knights and Heretics: Studies in Medieval English Social History*, Cambridge 1976, 216–20.

[45] Blanchard, 'Population Change', 435.

[46] *Duchy of Lancaster*, 16.

[47] N. Mayhew, 'Population, Money Supply and the Velocity of Circulation in England, 1300–1700', *EconHR*, xlviii (1995), 243–5.

it was so close to zero that arguments about whether it was rising, static or falling will never be resolved.

Population

The history of population between 1471 and 1529, like that of production, is problematic chiefly because any rate of change was slow. Much of the case for aggregate population growth has depended upon indirect economic evidence that needs to be handled with caution. Three types of evidence commonly used are inadequate to establish the point. One concerns vagrancy and unemployment, a second the wages of labour, and a third the movement of prices.

The level of unemployment was a matter of widespread comment in the early sixteenth century in the form of concern about vagrancy. There were no doubt some vagrants from towns such as Coventry and York that were suffering industrial contraction, and they can clearly be accounted for without postulating a growing population. The pattern of economic development suggests that regions where employment was growing were widely scattered, so there would be severe frictional employment in the movement of workers to hiring regions from firing regions, even without making allowance for any mismatching of skills. Similar unemployment would be created by the eviction of tenants from tenant holdings to create sheep pastures. This was not altogether an imaginary problem and presumably accounts for some observed destitution and vagrancy, though the number of attested cases before 1529 is small.[48] The most serious concern about vagrancy, however, arose from government preoccupations with political stability, law enforcement and the conservation of military resources. It is unnecessary to suppose that these essentially ideological innovations corresponded to any real increase in vagrancy at the time. Much of the anxiety about vagrancy was conceptually tied to the parallel concern about the enclosure of arable land. Some of the concern, too, was about internal security; anxiety about specifically Scottish vagrants, for example, reached a peak of intensity in 1490–1, at a time when Henry VII was preparing for war with France.[49]

---

[48] Cornwall, *Wealth and Society*, 237–8.
[49] R. W. Heinze, *The Proclamations of the Tudor Kings*, Cambridge 1976, 81; M. K. McIntosh, 'Local Change and Community Control in England, 1465–1500', *Huntington Library Quarterly*, xlix (1986), 227–33, C. M. Newman, 'Local Court Administration within the Liberty of Allertonshire, 1470–1540', *Archives*, xxii (1995), 21–3.

The history of wages in the period 1471–1529 does not suggest any significant restructuring of the labour market to accommodate population change. Having risen during the previous 100 years, wage rates were static. The well-known evidence of builders' wages from Brown and Hopkins shows a wage rate of 4d a day for labourers from 1412 to 1545 and of 6d a day for craftsmen from 1412 to 1532. Agricultural day wages around Oxford and Cambridge were 4d a day from 1450 to 1529, and they were almost as stable at Eton College, where there was an increase to 4½d in the 1520s. Essex carpenters' wages similarly show no change. Wage series from northern towns demonstrate the same stability in York and Hull; labourers earned 4d a day and craftsmen 6d.[50]

Any change in what these wages would buy was the result of changes in prices, which tended to move upwards from their late fifteenth-century level after about 1510. When commodity prices rise over periods of years this may be evidence that rising demand is causing competition for supplies amongst buyers and driving prices up. If then average incomes can be shown not to have changed, rising prices may in turn be evidence of population growth. The evidence of prices, so interpreted, suggests inflationary pressure rather earlier than the wage evidence. Prices began to rise from their later fifteenth-century level around 1510, and from 1520 a rising price level was associated with a pronounced shift in relative prices; at this point, unlike the preceding decade, cereal prices suddenly rose relative to wool (table 12.2). This suggests a particular pressure of demand on foodstuffs, as does the strong association of rising prices with harvest deficiencies up to the 1520s. In the 1520s most of the recorded inflation was attributable to temporarily severe climatic conditions, compounded with interrupted supplies from abroad in the first half of 1528.[51] Nevertheless a very gradual inflationary trend is apparent even if crisis years are omitted.

Though the early stages of inflation are compatible with a pressure on demand arising from population growth they require other evidence for the argument to be convincing. England was not a self-contained market for agricultural produce, and price movements had long been responsive to movements elsewhere in Europe. English producers are known to have been sensitive to market

[50] P. Bowden, 'Statistical Appendix', in J. Thirsk (ed.), The Agrarian History of England and Wales, IV: 1500–1640, Cambridge 1967, 864; H. P. Brown and S. V. Hopkins, A Perspective of Wages and Prices, London 1981, 11; Pᵣos, Rural Society, 211; Woodward, Men at Work, 263, 274.
[51] Gwyn, King's Cardinal, 455–9.

opportunities abroad, to the extent that governments sometimes regulated exports. Urban revival and growing population were pushing up prices in Antwerp in the second decade of the sixteenth century.[52] Market conditions on the continent inevitably affected the price of any imported supplies. The already- mentioned rise in the circulating currency over these years, which was higher than any likely estimate of growth of output in England, would imply that there was also a monetary stimulus to inflation in the domestic economy.

The fact that wages changed so sluggishly in response to rising prices between 1510 and 1529 is perhaps the strongest economic argument in favour of rising population, since it suggests that the bargaining power of wages-earners was weak, and that they were unable to defend their existing real wages. In the longer term such erosion of past living standards was undoubtedly a feature of sixteenth-century population growth. This evidence is compatible with rising population, but the strength of the argument is undermined by the conjunctural character of much unemployment in the 1520s. The evidence of falling real wages may be interpreted as the consequence of short-term deterioration in employment opportunities rather than the result of an increase in the workforce. Heavy unemployment would damp down pressures for higher money wages, even in the absence of any growth in the labour force.

Since the supposed economic evidence for population growth is so precarious, we are left with the hazardous task of interpreting the thin demographic evidence that is available. Not surprisingly, historians have come to conflicting conclusions, though most have allowed the possibility that there may have been slow growth. There was little severe impoverishment in this period, as opportunities for employment were good for much of the time, so the economic possibilities for population growth must be considered favourable. Indeed, there is definite evidence of growth in some specific locations. On the estates of the bishopric of Worcester the number of children in serf families implied some capacity for population to grow from the 1470s onwards, and the evidence there supports the idea that the increase was predominantly in the number of landless wage-earners. Population growth was particularly associated with growing industrial and commercial centres such as Kendal and Grasmere.[53]

[52] *Tudor Royal Proclamations*, i, 27; van der Wee, *Growth*, ii, 116–17.
[53] Dyer, *Lords and Peasants*, pp. 230–2, 243; Jones and Underwood, *King's Mother*, 123–4.

Meanwhile other direct evidence of population implies that population growth was not universal, and probably not widespread. The positive evidence of expansion in regions of industrial development must be set against evidence of contraction elsewhere resulting from economic deterioration. The best example of this is Coventry, where from a level of about 10,000 around 1440 numbers are calculated to have fallen to some 9000 in 1500, 7500 in 1520, 6000 in 1523 and 4000–5000 by 1550. Shrewsbury's population in 1525 was lower than in 1377, and probably continued to decline until 1540. In some rural areas, too, industrial contraction led to declining population, as in the lead-working villages of Derbyshire between 1490 and 1520. Scattered local evidence for population growth cannot, therefore, be safely generalized to describe the country as a whole.[54] Away from these areas of exceptional economic growth and economic decline, such evidence as we have implies little change either way. Statistical information from the Aquila honour in Sussex and from several Essex villages reveals a static population, with no upward swing before the 1530s.[55]

Evidently any potential for population growth arising from reasonably comfortable incomes was offset by other features of the period. One of these is not difficult to identify, especially before about 1500. The evidence for repeated setbacks to population growth resulting from crises of mortality has improved over the years, and with it the likelihood that some of these crises were enough to arrest population growth, and even to cause at least temporary reductions in the population of the kingdom. The monks of both Canterbury Cathedral Priory and Westminster Abbey experienced a declining expectation of life in the period 1450–80 to an extent it would be difficult to explain without some reference to a deterioration of life-expectancy outside the cloister walls. Repeated incidence of crisis mortality are much in evidence in the later fifteenth century. Amongst the Westminster monks there were high death rates in 1457–8, 1463–4, 1478–9, 1490–1. Even after 1500 there were crises of a similar kind. The monks of Westminster experienced another epidemic in 1529–30. On the

---

[54] I. S. W. Blanchard, 'Industrial Employment and the Rural Land Market, 1380–1520', in R. M. Smith (ed.), *Land, Kinship and Life Cycle*, Cambridge 1984, 251; Blanchard, 'Population Change', 427–45; W. A. Champion, 'The Shrewsbury Lay Subsidy of 1525', *Transaction of the Shropshire Archaeological Society*, 64 (1985), 38–9; Phythian-Adams, *Desolation*, 281.

[55] M. Mate, 'The Occupation of the Land: Kent and Sussex', in Miller, *Agrarian History*, 128; Poos, *Rural Society*, 96–103, 109.

estates of the bishopric of Worcester the years 1522–5 were some of the worst in the whole period for tenant deaths.[56]

Interpretations of this evidence vary, which is not surprising, given the diversities of recorded experience and the slightness of the aggregate changes that occurred. On one view of events, the period 1471–1529 saw a continuation of a earlier downward trend in population, temporarily offset by a period of recovery between about 1470 and the 1500s, but then reasserted in the 1510s under the impact of war, famine and disease until growth resumed again in the 1520s.[57] This argument, which is heavily tied into the evidence of economic fluctuations we have already discussed, would mean that the population, though not static, was perhaps no higher in 1529 than in 1471. This conclusion is easily credible, given a low estimate for English population of 1.8 million in 1522–5. Given that the poll-tax evidence suggests a figure of 2.75–3 million in 1377, it would take a remarkable interpretation of the century after 1377 to suppose that there could have been much growth of population between 1471 and 1529.[58]

An alternative argument, looking forward to later evidence, defines the early sixteenth century as a period of incipient growth. Since there is reason to suppose that the population of England approached 2.8 million by 1541,[59] it is argued, numbers are likely to have been rising already in the 1520s. There is therefore more reason to suppose that growth was occurring towards the end of the period 1471–1529 than at the beginning, especially given the pattern of mortality at Canterbury and Westminster. This argument postulates that for some reason as yet unexplained mortality rates fell from around 1500, permitting the population to grow once more.[60] The argument here would imply that population was probably somewhat larger in 1529 than in 1471, but that growth was recent and still only slight. This argument isolates changes in population from economic fluctuations more than the first argument, and postulates that numbers were increasing even in decades of economic recession after 1510.

---

[56] Dyer, Lords and Peasants, 223–5, 228; Harvey, Living and Dying, 122, 127–9; Hatcher, 'Mortality', 28–31.

[57] Blanchard, 'Population Change', 441.

[58] Campbell, 'Population', 145–54; Hatcher, Plague, Population and the English Economy, 14. The figure of 1.8 million is revised from an earlier estimate of 2.3 million, for which see Cornwall, 'English Population', 32–44.

[59] E. A. Wrigley and R. S. Schofield, The Population History of England, 1541–1871: A Reconstruction, London 1981, 208–9.

[60] Bailey, 'Demographic Decline', 16; D. Loschy and B. D. Childers, 'Early English Mortality', Journal of Interdisciplinary History, xxiv (1993), 85–97.

These two views of the evidence are unreconcilable, but they share some common features that are worth noting. Neither of them supposes that sustained recovery of population levels began as early as 1470; in the one argument any recovery in the period 1470–1500 was ephemeral, and in the other argument it was insignificant. Both the arguments suppose that growth was under way again by the 1520s, though the former sees growth as a new start then, while the latter view takes its beginning back a decade or two. Thirdly, the two arguments share the conclusion that there was little absolute population growth between 1471 and 1529, which is to some extent imposed by evidence for the small size of England's population in 1522–5. On both arguments, any population growth before the 1520s was mostly of only local consequence, and presumably taken up by the scattered centres of development that were noted in chapter 11. Both interpretations of population growth serve to strengthen the argument that the possibilities for sustained economic growth over the whole period were poor.

Conclusions

For much of the period 1471–1529, England presented no very impressive image to her neighbours. A kingdom that had deposed so many kings invited a certain mockery, even if European rulers had to take sitting tenants seriously. In September 1512, following the opening of war between France and England, the Poitevin poet Jean Bouchet wrote a lengthy poem in which Henry VII of England addresses his successor from the Elysian Fields, reproving him for his aggression against France. It was, he says, disloyal towards the dynasty which had put the Tudors on the throne, and could well lead to his losing crown and sceptre, 'seeing that your arrogant nation delights in change, and never wants a king to rule them very long, unless under compulsion'. The reference to recent historical events is plain enough. 'You have the title', he says,

> but not the authority of a king, for you are not obeyed in the same way as the king of France, who has no lack of men, gold nor silver. He is an emperor, not just a ruler, being master of both land and people. But you, my son, are so insignificant that your subjects can do as they please, to the extent that you are their servant, and can only be their king by observing their wishes and offering no resistance.[1]

By implication, Bouchet rejected the appropriateness of an imperial crown in the iconography of the English monarchy.

This portrait of England is distorted, but it is easy enough to

---

[1] J. Bouchet, Epistre envoyée du Champ Elisée par feu Henry, autrefois roy d'Angleterre', in Bouchet, *Epistres Morales*, fos. jʳ, vʳ·ᵛ. Bouchet was the anonymous author referred to by Antonovics, who discusses analogous contemporary comments: A. V. Antonovics, 'Henry VII, King of England, "By the Grace of Charles VIII of France"', in Griffiths and Sherborne (eds), *Kings and Nobles*, 169; J. J. Britnell, *Jean Bouchet*, Edinburgh 1986, 307–8.

see where its principal elements come from. It was twenty-seven
years since an English king had actually been turned off the throne,
but during the twenty-seven years before that it had happened five
times (in 1461, 1470, 1471, 1483 and 1485). Moreover, threats
to the Tudors' security from pretenders to the throne continued
after 1485. The Italian author of a description of England around
1500 commented on the volatility of English politics, again attribut-
ing it to English temperament. The English, he says, 'could muster
a very large army, were they as devoted to their crown as the Scotch
are, but from what I understand few of them are very loyal. They
generally hate their present and extol their dead sovereigns.'[2]
In writing about the insecurity of Henry VIII's throne in 1512,
Bouchet was probably aware of the claims of Richard de la Pole,
self-styled duke of Suffolk, whose title was recognized by Louis
XII of France during the period of warfare from 1512 to 1514.
The suggestion that Henry VIII risked losing his crown as a result
of the war was probably a direct reference to this.[3] It was not
obvious to the French that old days of dynastic chopping and
changing were over. Nor was this sense of ongoing insecurity
peculiar to wishful thinkers abroad. The concealment of Henry
VII's death for two days in 1509 gives support to the Spanish
ambassador's view that the kingdom was in jeopardy as a result
of it.[4] The panic over the duke of Buckingham in 1520–1 displays
nervousness concerning this same issue on the part of the king
and his leading minister. The vulnerability of the English crown,
exacerbated by the absence of a male heir to Henry VIII, was a
matter for dispassionate observation to the end of the period,
even if in retrospect Henry's position looks more secure than that
of his predecessors because of the absence of any effective challenge to his title. The other element in the picture of English royal
weakness was parliament, whose power was seen abroad to derog-
ate from the authority of the crown. Commynes had observed in
his *Mémoires* the inability of the king to impose taxes except for
war in France or Scotland, and the requirement that such taxes
should be approved in parliament.[5] Some Englishmen, notably
Sir John Fortescue, considered England to differ from France in
the extent to which the king's will was limited by parliament. In
retrospect these two elements of English history – susceptibility
to dynastic conflict, and the power of parliament – are necessarily

[2] *Relation*, 31–2.
[3] Bouchet, *Annales*, fos. 193ᵛ, 197ʳ.
[4] S. J. Gunn, 'The Accession of Henry VIII', *HR*, lxiv (1991), 279–81.
[5] Commynes, ii, 8, 76.

analysed separately by historians, but to Bouchet and his contemporaries abroad they went together as evidence of the weakness, and inferiority, of the English monarchy.

Though it was crude sociology to attribute the vulnerability of the monarchy to the temperament of the English people, it is a sort of crudity that remains familiar amongst the commonplaces of modern political analysis. In fact, so far from loving political change, the propensity of the nobility to support the monarchy was one of the striking features of English politics under the Tudors, and the notion that 'the English' loved change for its own sake was the reverse of the truth. Even though Henry VII's dealings with the nobility had become deeply resented by the time he died, there was no visible threat of resistance to his rule. The implications of political instability were spelled out in English interpretations of their recent past.

The biggest single cause of royal recovery was the result of the willingness of the nobility to close ranks in the interests of stability following the death of Richard III. In practice, this meant supporting the Tudors. Prominent men continued to be executed for treason – Stanley in 1495, Warwick in 1499, Buckingham in 1521 – but more on suspicion of what they might do than on the evidence of what they had done, and in each case the historian's hands are tied for want of convincing evidence that anything very serious was afoot. Those involved in actually causing trouble that can be documented and assessed were either impostors or claimants with nothing to lose because of their lack of resources or following. Even though there were credible Yorkist claimants to the throne – the earl of Warwick to 1499, the de la Poles thereafter – they had no significant following, and the great majority of former Yorkists were willing to accept the children of Elizabeth of York as the proper inheritors of the Yorkist claim.

Kings between 1471 and 1529 were able to effect a considerable measure of recovery from the low point of financial and political resources to which the crown had declined under Henry VI. This involved a certain amount of innovation in response to the particular problems they faced and the changing circumstances of the place of the English monarchy amongst the secular and lay powers of western Christendom. Some symbolic forms of kingship were developed, mostly imitated from other kingdoms, such as the use of the arched crown, the use of royal portraiture on coins, and the use of the expression 'his majesty'.[6] The development of

---

[6] Above, pp. 54, 56.

new forms of taxation, in discussion with representatives of the shires and boroughs in parliament, was a long-needed response to the ossification of the older system of levying fifteenths and tenths, but implies a growing willingness on the part of the commons to cooperate with the crown.[7] The less formal manner of summoning armies adopted by Henry VIII was seemingly a response to the growth of confidence in relations between the king and the nobility.[8] Although litigation before the king's council was always a very minor part of the total scene, its expansion under the Tudors represents a significant new development in the royal art of inducing respect for the law.[9]

As this last example demonstrates, however, the recovery of royal authority did not require or inspire any considerable alteration in the institutional structure of government and law. The task was to make existing institutions work. People were not impressed by new laws when they believed that what mattered was the enforcement of existing ones. Areas of controversial legislation, such as that against aristocratic retaining or against enclosures, were either building on earlier foundations, or proclaiming a conservative intent, or both. The kings of the period lacked the authority to introduce big innovations to enhance the power of the crown. Henry VII's attempts to bridle the nobility made use of existing institutions to new effect – the king's council, bonds of recognizance – but they did not amount to any lasting change in the apparatus of government. Henry VII's distinctive policy towards the nobility was a dead end, not a new beginning, and the slight institutional changes he had introduced to accommodate the activities of Empson and Dudley were dismantled after his death. Tudor government depended upon cooperation betwen crown and nobility in the internal government of the kingdom and in war in just the same ways as earlier governments had done. Nor was there any significant alteration between 1471 and 1529 in the capacity of parliament to check royal rapacity. The antagonism that Wolsey faced in raising a parliamentary subsidy in 1523 shows that to the end of the period the king's powers were heavily circumscribed, and that parliament was far from being a compliant stooge of government when the real interests of its members and the supposed interests of the commonwealth were in question. Widespread resistance to the Amicable Grant of 1525, and the manner in

---

[7] Above, p. 115.
[8] Above, p. 48.
[9] Above, pp. 172–3.

which the government backed down on that occasion, shows, too, the continuing vigour of popular politics, and the extent to which even the opinions of those who were not represented in parliament had to be taken into account in the government of the kingdom.[10]

Those who saw the volatility of late medieval English politics as the result of the character of the English people, rather than as the consequence of more transitory problems of government, ignored the extent to which, in reality, fundamental institutions of society and the beliefs associated with them favoured political stability. In particular, concepts of nation, church and law all accredited the authority of the king, and supplied rational and moral grounds for obedience. Henry V had exploited these resources with consummate brilliance. Even his unfortunate son had been able to depend upon them for most of his reign, though in the end his undoubted piety could not compensate in the eyes of his political enemies for his betrayal of national interests in France and his failure to maintain respect for the law. These old cultural resources were nevertheless there to be drawn upon by his successors. Nationalism, religion and law did not automatically inculcate respect for a king since each of them implied a set of principles in which a king was expected to operate, and a king, like Henry VI, who failed to do so was liable to lose friends. Awareness of religious and legal maxims throughout English society nevertheless supplied the potential for an elaborate use of rhetoric on behalf of the crown. Cardinal Wolsey is a particularly interesting figure in this respect, since he was in a strong position to articulate nationalist, religious and legal maxims in support of his administration. By the same token, the possibilities for criticism of governments were also richly structured along these same lines; Wolsey's critics, predictably, represented him as Francophile, irreligious and tyrannical.[11] The advantage in this situation lay with governments, who could control the balance of argument in their favour.

Although there was nothing before 1529 to suggest that a fundamental reshaping of relations between church and state was imminent, it is arguable that a growing sophistication amongst the laity concerning nationality, religion and law was a precondition for the events of the 1530s. Whatever feelings of regret the Henrician Reformation may have stirred up at parish level, the king did not

---

[10] Above, pp. 123–4.

[11] For conventional elements in the portrayal of Wolsey, see in particular G. Walker, *John Skelton and the Politics of the 1520s*, Cambridge 1988, 124–53.

impose his headship of the English church by arbitrary fiat, but by statute law made in parliament, and he depended on a high level of conceptualization of the issues by the nobility and commons to be able to do so. Nothing could demonstrate better than the Reformation, in fact, the ways in which nationhood, religion and law were capable of buttressing the power of the crown when they were effectively harnessed in the king's cause.

Those who came to England from abroad and judged its people by observation rather than by prejudice and surmise found much to interest them. In general the country seemed wealthy. There was nevertheless great scope for development. The Italian visitor who described England in 1500 commented on the slightness of the population in proportion to English resources of land, and thought that the English were characteristically lazy.[12] In spite of such potential, the economic development of the kingdom between 1471 and 1529 was narrowly based, and did not permit any very rapid change in what was produced or in standards of living. The growth of the woollen industry was the most dynamic aspect of the economy, and its effects were felt in many parts of the kingdom, from parts of Devon and Kent in the south to the Lake District in the north. As a result of the growing demand for wool, sheep-farming was the most profitable area of agriculture, and there was widespread investment in sheep-flocks and pastures.[13] Some aspects of this have been given particular prominence by writers wanting to see the period as one of transition to modernity. In particular, the enclosure of arable land to create sheep runs that so concerned the government has been seen as the work of a rising capitalist class. However, the government's interest was driven by an ideological commitment to the erroneous idea that enclosure was causing unemployment and depopulation rather than by any dependable analysis of its incidence and effects.[14] The government grossly exaggerated the depopulating effects of investment in sheep-flocks – indeed the period of greatest public concern coincided with the period when, after over a century of stagnation and decline, population was increasing. The enclosers included noblemen, bishops, abbots and gentry, so that it is impossible to define enclosure as the activity of any particular type of landlord. Nor was such investment new, though there was some acceleration in the amount of enclosure as cloth exports revived from the

---

[12] *Relation*, 10, 20, 28–9, 31, 39; *EHD*, 191.
[13] Above, pp. 235–6.
[14] Above, pp. 203–4.

1470s.[15] No one has yet given any reason for supposing that the investment in sheep in this period was any more distinctively capitalist than the build-up of sheep-flocks, with corresponding social conflicts concerning the use of common pastures, in the later twelfth and thirteenth centuries.

Arguments that represent the period 1471–1529 either as the closing of an old era or the beginning of a new one necessarily depend upon the selection of particular aspects for discussion. It is undeniable that these were the last decades of papal authority in England, and almost the last decades of monasticism, though there was little within the period itself to presage the turmoil of the 1530s. At the same time these decades saw the beginnings of a form of classical education that was to be important for centuries in the upbringing of the sons of the ruling elite. Such endings and beginnings are irrelevant to most aspects of the period, whose intellectual and social continuity has, in most respects, defied all attempts at identifying fundamental change.

[15] W. G. Hoskins, *The Age of Plunder: The England of Henry VIII, 1500–1547,* London 1976, 69–71.

Bibliography

A Sources

This section is arranged alphabetically by the abbreviated forms that are used in the footnotes.

Arrivall: *Historie of the Arrivall of Edward IV in England*, ed. J. Bruce, Camden Society, 1st ser., i, London 1838.

Barclay, *Eclogues*: A. Barclay, *The Eclogues*, ed. B. White, Early English Text Society, original ser., 175, London 1928.

Barclay, *St George*: A. Barclay, *The Life of St. George*, Early English Text Society, ccxxx, London 1955.

Basin: T. Basin, *Histoire de Louis XI*, ed. C. Samaran and M.-C. Garand, 3 vols, Paris 1963–72.

Boke of Justices of Peas: *The Boke of Justices of Peas, 1506*, ed. P. R. Glazebrook, Classical English Law Texts, London 1972.

Boke of Noblesse: *The Boke of Noblesse Addressed to King Edward the Fourth on his Invasion of France in 1475*, ed. J. G. Nichols, Roxburghe Club 1860.

Bouchet, *Annales*: J. Bouchet, *Les Annales d'Aquitaine*, 6th major edn, Poitiers 1557.

Bouchet, *Epistres morales*: J. Bouchet, 'Epistre envoyée du Champ Élisée par feu Henry, autrefois roy d'Angleterre', in J. Bouchet, *Epistres morales et familières du Traverseur*, Poitiers 1545, reprinted with introduction by J. Beard, Wakefield, New York and Paris 1969.

Calisto and Melebea: *Calisto and Melebea*, Malone Society Reprints, London 1908.

Catholic England: *Catholic England: Faith, Religion and Observance before the Reformation*, trans. and ed. R. N. Swanson, Manchester 1993.

Cavendish: G. Cavendish, *The Life and Death of Cardinal Wolsey*, ed. R. S. Sylvester, Early English Text Society, ccxliii, Oxford 1959.

Caxton: *Caxton's Own Prose*, ed. N. F. Blake, London 1973.

Clifford Letters: *Clifford Letters of the Sixteenth Century*, ed. A. G. Dickens, Surtees Society, clxxii, Durham 1962.

Commynes: P. de Commynes, *Mémoires*, ed. J. Calmette, 3 vols, Paris 1924–5.

Coventry LB: *The Coventry Leet Book*, ed. M. D. Harris, Early English Text Society, cxxxiv, cxxxv, cxxxviii, cxlvi, London 1907–13.

Crowland Continuations: *The Crowland Chronicle Continuations, 1459–1486*, ed. N. Pronay and J. Cox, Gloucester 1986.

Documents: *Documents Illustrative of the Continental Reformation*, ed. B. J. Kidd, Oxford 1911.

Domesday of Enclosures: *The Domesday of Enclosures, 1517–18*, ed. I. S. Leadam, 2 vols, Royal Historical Society, London 1897.

Duchy of Lancaster: *Duchy of Lancaster Estates in Derbyshire, 1485–1540*, ed. I. S. W. Blanchard, Derby Archaeological Society Record Series, iii, Derby 1971.

Dudley: E. Dudley, *The Tree of Commonwealth*, ed. D. M. Brodie, Cambridge 1948.

EHD, 1485–1558: *English Historical Documents, 1485–1558*, ed. C. H. Williams, London 1967.

Erasmus, *Op. Ep.*: Erasmus of Rotterdam, *Opus Epistolarum*, ed. P. S. Allen and H. M. Allen, 12 vols, Oxford 1906–58.

Fish: S. Fish, *A Supplicacyon for the Beggers*, ed. F. J. Furnivall, Early English Text Society, extra ser., xiii, London 1871.

Fitzherbert: J. Fitzherbert, *The Book of Husbandry by Master Fitzherbert*, ed. W. W. Skeat, English Dialect Society, London 1882.

Foedera: *Foedera, Conventiones, Literae et Cujuscunque Generis Acta Publica*, ed. T. Rymer, 3rd edn, 10 vols, The Hague 1739–45.

Fortescue, *De Laudibus*: J. Fortescue, *De Laudibus Legum Anglie*, ed. S. B. Chrimes, Cambridge Studies in English Legal History, xii, Cambridge 1942.

Fortescue, *Governance*: J. Fortescue, *The Governance of England*, ed. C. Plummer, Oxford 1885.

Great Chronicle: *The Great Chronicle of London*, ed. A. H. Thomas and I. D. Thornley, London 1938.

Hall: E. Hall, *Chronicle: The Union of the Two Noble and Illustre Famelies of Lancastre and Yorke*, London 1809.

Harley 433: *British Library Harleian Manuscript 433*, ed. R. Horrox and P. W. Hammond, 4 vols, Gloucester and London 1979–83.

Hawes: S. Hawes, *The Minor Poems*, Early English Text Society, cclxxi, London 1974.

Household of Edward IV: *The Household of Edward IV: The Black Book and the Ordinance of 1478*, ed. A. R. Myers, Manchester 1959.

Household of Elizabeth Woodville: 'The Household of Queen Elizabeth Woodville, 1466–7', ed. A. R. Myers, *Bulletin of the John Rylands Library, Manchester*, 50 (1967–8), 207–35, 443–81.

John Vale's Book: *The Politics of Fifteenth Century England: John Vale's Book*, ed. M. L. Kekewich, C. Richmond, A. F. Sutton, L. Visser-Fuchs and J. L. Watts, Stroud 1995.

Leeds Documents: *The Manor and Borough of Leeds, 1425–1662: An Edition of Documents*, ed. J. W. Kirby, Thoresby Society, lvii, Leeds 1983.

LP: *Letters and Papers, Foreign and Domestic, of the Reign of Henry VIII*, ed. J. S. Brewer, J. Gairdner and R. H. Brodie, 2nd edn, 23 vols in 38, London 1862–1932.

LP, Richard III and Henry VII: *Letters and Papers Illustrative of the Reigns of Richard III and Henry VII*, ed. J. Gairdner, 2 vols, Rolls Series, London 1861–3.

Mancini: D. Mancini, *The Usurpation of Richard III*, ed. C. A. J. Armstrong, 2nd edn, Gloucester 1969.

Marcher Lordships: *The Marcher Lordships of South Wales, 1415–1536*, ed. T. B. Pugh, Board of Celtic Studies, University of Wales, Cardiff 1963.

Mary of Nemmegen: *Mary of Nemmegen*, ed. J. S. McKinnell, Durham 1993.

Medwall: *The Plays of Henry Medwall*, ed. A. H. Nelson, Cambridge 1980.

Milanese Papers: *Calendar of Milanese Papers, 1385–1618*, London 1912.

More, *Correspondence*: T. More, *The Correspondence*, ed. E. F. Rogers, Princeton 1947.

More, *Richard III*: T. More, *The History of Richard III and Selections from the English and Latin Poems*, ed. R. S. Sylvester, New Haven and London 1976.

More, *Utopia*: T. More, *Utopia*, ed. and trans. G. M. Logan and R. M. Adams, Cambridge 1989.

Old Tenure: *The Old Tenure (c.1515) and The Old Natura Brevium (c.1518)*, ed. M. S. Arnold, Classical English Law Texts, London 1974.

Paston Letters: *Paston Letters and Papers of the Fifteenth Century*, ed. N. Davis, 2 vols, Oxford 1971–6.

Plumpton Correspondence: *Plumpton Correspondence*, ed. T. Stapleton, Camden Society, 1st ser., iv, London 1839.

Privy Purse: *Privy Purse Expenditure of Elizabeth of York*, ed. N. H. Nicolas, London 1830.

Register of Thetford Priory: *The Register of Thetford Priory*, ed. D. Dymond, 2 vols, British Academy, Oxford 1995–.

Relation: *A Relation of the Island of England about the Year 1500*, ed. C. A. Sneyd, Camden Society, 1st ser., xxxvii, London 1847.

Rot. Parl.: *Rotuli Parliamentorum*, Record Commission, 6 vols, London 1783.

Rous: J. Rous, *Historia Regum Angliae*, ed. T. Hearne, 2nd edn, Oxford 1745.

Skelton: J. Skelton, *The Complete English Poems*, ed. J. Scattergood, Harmondsworth 1983.

Spelman: *The Reports of Sir John Spelman*, ed. J. H. Baker, 2 vols, Selden Society, xciii, xciv, London 1977.

SP: *State Papers of the Reign of Henry VIII*, 11 vols, Record Commission, London 1830–52.

SR: *Statutes of the Realm (1101–1713)*, ed. A. Luders, T. E. Tomlins, J. France, W. E. Taunton and J. Raithby, 11 vols, Record Commission, London 1808–28.

Stonor Letters: *Kingsford's Stonor Letters and Papers*, ed. C. Carpenter, Cambridge 1996.

Tudor Economic Documents: *Tudor Economic Documents*, ed. R. H. Tawney and E. Power, 3 vols, London 1924.

Tudor Royal Proclamations: *Tudor Royal Proclamations*, ed. P. L. Hughes and J. F. Larkin, 3 vols, New Haven 1964–9.

Vergil: P. Vergil, *Anglica Historia, A.D. 1485–1537*, ed. D. Hay, Royal Historical Society, Camden 3rd ser., lxxiv, London 1950.

Warkworth: J. Warkworth, *A Chronicle of the First Thirteen Years of King Edward the Fourth*, ed. J. O. Halliwell, Camden Society, 1st ser., x, London 1839.

Waurin: J. Waurin, *Receuil des Chroniques*, ed. W. Hardy and E. L. C. P. Hardy, 5 vols, Rolls Series, London 1864–91.

York House Books: *York House Books, 1461–1490*, ed. L. C. Attreed, 2 vols, Stroud 1991.

B General and narrative works

This section includes the abbreviations used in the footnotes and chapter bibliogaphies for journal titles.

AHR: Agricultural History Review.

Archer, R. E. and Walker, S. (eds), *Rulers and Ruled in Late Medieval England: Essays presented to Gerald Harriss*, London and Rio Grande 1995.

Arthurson, I., *The Perkin Warbeck Conspiracy, 1491–99*, Stroud 1994.

Bennett, M. J., *Lambert Simnel and the Battle of Stoke*, Gloucester 1987.

Bernard, G. W. (ed.), *The Tudor Nobility*, Manchester 1992.

BIHR: Bulletin of the Institute of Historical Research.

Britnell, R. H. and Pollard, A. J. (eds), *The McFarlane Legacy: Studies in Late Medieval Politics and Society*, Stroud 1995.

Chrimes, S. B., *English Constitutional Ideas in the Fifteenth Century*, Cambridge 1936.

Chrimes, S. B., *Henry VII*, London 1972.

Colvin, H. M. (ed.), *The History of the King's Works*, 6 vols, London 1963–82.

Cornwall, J. C. K., *Wealth and Society in Early Sixteenth-Century England*, London 1988.

EconHR: Economic History Review.

EHR: English Historical Review.

Elton, G. R., *Studies in Tudor and Stuart Politics and Government*, 4 vols, Cambridge 1974–92.

G. E. C., *Complete Peerage*: G. E. C[okayne], *Complete Peerage of England, Scotland, Ireland, Great Britain and United Kingdom*, new edn, ed. V. Gibbs and others, 12 vols, London 1910–59.

Grant, A., *Henry VII*, London 1985.

Griffiths, R. A. and Sherborne, J. (eds), *Kings and Nobles in the Later Middle Ages*, Gloucester and New York 1986.

Griffiths, R. A. and Thomas, R. S., *The Making of the Tudor Dynasty*, Gloucester 1985.

Gunn, S. J., *Charles Brandon, Duke of Suffolk, 1484–1545*, Oxford 1988.

Gunn, S. J., *Early Tudor Government, 1485–1558*, London 1995.

Gunn, S. J. and Lindley, P. G. (eds), *Cardinal Wolsey: Church, State and Art*, Cambridge, 1991.

Guy, J. A., *The Public Career of Sir Thomas More*, New Haven and London 1980.

Guy, J. A., *Tudor England*, Oxford 1988.

Gwyn, P., *The King's Cardinal: The Rise and Fall of Thomas Wolsey*, London 1990.

Hammond, P. W., *The Battles of Barnet and Tewkesbury*, Gloucester 1990.

Hammond, P. W. (ed.), *Richard III: Loyalty, Lordship and Law*, London 1986.

Harris, B. J., *Edward Stafford, Third Duke of Buckingham, 1478–1521*, Stanford 1986.

Hicks, M. A., *False, Fleeting, Perjur'd Clarence: George Duke of Clarence, 1449–78*, Gloucester 1980.

Hicks, M. A., *Richard III and his Rivals: Magnates and their Motives in the Wars of the Roses*, London 1991.

HJ: Historical Journal.

Horrox, R. E., *Richard III: A Study of Service*, Cambridge 1989.

Ives, E. W., *Anne Boleyn*, Oxford 1986.

JBS: Journal of British Studies.

JMH: Journal of Medieval History.

Jones, M. K. and Underwood, M. G., *The King's Mother: Lady Margaret Beaufort, Countess of Richmond and Derby*, Cambridge 1992.

Lander, J. R., *Crown and Nobility, 1450–1509*, London 1976.

Lander, J. R., *Government and Community: England, 1450–1509*, London 1980.

Lander, J. R., *The Limitations of the English Monarchy in the Later Middle Ages*, Toronto 1989.

MacCulloch, D. (ed.), *The Reign of Henry VIII: Politics, Policy and Piety*, London 1995.

NH: Northern History.

OED: Oxford English Dictionary, ed. J. A. H. Murray and others, 10 vols in 13, Oxford 1888–1928.

P&P: Past and Present.

Pollard, A. F., *Wolsey*, illustrated edn, London 1953.

Pollard, A. J., *North-Eastern England during the Wars of the Roses*, Oxford 1990.

Ross, C., *Edward IV*, London 1974.

Ross, C., *Richard III*, London 1981.

Scarisbrick, J. J., *Henry VIII*, London 1968.

Scattergood, V. J., *Politics and Poetry in the Fifteenth Century*, London 1971.

Scofield, C. L., *The Life and Reign of Edward the Fourth*, 2 vols, London 1923.

Thompson, J. A. F., *The Transformation of Medieval England, 1370–1529*, London 1983.

TRHS: Transactions of the Royal Historical Society.

VCH: The Victoria History of the Counties of England, ed. H. A. Doubleday, W. Page, L. F. Salzman and R. B. Pugh, numerous volumes, London and Westminster 1900–34, then London, 1935–.

Weightman, C., *Margaret of York, Duchess of Burgundy, 1446–1503*, New York and Gloucester 1989.

Williams, G., *Recovery, Reorientation and Reformation: Wales, c.1415–1642*, Oxford 1987.

C Chapter bibliographies

This section lists a selection of titles cited in the footnotes. Details of references not included in the bibliography for a chapter are given at the first citation in that chapter, unless they occur in sections A or B. For the abbreviations of journal titles, see section B.

Chapter 1: Kings

Arthurson, I., *The Perkin Warbeck Conspiracy, 1491–99*, Stroud 1994.

Bennett, M., *Lambert Simnel and the Battle of Stoke*, New York and Gloucester 1987.

Chrimes, S. B., *Henry VII*, London 1972.

Griffiths, R. A. and Thomas, R. S., *The Making of the Tudor Dynasty*, Gloucester 1985.

Harris, B. J., *Edward Stafford, Third Duke of Buckingham, 1478–1521*, Stanford 1986.

Helmholz, R. H., 'The Sons of Edward IV: A Canonical Assessment of the Claim that they were Illegitimate', in Hammond (ed.), *Richard III: Loyalty, Lordship and Law*, 91–103.

Hicks, M. A., *False, Fleeting, Perjur'd Clarence: George Duke of Clarence, 1449–78*, Gloucester 1980.

Hicks, M. A, *Richard III and his Rivals: Magnates and their Motives in the Wars of the Roses*, London 1991.

Horrox, R. E., *Richard III: A Study of Service*, Cambridge 1989.

Ives, E. W., *Anne Boleyn*, Oxford 1986.

Jones, M. K. and Underwood, M. G., *The King's Mother: Lady*

Margaret Beaufort, Countess of Richmond and Derby, Cambridge 1992.

Pollard, A. J., *Richard III and the Princes in the Tower*, Stroud 1991.

Ross, C., *Edward IV*, London 1974.

Ross, C., *Richard III*, London 1981.

Scarisbrick, J. J., *Henry VIII*, London 1968.

Chapter 2: Neighbours

Arthurson, I., *The Perkin Warbeck Conspiracy, 1491–99*, Stroud 1994.

Bernard, G. W., *War, Taxation and Rebellion in Tudor England: Henry VIII, Wolsey and the Amicable Grant of 1525*, Brighton 1986.

Chambers, D. S., 'Cardinal Wolsey and the Papal Tiara', BIHR, xxxviii (1965), 20–30.

Cruikshank, C., *The English Occupation of Tournai, 1513–19*, Oxford 1971.

Cruikshank, C., *Henry VIII and the Invasion of France*, Stroud 1990.

Giry-Deloison, C., 'A Diplomatic Revolution? Anglo-French Relations and the Treaties of 1527', in D. Starkey (ed.), *Henry VIII: A European Court in England*, London 1991, 77–83.

Gunn, S. J., 'The Duke of Suffolk's March on Paris in 1523', EHR, ci (1986), 596–634.

Gunn, S. J., 'The French Wars of Henry VIII', in J. M. Black (ed.), *The Origins of War in Early Modern Europe*, London 1987, 28–51.

Gwyn, P., 'Wolsey's Foreign Policy: The Conferences at Calais and Bruges Reconsidered', HJ, xxiii (1980), 755–72.

Nicholson, R., *Scotland: The Later Middle Ages*, Edinburgh 1974.

Potter, D., 'Foreign Policy', in MacCulloch (ed.), *Reign of Henry VIII*, 101–33.

Ross, C., *Edward IV*, London 1974.

Russell, J. G., *Diplomats at Work: Three Renaissance Studies*, Stroud 1992.

Russell, J. G., *Peacemaking in the Renaissance*, London 1986.

Wernham, R. B., *Before the Armada: the Growth of English Foreign Policy, 1485–1588*, London 1966.

Chapter 3: Kingship

Anglo, S., 'The Court Festivals of Henry VII: A Study Based upon the Account Books of John Heron, Treasurer of the Chamber', *Bulletin of the John Rylands Library*, xliii (1960), 12–45.

Anglo, S., *Images of Tudor Kingship*, London 1992.

Challis, C. E., *The Tudor Coinage*, Manchester 1978.

Cruikshank, C., *Henry VIII and the Invasion of France*, Stroud 1990.

Fox, A., *Politics and Literature in the Reigns of Henry VII and Henry VIII*, Oxford 1989.

Goodman, A., *The Wars of the Roses: Military Activity and English Society, 1452–97*, London 1991.

Goring, J. J., 'The General Proscription of 1522', EHR, lxxxvi (1971), 681–705.

Gunn, S. J., *Early Tudor Government, 1485–1558*, London 1995.

Hoak, D., 'The Iconography of the Crown Imperial', in D. Hoak (ed.), *Tudor Political Culture*, Cambridge 1995, 54–103.

Hoyle, R., 'War and Public Finance', in MacCulloch (ed.), *Reign of Henry VIII*, 75–99.

Knecht, R. J., *Renaissance Warrior and Patron: The Reign of Francis I*, Cambridge 1994.

Samman, N., 'The Progresses of Henry VIII', in MacCulloch (ed.), *Reign of Henry VIII*, 59–73.

Thurley, S., *The Royal Palaces of Tudor England*, New Haven and London 1993.

Wolffe, B. P., *The Crown Lands, 1461–1536*, London 1970.

Wolffe, B. P., *The Royal Demesne in English History: The Crown Estate in the Governance of the Realm from the Conquest to 1509*, London 1971.

Chapter 4: Court and Council

Bernard, G. W., 'Politics and Government in Tudor England', HJ, xxi (1988), 159–82.

Condon, M., 'Ruling Elites in the Reign of Henry VII', in C. Ross (ed.), *Patronage, Pedigree and Power in Late Medieval England*, Gloncester 1979, 109–42.

Gunn, S. J., 'The Courtiers of Henry VII', EHR, cviii (1993), 23–49.

Gunn, S. J., 'The Structure of Politics in Early Tudor England', TRHS, 6th ser., v (1995), 59–90.

Ives, E. W., 'The Fall of Wolsey', in Gunn and Lindley (eds), *Cardinal Wolsey*, 286–315.

Loades, D., *The Tudor Court*, 2nd edn, Bangor 1992.

Samman, N., 'The Progresses of Henry VIII', in MacCulloch (ed.), *Reign of Henry VIII*, 59–73.

Starkey, D., 'Court, Council and Nobility in Tudor England', in R. G. Asch and A. M. Birke, *Princes, Patronage and the Nobility: The Court at the Beginning of the Modern Age*, Oxford 1991, 175–203.

Starkey, D., 'Court and Government', in Starkey (ed.), *Revolution Reassessed*, 29–58.

Starkey, D. *The Reign of Henry VIII: Personalities and Politics*, London 1985.

Starkey, D. (ed.), *The English Court from the Wars of the Roses to the Civil War*, London 1987.

Starkey, D. (ed.), *Henry VIII: A European Court in England*, London 1991.

Starkey, D. (ed.), *Revolution Reassessed: Revisions in the History of Tudor Government and Administration*, Oxford 1986.

Thurley, S., *The Royal Palaces of Tudor England*, New Haven and London, 1993.

Wolffe, B. P., *The Crown Lands, 1461–1536*, London 1970.

Chapter 5: Country Politics

Bernard, G. W. (ed.), *The Tudor Nobility*, Manchester 1992.

Carpenter, M. C. 'Gentry and Community in Medieval England', *JBS*, xxxiii (1994), 340–80.

Carpenter, M. C., *Locality and Polity: A Study of Warwickshire Landed Society, 1401–1499*, Cambridge 1992.

Carpenter, M. C., 'The Stonor Circle in the Fifteenth Century', in Archer and Walker (eds), *Rulers and Ruled*, 175–200.

Ellis, S. G., *Tudor Frontiers and Noble Powers: The Making of the British State*, Oxford 1995.

Gunn, S. J., 'The Regime of Charles, Duke of Suffolk, in North Wales and the Reform of Welsh Government, 1509–25', *Welsh History Review*, xii (1984–5), 461–94.

Guy, J., 'Wolsey and the Tudor Polity', in Gunn and Lindley (eds), *Cardinal Wolsey*, 54–75.

Horrox, R. E., *Richard III: A Study of Service*, Cambridge 1989.

James, M., *Society, Politics and Culture: Studies in Early Modern England*, Cambridge 1986.

Lander, J. R., *English Justices of the Peace, 1461–1509*, Gloucester 1989.

Luckett, D., 'Crown Officers and Licensed Retinues in the Reign of Henry VII', in Archer and Walker (eds), *Rulers and Ruled*, 223–38.

Luckett, D., 'Patronage, Violence and Revolt in the Reign of

Henry VII', in R. E. Archer (ed.), *Crown, Government and People in the Fifteenth Century*, Stroud 1995, 145–60.

Miller, H., *Henry VIII and the English Nobility*, Oxford 1986.

Pollard, A. J., *North-Eastern England during the Wars of the Roses*, Oxford 1990.

Pollard, A. J., 'The Tyranny of Richard III', *JMH*, iii (1977), 147–65.

Wright, S. M., *The Derbyshire Gentry in the Fifteenth Century*, Derbyshire Record Society, Chesterfield 1983.

Chapter 6: *Parliament and Popular Politics*

Arthurson, I., 'The Rising of 1497: A Revolt of the Peasantry?', in J. Rosenthal and C. Richmond (eds), *People, Politics and Community in the Later Middle Ages*, Gloucester 1987, 1–18.

Bennett, M. J., 'Henry VII and the Northern Rising of 1489', *EHR*, cv (1990), 34–59.

Bernard, G. W., *War, Taxation and Rebellion in Early Tudor England*, Brighton 1986.

Bindoff, S. T. (ed.), *The House of Commons, 1509–1558*, 3 vols, London 1982.

Bush, M., 'Tax Reform and Rebellion in Early Tudor England', *History*, 76 (1991), 379–400.

Butt, R., *A History of Parliament: The Middle Ages*, London 1989.

Graves, M. A. R., *The Tudor Parliaments: Crown, Lords and Commons, 1485–1603*, London 1985.

Guy, J. A., 'Wolsey and the Parliament of 1523', in C. Cross, D. Loades and J. J. Scarisbrick (eds), *Law and Government under the Tudors: Esays Presented to Geoffrey Elton*, Cambridge 1988, 1–18.

Harvey, I. M. W., 'Was There Popular Politics in Fifteenth-Century England?', in Britnell and Pollard (eds), *McFarlane Legacy*, 155–74.

Lehmberg, S. E., *The Reformation Parliament, 1529–1536*, Cambridge 1970.

Loach, J., *Parliament under the Tudors*, Oxford 1991.

Roskell, J., *The Commons and their Speakers in English Parliaments, 1376–1523*, Manchester 1965.

Schofield, R. S., 'Taxation and the Political Limits of the Tudor State', in C. Cross, D. M. Loades and J. J. Scarisbrick (eds), *Law and Government under the Tudors*, Cambridge 1988, 227–55.

Wedgwood, J. C., *History of Parliament: Biographies of the Membes of the Commons House, 1439–1509*, 2 vols, London 1936–8.

Chapter 7: Nationhood

Blake, N. F., *Caxton and his World*, London 1969.

Blake, N. F., *William Caxton and English Literary Culture*, London and Rio Grande 1991.

Davis, N., 'Notes on Grammar and Spelling in the Fifteenth Century', in D. Gray (ed.), *The Oxford Book of Late Medieval Verse and Prose*, Oxford 1985, 493–508.

Griffiths, R. A., *Conquerors and Conquered in Medieval Wales*, New York and Stroud 1994.

Griffiths, R. A., *King and Country: England and Wales in the Fifteenth Century*, London 1991.

Gunn, S. J. and Lindley, P. G. (eds), *Cardinal Wolsey: Church, State and Art*, Cambridge, 1991.

Harvey, J., *The Perpendicular Style*, London 1978.

Orme, N., *Education and Society in Medieval and Renaissance England*, London and Ronceverte 1989.

Pollard, A. J., *North-Eastern England during the Wars of the Roses*, Oxford 1990.

Russell, J. G., 'Language: A Barrier or a Gateway?', in J. G. Russell, *Diplomats at Work: Three Renaissance Studies*, Stroud 1992, 1–50.

Schubert, H. R., *History of the British Iron and Steel Industry from c.450 B.C. to A.D. 1775*, London 1957.

Thurley, S., *The Royal Palaces of Tudor England*, New Haven and London 1993.

Williams, G., *Recovery, Reorientation and Reformation: Wales, c.1415–1642*, Oxford 1987.

Chapter 8: The Church

Aston, M., *Lollards and Reformers: Images and Literacy in Late Medieval Religion*, London 1984.

Brigden, S., *London and the Reformation*, Oxford 1989.

Catto, J. I. and Evans, R. (eds), *The History of the University of Oxford, II: Late Medieval Oxford*, Oxford 1992.

Duffy, E., *The Stripping of the Altars: Traditional Religion in England, 1400–1580*, New Haven and London 1992.

Harvey, B., *Living and Dying in England, 1100–1540: The Monastic Experience*, Oxford 1993.

Hudson, A., *The Premature Reformation: Wycliffite Texts and Lollard History*, Oxford 1988.

Hutton, R., *The Rise and Fall of Merry England: The Ritual Year, 1400–1700*, Oxford 1994.

Rex, R., 'The English Campaign against Luther in the 1520s', *TRHS*, 5th ser., xxxix (1989), 85–106.

Rubin, M., *Corpus Christi: The Eucharist in Late Medieval Culture*, Cambridge 1991.

Scarisbrick, J. J., 'Clerical Taxation in England, 1485 to 1547', *Journal of Ecclesiastical History*, xi (1960), 41–54.

Swanson, R. N., *Church and Society in Late Medieval England*, Oxford 1989.

Tanner, N. P., *The Church in Late Medieval Norwich, 1370–1532*, Toronto 1984.

Thomson, J. A. F., *The Early Tudor Church and Society, 1485–1529*, London 1993.

Chapter 9: The Law

Abbott, L. W., *Law Reporting in England, 1485–1585*, London 1973.

Baker, J. H., 'Introduction', in *Spelman*, ii, 23–396.

Baker, J. H., *The Legal Profession and the Common Law: Historical Essays*, London 1986.

Bellamy, J. G., *Bastard Feudalism and the Law*, London 1989.

Blatcher, M., *The Court of King's Bench, 1450–1550: A Study in Sef-Help*, London 1978.

Brooks, C. W., *Pettyfoggers and Vipers of the Commonwealth: The 'Lower Branch' of the Legal Profession in Early Modern England*, Cambridge 1986.

Gunn, S. J., *Early Tudor Government, 1485–1558*, London 1995.

Guth, D. J., 'Enforcing Late Medieval Law: Patterns in Litigation during Henry VII's Reign', in J. H. Baker (ed.), *Legal Records and the Historian*, London 1978, pp. 80–96.

Guth, D. J., 'Notes on the Early Tudor Exchequer of Pleas', in A. J. Slavin (ed.), *Tudor Men and Institutions: Studies in English Law and Government*, Louisiana 1972, 101–22.

Guy, J. A., *The Cardinal's Court: The Impact of Thomas Wolsey in Star Chamber*, Hassocks 1977.

Hastings, M., *The Court of Common Pleas in Fifteenth Century England*, Ithaca 1947.

Heinze, R. W., *The Proclamations of the Tudor Kings*, Cambridge 1976.

Ives, E. W., 'The Common Lawyers', in C. H. Clough (ed.), *Profession, Vocation and Culture in Later Medieval England: Essays*, Liverpool 1982, 181–217.

Ives, E. W., *The Common Lawyers of Pre-Reformation England*, Cambridge 1983.

Simpson, A. W. B., *Legal Theory and Legal History: Essays on the Common Law*, London 1987.

Chapter 10: Social Order

Bernard, G. W. (ed.), *The Tudor Nobility*, Manchester 1992.

Blanchard, I. S. W., 'Social Structure and Social Organization in an English Village at the Close of the Middle Ages: Chewton, 1526', in E. B. DeWindt (ed.), *The Salt of Common Life: Individuality and Choice in the Medieval Town, Countryside and Church*, Kalamazoo 1995, 307–39.

Carpenter, M. C., *Locality and Polity: A Study of Warwickshire Landed Society, 1401–1499*, Cambridge 1992.

Cornwall, J. C. K., *Wealth and Society in Early Sixteenth-Century England*, London 1988.

Dyer, C., 'The English Medieval Village Community and its Decline', *JBS*, xxxiii (1994), 407–29.

Dyer, C., *Standards of Living in the Later Middle Ages: Social Change in England, c.1200–1520*, Cambridge 1989.

Goldberg, P. J. P., *Women, Work and Life Cycle in a Medieval Economy: Women in York and Yorkshire, c.1300–1520*, Oxford 1992.

Holt, R. and Rosser, G. (eds), *The Medieval Town: A Reader in Urban History, 1200–1540*, London 1990.

Horrox, R. E. (ed.), *Fifteenth-Century Attitudes: Perceptions of Society in Late Medieval England*, Cambridge 1994.

Horrox, R. E., 'The Urban Gentry in the Fifeenth Century', in J. A. F. Thomson (ed.), *Towns and Townspeople in the Fifteenth Century*, Gloucester 1988, 22–44.

James, M., 'Ritual, Drama and Social Body in the Late Medieval English Town', in M. James, *Society, Politics and Culture: Studies in Early Modern England*, Cambridge 1988, 16–47.

Phythian-Adams, C., *Desolation of a City: Coventry and the Urban Crisis of the Late Middle Ages*, Cambridge 1979.

Rigby, S. H., *English Society in the Later Middle Ages: Class, Status and Gender*, London 1995.

Thirsk, J., 'Enclosing and Engrossing', in J. Thirsk (ed.), *The*

Agrarian History of England and Wales, iv: 1500–1640, Cambridge 1967, 200–55.

Thompson, M. W., *The Decline of the Castle*, Cambridge 1987.

Chapter 11: The Market Economy

Blanchard, I. S. W., 'Industrial Employment and the Rural Land Market, 1380–1520', in R. M. Smith (ed.), *Land, Kinship and Life Cycle*, Cambridge 1984, 227–75.

Blanchard, I. S. W., 'The Miner and the Agricultural Community in Medieval England', *AHR*, xx (1972), 93–196.

Carus-Wilson, E. M., *Medieval Merchant Venturers*, 2nd edn, London 1967.

Carus-Wilson, E. M., 'The Woollen Industry before 1550', *The Victoria County History of Wiltshire*, iv, 115–47.

Cornwall, J. C. K., *Wealth and Society in Early Sixteenth-Century England*, London 1988.

Dyer, C., *Lords and Peasants in a Changing Society: The Estates of the Bishopric of Worcester, 680–1540*, Cambridge 1980.

Hanham, A., *The Celys and their World: An English Merchant Family in the Fifteenth Century*, Cambridge 1985.

Hatcher, J., *English Tin Production and Trade before 1550*, Oxford 1973.

Kermode, J., 'Money and Credit in the Fifteenth Century: Some Lessons from Yorkshire', *Business History Review*, lxv (1991), 475–501.

Miller, E. (ed.), *The Agrarian History of England and Wales, iii: 1348–1500*, Cambridge 1991.

Moreton, C. E., *The Townshends and their World: Gentry, Law and Land in Norfolk, c.1450–1551*, Oxford 1992.

Palliser, D. M., *Tudor York*, Oxford 1979.

Phythian-Adams, C., *Desolation of a City: Coventry and the Urban Crisis of the Late Middle Ages*, Cambridge 1979.

Swanson, H., *Medieval Artisans*, Oxford 1989.

Thirsk, J. (ed.), *The Agrarian History of England and Wales, iv: 1500–1640*, Cambridge 1967.

Watkins, A., 'Cattle-Grazing in the Forest of Arden in the Later Middle Ages', *AHR*, xxxvii (1989), 12–25.

Chapter 12: Economic Development

Bailey, M., 'Demographic Decline in Late Medieval England: Some Thoughts on Recent Reearch', *EconHR*, xlix (1996), 1–19.

Blanchard, I. S. W., 'Commercial Crisis and Change: Trade and the Industrial Economy of the North East, 1509–1532', *NH*, viii (1973), 71–85.

Blanchard, I. S. W., 'Population Change, Enclosure and the Early Tudor Economy', *EconHR*, 2nd ser., xxiii (1970), 427–45.

Campbell, B. M. S., 'The Population of Early Tudor England: A Re-Evaluation of the 1522 Muster Returns and 1524 and 1525 Lay Subsidies', *Journal of Historical Geography*, vii (1981), 145–54.

Childs, W. R., 'Devon's Overseas Trade in the Late Middle Ages', in M. Duffy, S. Fisher, B. Greenhill, D. J. Starkey and J. Youings (eds), *The New Maritime History of Devon*, 2 vols, Exeter 1992–, i, 79–89.

Cornwall, J. C. K., 'English Population in the Early Sixteenth Century', *EconHR*, 2nd ser., xxiii (1970), 32–44.

Cornwall, J. C. K., *Wealth and Society in Early Sixteenth-Century England*, London 1988.

Dyer, C., *Lords and Peasants in a Changing Society: The Estates of the Bishopric of Worcester, 680–1540*, Cambridge 1980.

Fisher, F. J., 'Commercial Trends and Policy in Sixteenth-Century England', *EconHR*, x (1939–40), 95–117.

Hare, J. N., 'Durrington: A Chalkland Village in the Later Middle Ages', *Wiltshire Archaeological Magazine*, lxxiv/lxxv (1981), 137–47.

Harvey, B., *Living and Dying in England, 1100–1540: The Monastic Experience*, Oxford 1993.

Hatcher, J., *English Tin Production and Trade before 1550*, Oxford 1973.

Hatcher, J., 'Mortality in the Fifteenth Century: Some New Evidence', *EconHR*, 2nd ser., xxxix (1986), 19–38.

Hoyle, R., 'War and Public Finance', in D. MacCulloch (ed.), *The Reign of Henry VIII: Politics, Policy and Piety*, London 1995, 75–99.

Poos, L. R., *A Rural Society after the Black Death: Essex 1350–1525*, Cambridge 1991.

Index

Places in England are located according to the medieval county divisions that remained more or less in place up to 1971, as represented in the map on p. 86. Places in Wales are located by the county divisions imposed in 1536. Peers of England and Scotland are identified in accordance with the information in G.E.C., *Complete Peerage*, except in the case of the earls of Northumberland who are numbered, following common convention, from the first Percy earl.

Printed in the United States
31665LVS00004B/231

DATE DUE
